COMPREHENSIVE GUIDE TO HERBAL DRUG TECHNOLOGY

PRINCIPLES, PRACTICES, AND APPLICATIONS

PROF. Y. RAJENDRA PRASAD, DR. L. SURENDRA BABU, DR. BUSI. SUNIL KUMAR

Contents

Comprehensive Guide To Herbal Drug Technology

Principles, Practices, and Applications

Prof. Y. Rajendra Prasad
Professor,
Department of Pharmaceutical Chemistry,
AU College of Pharmaceutical Sciences,
Andhra University,
Visakhapatnam-530003, Andhra Pradesh, India

Dr. L. Surendra Babu
Assistant Professor,
Pharmaceutical Chemistry Division,
Adikavi Nannaya University College of Pharmaceutical
Sciences,
Tadepalligudem-534101, Andhra Pradesh, India

Dr. Busi Sunil Kumar
Professor & Head, Department of Pharmaceutical
Chemistry,
VJ'S College of Pharmacy,
Rajahmundry, Andhra Pradesh, India

Published by Notion Press
Notion Press, Inc.
800, West El Camino Real #180,
California, USA 94040

Notion Press Media Pvt Ltd
#7, Red Cross Road,

Egmore, Chennai, Tamil Nadu 600008
Email ID: publish@notionpress.com
Phone Number: +91 44 46315631

Preface

Herbal medicine has been an integral part of healthcare systems across the world for centuries, with a rich history of use in traditional systems such as Ayurveda, Unani, and Traditional Chinese Medicine. In recent years, herbal drugs have regained prominence due to growing awareness about the benefits of natural remedies and the increasing interest in alternative and complementary medicines. However, the field of herbal drug technology is complex and requires a structured understanding of both traditional practices and modern scientific advancements.

"Comprehensive Guide to Herbal Drug Technology: Principles, Practices, and Applications" is written to provide a clear and thorough understanding of the key concepts, processes, and applications involved in herbal drug technology. This book is designed to meet the educational needs of pharmacy students and professionals, specifically aligning with the Pharmacy Council of India (PCI) syllabus. Our aim is to present an academic resource that not only imparts knowledge but also encourages critical thinking and innovation in the field of herbal drug research and development.

The content of this book has been carefully curated to cover a wide spectrum of topics, ranging from the identification and authentication of herbal materials to the preparation and standardization of Ayurvedic formulations. Special emphasis has been placed on Good Agricultural Practices (GAP), quality control, and the standardization of herbal products to ensure consistency, safety, and efficacy. Furthermore, the book addresses key challenges faced by the herbal drug industry, including herbal adulteration, contamination, and the need for rigorous phytochemical analysis.

As authors, we have drawn on our extensive academic and professional experiences to offer practical insights and real-world examples that will benefit students, researchers, and practitioners alike. We hope this book serves as a reliable guide not only for mastering the fundamentals of herbal drug technology but also for applying this knowledge to advance the field and contribute to the healthcare industry.

We express our sincere gratitude to our colleagues, students, and the institutions that supported us throughout the writing of this book. We also extend our thanks to the numerous herbalists, pharmacists, and researchers whose work has helped shape this comprehensive text.

We invite readers to immerse themselves in the world of herbal drug technology, and we hope that this book will inspire future generations to continue exploring the vast potential of medicinal plants in healthcare.

Prof. Y. Rajendra Prasad

Dr. L. Surendra Babu

Dr. Busi Sunil Kumar

Contents

- 2.3.1 Dietary supplements
- 2.3.2 Functional foods
- 2.3.3 Medical foods

2.4 Health Benefits of Nutraceuticals

- 2.4.1 Role in managing chronic diseases:

  - 2.4.1.1 Diabetes
  - 2.4.1.2 Cardiovascular diseases
  - 2.4.1.3 Cancer
  - 2.4.1.4 Gastrointestinal disorders

2.5 Study of Herbs as Health Foods

- 2.5.1 **Alfalfa** – Rich source of vitamins and minerals
- 2.5.2 **Chicory** – Digestive health benefits
- 2.5.3 **Ginger** – Anti-inflammatory properties
- 2.5.4 **Fenugreek** – Anti-diabetic effects
- 2.5.5 **Garlic** – Cardiovascular benefits
- 2.5.6 **Honey** – Antioxidant and antimicrobial properties
- 2.5.7 **Amla** – Rich in Vitamin C
- 2.5.8 **Ginseng** – Adaptogenic herb
- 2.5.9 **Ashwagandha** – Stress-relieving herb
- 2.5.10 **Spirulina** – Protein-rich superfood

2.6 Herbal-Drug and Herb-Food Interactions

- 2.6.1 General introduction to herbal interactions
- 2.6.2 Classification of herb-drug and herb-food interactions
- 2.6.3 Case studies of key herbs and their side effects

  - 2.6.3.1 **Hypericum (St. John's Wort)**
  - 2.6.3.2 **Kava-Kava**
  - 2.6.3.3 **Ginkgo Biloba**
  - 2.6.3.4 **Ginseng**
  - 2.6.3.5 **Garlic**
  - 2.6.3.6 **Pepper**

CONTENTS

CHAPTER I

Herbs as Raw Materials

1.1 Definition of Herb and Herbal Products

Herbs are plants or plant parts valued for their medicinal, culinary, aromatic, or therapeutic properties. The term **herb** refers to any plant with leaves, seeds, or flowers used for flavoring, food, medicine, or fragrance. In botanical terms, herbs are non-woody plants, but in broader applications, they include shrubs and even trees whose leaves or bark are used for medicinal purposes. Herbal products, derived from herbs, encompass a wide range of **preparations** including extracts, powders, tinctures, and dried plant material, formulated to deliver the active components to the human body for various therapeutic benefits. Herbs are rich in **bioactive compounds** such as alkaloids, flavonoids, glycosides, and essential oils, which contribute to their medicinal properties. Examples include **Tulsi (Ocimum sanctum)**, widely used in Indian traditional medicine, and **Ginkgo biloba**, known for its effects on cognitive health.

1.1.1 Definition of Herb

A **herb** is generally defined as a plant or plant part that is used for its flavor, scent, or therapeutic properties. While herbs are most commonly thought of as plants, in medicinal and culinary contexts, they often refer to specific parts of the plant, such as leaves or roots, used to prepare medicines, teas, or foods. **Botanical herbs**, such as basil or mint, are widely recognized in cooking, whereas **medicinal herbs**, like ashwagandha or turmeric, are valued for their healing properties. Historically, herbs have played a pivotal role in medicine, especially within systems such as Ayurveda and Traditional Chinese Medicine (TCM). According to the **World Health Organization (WHO)**, over 80% of the world's population relies on herbal medicine as part of their primary healthcare.

1.1.2 Herbal Medicine vs. Herbal Medicinal Product

The distinction between **herbal medicine** and **herbal medicinal products** lies in their usage and regulation. **Herbal medicine** refers to the use of plants or plant extracts in the treatment of diseases and maintenance of health, often as part of traditional practices such as **Ayurveda** or **Traditional Chinese Medicine (TCM)**. These practices have been used for centuries and are still prevalent today, especially in rural areas and developing countries. **Herbal medicinal products**, on the other hand, are standardized preparations made from herbs that are subjected to regulatory approval and quality control, ensuring consistency in their **therapeutic efficacy**. Herbal medicinal products are often sold as over-the-counter remedies in pharmacies and are regulated to meet safety and efficacy standards. In India, for example, herbal products must comply with the **Drugs and Cosmetics Act (1940)** to ensure their quality and authenticity before they can be marketed.

1.1.3 Herbal Drug Preparation Methods

Herbal drug preparation methods are essential in ensuring that medicinal herbs are processed in a way that preserves their **therapeutic efficacy** and maximizes the extraction of their active compounds. These preparation methods have been used for centuries in **traditional systems of medicine** like Ayurveda, Siddha, and Unani. The methods vary depending on the type of plant material used, the specific active compounds to be extracted, and the intended use of the herbal formulation. The following are some of the most common **herbal drug preparation methods**, each of which plays a vital role in creating effective medicinal products from herbs.

Infusion

An **infusion** is one of the simplest and most widely used methods of preparing herbal remedies, particularly for herbs that contain **volatile** and **water-soluble** compounds. The process involves steeping the herb, typically in dried form, in **hot water** to extract its active constituents. Infusions are most commonly used for **soft plant parts** like leaves, flowers, and stems.

To prepare an infusion, about **5-10 grams** of dried herb or **15-30 grams** of fresh herb are typically added to **200-250 mL** of boiling water. The herb is allowed to steep for **5-10 minutes**, and the liquid is then strained before use. Infusions are often consumed as **herbal teas**, making them a popular method for administering remedies for conditions such as **mild digestive issues, cold symptoms,** or **stress relief.** Herbs like **peppermint** (Mentha piperita) and **chamomile** (Matricaria chamomilla) are frequently prepared as infusions due to their calming and digestive properties.

Decoction

A **decoction** is a more intensive preparation method, primarily used for extracting medicinal compounds from **hard plant materials** such as **roots, bark, seeds,** and **stems.** This method involves **boiling** the plant material in water for an extended period to break down the tough fibers and release the active ingredients into the water.

To prepare a decoction, typically about **10-15 grams** of dried herb are added to **500 mL** of cold water. The mixture is brought to a boil and then simmered for **20-30 minutes**. After simmering, the liquid is strained and used either internally or externally, depending on the condition being treated. Decoctions are often stronger than infusions due to the longer extraction process, and they are used to treat more **chronic conditions** or issues requiring potent therapeutic effects, such as **arthritis, inflammation,** or **respiratory problems.** For example, **ashwagandha** (Withania somnifera) root and **licorice** (Glycyrrhiza glabra) are often prepared as decoctions due to the hard nature of their plant parts and the need to extract their active constituents more effectively.

Maceration

Maceration involves soaking plant materials in a **cold solvent**, usually **water, alcohol**, or **oil**, for an extended period to extract active compounds without applying heat. This method is particularly useful for herbs that contain compounds that are sensitive to heat or volatile oils that might evaporate during boiling. Maceration is often used to prepare **tinctures** and **oils**, where the active constituents are dissolved in a solvent that can be preserved for longer periods.

To prepare a maceration, typically about **100 grams** of dried herb are soaked in **1 liter** of solvent. The mixture is allowed to sit for **several days** to weeks, depending on the strength desired. The process involves periodic stirring to ensure even extraction of the active compounds. Once the maceration process is complete, the mixture is strained to remove the solid plant material, and the liquid extract is stored for use. **Tinctures** prepared through maceration are often more **concentrated** than teas or decoctions and are used in small doses to treat a variety of conditions, such as **stress, digestive disorders,** and **immune support.** For instance, **Echinacea** tinctures are commonly prepared using this method due to the plant's immune-boosting properties.

Percolation

Percolation is a method of preparing **herbal extracts** by allowing a **solvent,** usually alcohol or water, to pass through a bed of finely powdered herbs in a **percolator.** This method is similar to maceration but is quicker and more efficient in extracting active compounds. The percolator ensures that the solvent passes through the herb continuously, extracting the active ingredients as it moves.

To perform percolation, the herbs are first finely powdered and moistened with a small amount of solvent. The herb powder is then packed into the percolator, and more solvent is added slowly. The percolation process typically takes **hours to a few days**, depending on the desired potency. The liquid extract that drips out is collected and stored for medicinal use. This method is particularly useful for making **fluid extracts**, which are highly concentrated herbal products used in small doses. **Ginseng** (Panax ginseng) and **goldenseal** (Hydrastis canadensis) are often prepared using this method because they require efficient extraction of their bioactive compounds, such as ginsenosides and alkaloids.

Powdering

Powdering is another fundamental preparation method in herbal medicine, where herbs are ground into a fine powder that can be used in **capsules, tablets,** or **teas**. The powdered form of the herb allows for ease of use, especially when creating **herbal supplements** that are standardized for specific dosages.

The powdering process begins with **drying** the herb to ensure that no moisture is present, as this could affect the **shelf life** and **potency** of the final product. The dried herb is then ground using a **mortar and pestle** or a **grinder**. The powder is often sifted through fine mesh to ensure consistency in particle size. Herbs like **turmeric** (Curcuma longa) and **ginger** (Zingiber officinale) are frequently used in powdered form because their bioactive compounds, like **curcumin** and **gingerol**, are stable and effective when consumed as powders.

Powdered herbs are commonly added to **capsules**, allowing for **precise dosages** of the herb to be consumed without the need for preparation. They can also be mixed into liquids or foods, making them a versatile option for herbal remedies.

The preparation methods of **herbal drugs** play a crucial role in ensuring that the therapeutic properties of the herbs are effectively extracted and preserved. Techniques such as **infusion, decoction, maceration, percolation,** and **powdering** are carefully chosen based on the nature of the herb and the desired medicinal outcome. These methods have been refined over centuries in traditional medicine and continue to be vital in modern herbal practices, ensuring that herbs are used effectively to promote health and well-being

1.2 Sources of Herbs

The sources of **herbs** play a significant role in determining their **quality, potency,** and **therapeutic efficacy**. Herbs can be classified broadly into two categories based on their source: **wild herbs** and **cultivated herbs**. The origin and environmental conditions under which herbs grow greatly affect their **chemical composition** and **bioactive constituents**. Wild herbs are often considered to have a richer concentration of natural compounds due to the lack of human intervention in their growth process. On the other hand, cultivated herbs provide a controlled environment, which allows for the consistent production of specific phytochemicals and easier standardization.

1.2.1 Wild Herbs vs. Cultivated Herbs

Wild herbs are those that grow naturally in the wild without any human intervention. They thrive in their natural habitats, which can vary from forests and mountains to grasslands and wetlands. Wild herbs are generally more **resilient**, adapting to diverse environmental conditions, which may lead to higher concentrations of **bioactive compounds**. For instance, wild-harvested **Ginseng (Panax ginseng)** is known to have higher levels of **ginsenosides**, the active compounds responsible for its medicinal properties, compared to cultivated varieties. However, wild herbs face challenges such as over-harvesting, leading to **depletion of resources** and **environmental degradation**.

Cultivated herbs, on the other hand, are grown systematically in controlled agricultural settings. This allows for **standardization** of growth conditions such as soil quality, water supply, and use of **organic farming practices**. Cultivation also ensures the availability of herbs throughout the year and reduces the risk of **adulteration** and **contamination**. For example, **Tulsi (Ocimum sanctum)**, a widely used herb in Ayurveda, is cultivated on a large scale in India to meet the demand for both domestic and global markets. Cultivated herbs can also be selectively bred to enhance their **medicinal properties** or resistance to pests and diseases.

Characteristic	Wild Herbs	Cultivated Herbs
Growth Conditions	Grows naturally in wild environments	Cultivated in controlled environments
Biodiversity	High biodiversity, natural selection	Lower biodiversity, human intervention
Availability	Seasonal and unpredictable	Year-round and predictable
Sustainability	More sustainable due to natural regeneration	May require pesticides and fertilizers
Nutritional Value	May be richer in nutrients due to diverse soil	Nutritional value depends on cultivation practices
Harvesting	Harvested in small quantities, challenging	Easier to harvest in bulk

Comparison of Wild Herbs vs Cultivated Herbs: Growth, Sustainability, and Nutritional Aspects

1.2.2 Sourcing Considerations for Herbal Drug Production

Sourcing herbs for **herbal drug production** requires careful consideration of multiple factors to ensure the **purity, efficacy,** and **safety** of the final product. The first and most important aspect is the **geographical location** of the herb's origin. The **soil quality, climatic conditions,** and **altitude** at which a herb is grown can significantly influence its chemical composition. For example, **Saffron (Crocus sativus)** sourced from Kashmir is considered of higher quality due to the region's specific environmental conditions.

The second consideration is whether the herb is **wild-harvested** or **cultivated.** While wild-harvested herbs may have stronger medicinal properties, cultivated herbs provide more **consistency** in terms of supply and **quality control.** It's also essential to ensure that the herbs are sourced ethically, particularly when wild-harvesting, to prevent **over-exploitation** and ensure **sustainability.** Moreover, the use of **pesticides, herbicides,** or chemical fertilizers in cultivated herbs must be carefully monitored, as residues can affect the **safety** of herbal products.

1.3 Selection, Identification, and Authentication of Herbal Materials

The **selection, identification, and authentication** of herbal materials are critical processes in ensuring the safety, efficacy, and consistency of **herbal medicines.** Proper identification of herbs is essential to avoid contamination, adulteration, or misidentification, which can lead to therapeutic failure or harmful effects. Various methods are used to identify herbs based on their **botanical, morphological,** and **chemical** characteristics. These methods ensure that the correct herb is selected, and its medicinal properties are preserved for therapeutic use.

1.3.1 Methods of Herb Identification (Botanical, Morphological, Chemical)

The identification of herbal materials involves using a combination of methods that include **botanical, morphological,** and **chemical techniques.** Each method has its specific focus and importance, and they are often used together to confirm the identity and quality of the herbs.

Botanical Identification

Botanical identification is one of the first and most fundamental steps in recognizing a herb. It relies on the study of **taxonomic characteristics** and **nomenclature** to identify the plant species accurately. The **taxonomy** of a plant involves classifying it into a **family, genus,** and **species.** The botanical name of a plant follows the **binomial nomenclature** system, which provides a universal standard to ensure clarity in the identification process.

Botanical identification involves observing the overall characteristics of the plant, including its growth patterns, habitat, and flowering seasons. Botanists typically use **herbarium specimens, botanical keys,** and **reference texts** to compare unknown plants with known species. This method is especially useful for identifying medicinal plants in their **natural environments** and for ensuring that only the correct species is harvested for medicinal purposes. For example, the **botanical family Rutaceae** includes the well-known medicinal plant **Aegle marmelos** (Bael), which is easily identifiable through botanical classification based on its **leaves, fruits, and flowers.**

Morphological Identification

Morphological identification focuses on the **physical appearance** and **external features** of a plant. This method is useful for identifying whole or **unprocessed herbs,** especially in traditional medicine, where visual cues are relied upon to recognize specific plants. Morphological identification studies the **shape, size, color, texture,** and **structural characteristics** of the plant parts, such as the leaves, stems, roots, flowers, and seeds.

For example, the leaves of **Azadirachta indica** (Neem) are **serrated, elongated,** and **opposite,** making it easy to distinguish from other plants. Similarly, the characteristic yellow-orange color and **tuberous root** of **Curcuma longa** (Turmeric) make it identifiable through simple morphological examination. In the case of **Zingiber officinale** (Ginger), the **knobby rhizomes** with a pungent smell and taste are key markers for identification.

Morphological features can vary based on the plant's **maturity** or **environment**, so it is important to compare the observed plant with standard references. This method is often the first step in identifying raw herbal materials before proceeding to more sophisticated testing methods.

Visual Guide to Morphological Identification in Herbal Medicine

Chemical Identification

Chemical identification is a more precise method used to authenticate herbs by analyzing their **chemical composition**. This method is particularly important when herbs need to be processed into **medicinal extracts, tinctures**, or **capsules**, as the active compounds must be verified for **therapeutic efficacy. Phytochemical analysis** is carried out to detect the presence of specific **bioactive compounds** such as **alkaloids, flavonoids, terpenoids, glycosides**, and **polyphenols**, which are responsible for the medicinal properties of the herb.

Advanced techniques such as **Thin-Layer Chromatography (TLC), High-Performance Liquid Chromatography (HPLC)**, and **Gas Chromatography-Mass Spectrometry (GC-MS)** are commonly used for chemical identification. These methods allow for the separation, detection, and quantification of the active compounds in an herbal sample. For example, **Curcumin**, the main bioactive compound in **Turmeric** (Curcuma longa), can be detected using **HPLC**, confirming the herb's identity and ensuring its quality for medicinal use.

In TLC, plant extracts are applied to a **silica-coated plate** and developed using a solvent, separating the compounds into distinct bands. The position and color of these bands are compared with reference standards to confirm the identity of the herb. In HPLC, the herbal extract is injected into a chromatographic column, and the active compounds are detected based on their retention time and spectral properties.

Chemical fingerprinting is another method where the entire chemical profile of a herb is compared with a reference standard to ensure its authenticity. This is particularly useful in differentiating between similar species or detecting **adulterants** or **substitutes** in herbal preparations. For instance, **Panax ginseng** and its related species, **Panax quinquefolius**, can be differentiated by their specific **ginsenoside** profiles using HPLC.

Chemical identification methods are critical not only for confirming the identity of the herb but also for ensuring its **purity, potency**, and **safety** for medicinal use. It is especially valuable in modern herbal medicine, where **standardization** and **quality control** are required for regulatory compliance.

The **selection, identification**, and **authentication** of herbal materials require a combination of **botanical, morphological**, and **chemical methods** to ensure that the correct herb is used and that it is free from adulteration or contamination. Botanical methods provide a broad classification of the herb, while morphological methods offer insight into its physical features. Chemical identification allows for the precise analysis of its active constituents, ensuring that the herb has the required therapeutic properties. These methods collectively ensure the efficacy and safety of herbal medicines, playing a crucial role in both traditional and modern systems of herbal medicine.

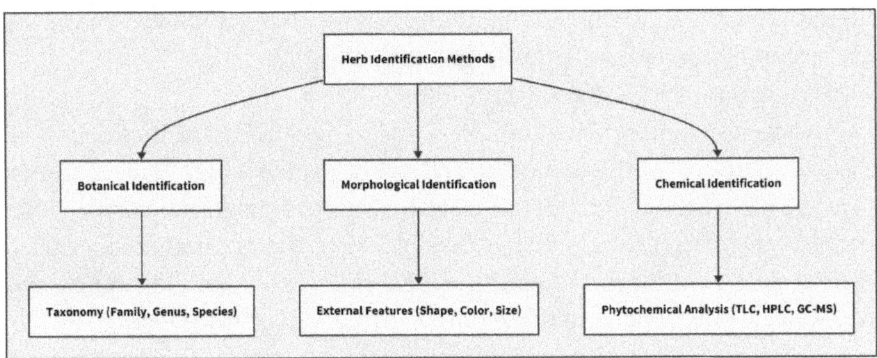

Overview of Herb Identification Methods

1.3.2 Techniques for Authentication of Raw Materials

Authentication of raw materials in herbal medicine is a critical step in ensuring the **quality, safety,** and **efficacy** of the final product. The use of authentic, uncontaminated herbs is essential to avoid therapeutic failures and prevent adverse effects that may arise from the use of **misidentified** or **adulterated materials.** Several techniques have been developed to authenticate raw herbal materials, utilizing **macroscopic, microscopic, phytochemical, chromatographic,** and **molecular** methods. Each technique serves a unique role in verifying the identity and quality of the raw material before it is processed into **herbal drugs.**

Macroscopic Techniques

Macroscopic authentication involves the visual examination of the **external characteristics** of the raw material. This method is often the first line of defense in authenticating herbs in their **whole** or **crude form.** Macroscopic techniques focus on the **physical attributes** of the plant parts, such as **size, shape, color, texture,** and **fragrance.**

For example, the leaves of **Ocimum sanctum** (Holy Basil) have an easily identifiable **oval shape, toothed edges,** and a distinct **aromatic odor.** The root of **Withania somnifera** (Ashwagandha) is characterized by its **thick, fleshy structure** and a pale yellow color. These visual cues help identify and differentiate herbs from **adulterants** or **substitutes**. Macroscopic examination also includes observing any signs of **damage, contamination,** or **fungal growth** that could affect the quality of the herb.

Although macroscopic techniques are useful for quick identification, they may not always be reliable, especially for powdered or processed herbs. Therefore, more advanced methods are often employed alongside macroscopic inspection for thorough authentication.

Microscopic Techniques

Microscopic authentication involves a detailed examination of the **cellular structure** of the plant material under a **microscope**. This technique is especially useful for identifying herbs in **powdered form**, where macroscopic features are no longer visible. Microscopic analysis focuses on **cellular patterns**, such as **stomata, trichomes, vessels, fibers,** and **calcium oxalate crystals**, which are often unique to specific plant species.

For example, the powdered root of **Curcuma longa** (Turmeric) can be identified microscopically by the presence of **starch granules** and **oil cells** that are characteristic of the plant. Similarly, the **unicellular trichomes** on the leaves of **Mentha piperita** (Peppermint) are easily distinguishable under a microscope, aiding in its authentication.

Microscopic techniques also help detect **foreign matter** or **adulterants** that may have been mixed with the raw material. For instance, the detection of **foreign starch granules** or **non-native trichomes** could indicate contamination or intentional substitution of the herb. Microscopy is particularly important in the quality control of **powdered herbs** and **granular formulations**, ensuring that the material is pure and consistent with its intended identity.

Phytochemical Techniques

Phytochemical authentication involves the analysis of the **bioactive compounds** or **chemical markers** that are unique to a particular herb. These compounds, which include **alkaloids, flavonoids, terpenoids, glycosides,** and **polyphenols,** are responsible for the medicinal properties of the plant. **Phytochemical screening** tests are often conducted to detect the presence or absence of these markers, providing a chemical fingerprint for the herb.

Various chemical tests are used in phytochemical analysis. For example, the **Dragendorff's reagent** is used to detect the presence of **alkaloids** in herbs like **Rauwolfia serpentina** (Indian Snakeroot). The **Shinoda test** is used to confirm the presence of **flavonoids** in plants such as **Camellia sinensis** (Green Tea). These simple colorimetric or precipitation reactions help identify key compounds and confirm the authenticity of the herb.

Phytochemical authentication is particularly important for ensuring that **active constituents** are present in the correct concentration, especially for herbs used in standardized herbal formulations. It also aids in identifying **adulterants** that may lack the expected phytochemical profile.

Chromatographic Techniques

Chromatographic techniques are widely used for the authentication of herbal raw materials due to their precision in separating and analyzing complex **chemical mixtures**. Techniques such as **Thin-Layer Chromatography (TLC)**, **High-Performance Liquid Chromatography (HPLC)**, and **Gas Chromatography-Mass Spectrometry (GC-MS)** are commonly used to obtain a **chemical fingerprint** of the herb and compare it with a reference standard.

In **TLC**, the herbal extract is applied to a thin layer of silica gel, and the plate is developed using a solvent. The separation of compounds produces distinct bands or spots on the plate, which are then visualized under **UV light** or after applying chemical reagents. The resulting **TLC profile** is compared with standard profiles of the herb, helping to confirm its authenticity. TLC is frequently used for detecting **secondary metabolites** like **flavonoids** and **alkaloids**.

HPLC provides a more detailed analysis, where the herbal extract is passed through a column under high pressure, separating the compounds based on their **polarity** and **molecular weight**. The separated compounds are then detected using a **UV detector** or **mass spectrometer**. HPLC is particularly useful for herbs with complex mixtures of bioactive compounds, such as **Ginseng** (Panax ginseng) or **Ginkgo biloba**, where it is important to quantify the active constituents like **ginsenosides** or **flavonol glycosides**.

GC-MS is used for herbs containing **volatile oils** and other compounds that can be vaporized. In this method, the herbal sample is heated, and the vaporized compounds are separated in the gas phase and analyzed by a mass spectrometer. GC-MS is commonly used for herbs like **Lavandula angustifolia** (Lavender) and **Mentha piperita** (Peppermint), where the volatile oil profile is a key marker of quality.

Chromatographic techniques are essential for detecting **adulteration**, identifying **active compounds**, and ensuring the **purity** of herbal materials, especially in commercial formulations.

Molecular Techniques

Molecular techniques are the most advanced methods of herbal authentication and involve the analysis of the plant's **genetic material (DNA)**. **DNA barcoding** and **polymerase chain reaction (PCR)** are commonly used molecular methods for identifying and authenticating plant species.

In **DNA barcoding**, a short DNA sequence from a specific region of the plant genome, such as the **rbcL** or **ITS region**, is amplified using PCR. This sequence is then compared with a reference database of known plant species to confirm the identity of the herb. DNA barcoding is particularly useful in differentiating between closely related species or detecting **adulterants** that may not be distinguishable through traditional methods.

For example, DNA barcoding can easily differentiate between **Panax ginseng** and the adulterant **Panax quinquefolius**, which may appear similar morphologically. Similarly, molecular techniques can detect the presence of **non-native species** or substitutes in **multi-herb formulations**, ensuring that the correct species are used.

Molecular authentication is highly reliable and provides **unambiguous identification**, making it a critical tool in modern herbal quality control, particularly in ensuring **genetic purity**.

The **authentication of raw materials** in herbal medicine relies on a combination of **macroscopic, microscopic, phytochemical, chromatographic**, and **molecular techniques** to ensure the **quality, purity**, and **safety** of the herbs used in medicinal formulations. Each technique offers unique advantages, and when used together, they provide a comprehensive approach to confirming the identity of herbal materials and detecting any **adulteration** or **contamination**. Accurate authentication is essential for maintaining the efficacy of herbal medicines and upholding the standards of traditional and modern herbal practices.

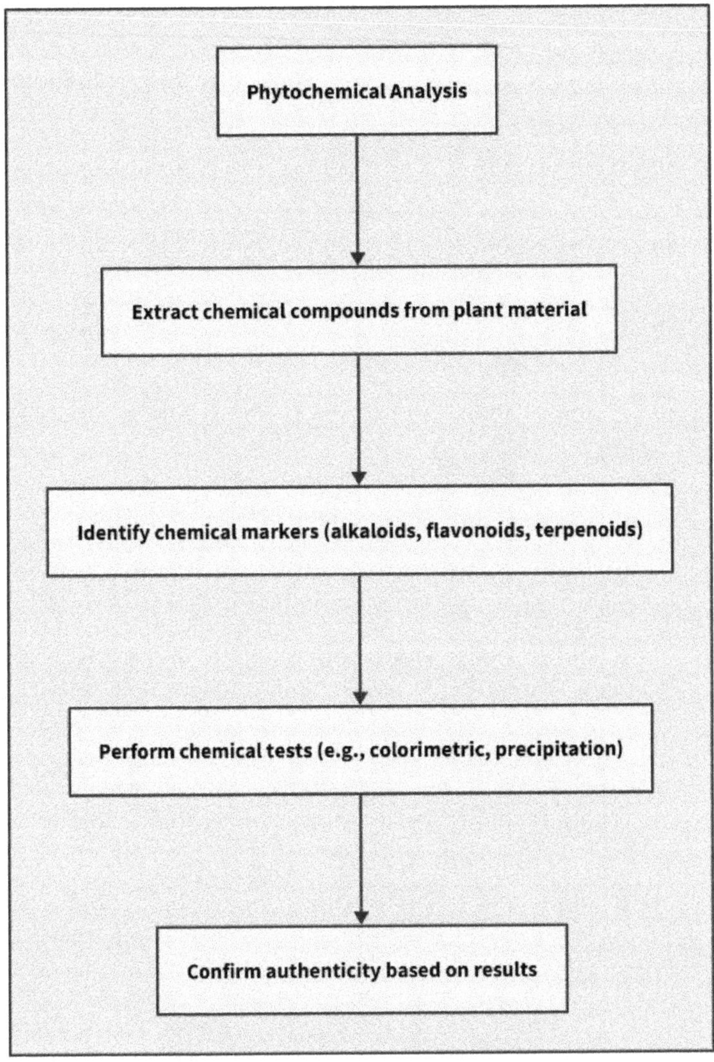

Phytochemical Analysis for Authentication

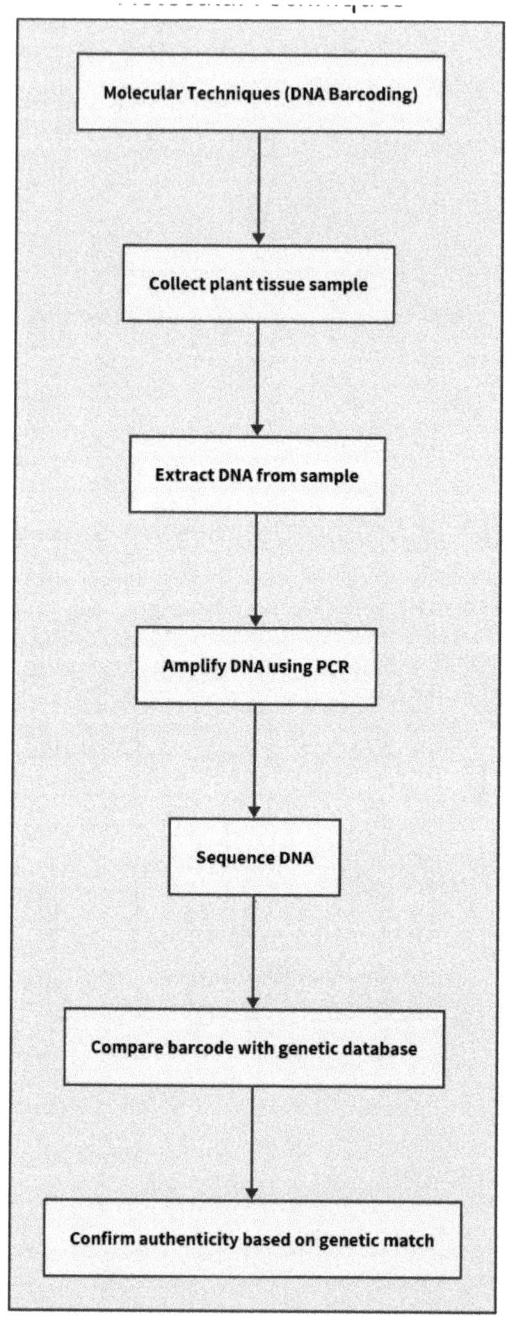

DNA barcoding, used for authenticating raw herbal materials

1.3.3 Common Adulterations and Their Detection

Adulteration of herbal materials is a significant concern in both traditional and modern herbal medicine practices. It refers to the deliberate or accidental inclusion of **inferior** or **substitute materials**, non-therapeutic parts of a plant, or contaminants in herbal products. Adulteration can reduce the **efficacy** of the herbal product and may even pose serious **health risks** to consumers. Adulterants are often introduced due to **economic reasons**, such as scarcity of the authentic material or the desire to reduce production costs. Identifying and detecting adulteration is therefore crucial for ensuring the **quality, safety,** and **therapeutic value** of herbal medicines. Several methods are employed to detect adulteration in herbal materials, including **botanical, microscopic, phytochemical, chromatographic,** and **molecular techniques.**

Common Types of Adulteration

1. **Substitution with Similar-Looking Plants**: One of the most frequent forms of adulteration occurs when a less expensive or more readily available plant that looks similar to the desired herb is used as a substitute. For example, **Curcuma zedoaria** (white turmeric) is sometimes substituted for **Curcuma longa** (true turmeric), despite the former having inferior medicinal properties. Such substitutions can significantly alter the **therapeutic efficacy** of the final product.

2. **Addition of Inferior Plant Parts**: Another common practice involves the addition of **non-therapeutic parts** of the same plant. For instance, the stems or leaves of **Withania somnifera** (Ashwagandha) may be added to its root powder, even though the root is the primary medicinal part with well-documented benefits. This adulteration lowers the overall potency of the herb.

3. **Contamination with Foreign Substances**: Herbal products may also be contaminated with **foreign materials** such as **sand, soil, metal shavings,** or **synthetic chemicals** to increase weight. For example, the addition of **yellow dyes** to **turmeric powder** to enhance its appearance is a known issue in the market.

4. **Mixing with Synthetic Compounds**: In some cases, herbal materials may be adulterated with **synthetic compounds** to enhance their effects or mimic the appearance of authentic products. An example is the addition of **synthetic curcumin** to turmeric powder, which compromises

the natural purity of the herb.

5. **Adulteration with Non-native Species:** Some herbs are adulterated with related species that are not native to the region where the herb is traditionally grown. For example, **Panax quinquefolius** (American ginseng) is often substituted for **Panax ginseng** (Asian ginseng), despite differences in their therapeutic properties.

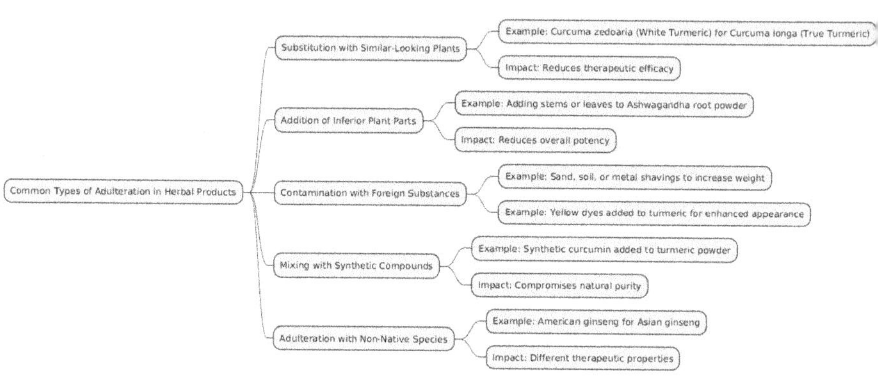

Detection Methods

Macroscopic and Organoleptic Methods

Macroscopic examination and **organoleptic evaluation** are the first line of defense against adulteration. These methods rely on **visual inspection, touch, smell,** and **taste** to detect abnormalities in the herbal material.

- **Macroscopic inspection:** The size, shape, color, and texture of the plant material are compared with the standard characteristics of the authentic herb. For example, authentic **Piper nigrum** (black pepper) has a wrinkled, dark brown appearance, while an adulterated sample may appear smoother or have a different color.
- **Organoleptic evaluation:** This involves assessing the **taste** and **aroma** of the herb. Authentic **Mentha piperita** (peppermint) leaves have a strong, characteristic minty smell, which can be used to detect the presence of substitutes that lack this distinct aroma.

These methods are useful for detecting **gross adulteration** but are less effective when dealing with powdered or highly processed materials.

Microscopic Techniques

Microscopic examination is a powerful tool for detecting adulteration in **powdered herbs** or materials where macroscopic inspection is insufficient. It involves the observation of **cellular structures**, such as **epidermal cells, stomata, trichomes**, and **calcium oxalate crystals**, which are often species-specific.

- **Starch grains:** For example, the microscopic examination of turmeric powder can reveal the presence of foreign starch grains that are not characteristic of **Curcuma longa.** This would indicate adulteration with other plant parts or unrelated materials.
- **Trichomes and fibers:** Similarly, the presence of distinct **unicellular trichomes** in **peppermint** (Mentha piperita) can help confirm the identity of the herb and detect adulteration with other mint species.

Microscopic analysis can also reveal **inorganic impurities** such as sand or silica, which might have been added to increase the weight of the product.

Phytochemical Tests

Phytochemical screening is used to detect the presence of specific **bioactive compounds** or **chemical markers** that are unique to the authentic herb. These tests often involve simple **colorimetric reactions** or **precipitation tests.**

- **Alkaloid tests:** For example, the presence of **alkaloids** in **Rauwolfia serpentina** (Indian Snakeroot) can be confirmed using **Dragendorff's reagent**, which causes a characteristic orange precipitate in the presence of alkaloids. The absence of this reaction would suggest adulteration.
- **Flavonoid tests:** Similarly, the **Shinoda test** is used to detect **flavonoids** in herbs like **Chamomile** (Matricaria chamomilla). A change in color indicates the presence of flavonoids, and its absence may suggest adulteration or substitution with non-flavonoid-containing herbs.

These qualitative phytochemical tests provide a quick and inexpensive method for screening raw materials, although they are not as precise as chromatographic methods.

Chromatographic Techniques

Chromatographic techniques such as **Thin-Layer Chromatography (TLC)** and **High-Performance Liquid Chromatography (HPLC)** are among the most effective methods for detecting adulteration. These methods allow for the **separation** and **identification** of individual chemical constituents based on their **polarity, molecular size**, and **chemical properties**.

- **TLC:** In **TLC**, herbal extracts are applied to a silica-coated plate, and the components are separated based on their interaction with a solvent. Each compound produces a distinct spot, which can be compared to a reference standard for the authentic herb. For example, in TLC, **Curcuma longa** (Turmeric) produces a distinct yellow spot for **curcumin**, while the absence or alteration of this spot indicates adulteration.
- **HPLC:** **HPLC** is even more precise, allowing for the quantification of bioactive compounds. For example, HPLC is commonly used to quantify **ginsenosides** in **Panax ginseng**. A lower concentration of these compounds could indicate substitution with an inferior species or the use of non-therapeutic parts.

These techniques are highly reliable and are widely used in the **quality control** of herbal products to detect both **qualitative** and **quantitative** deviations from the authentic herb profile.

Molecular Techniques

Molecular techniques such as **DNA barcoding** and **Polymerase Chain Reaction (PCR)** are the most advanced methods for detecting adulteration, especially when dealing with closely related species or highly processed materials. These methods analyze the **genetic material** of the plant to ensure species authenticity.

- **DNA barcoding:** This method involves extracting and amplifying a specific region of the plant's DNA, such as the **rbcL** or **ITS region**, which is unique to each species. The resulting DNA sequence is then compared with a reference database. DNA barcoding is particularly useful for detecting adulteration in multi-herb formulations or powdered herbs, where traditional methods may not be effective. For instance, it can easily distinguish between **Panax ginseng** and **Panax quinquefolius**, which are often substituted for each other.

- **PCR**: PCR-based methods can detect the presence of **non-native species** or **contaminants** in herbal formulations. These techniques are highly accurate and provide definitive results regarding the species composition of the product.

Adulteration of herbal materials remains a challenge in the herbal medicine industry, but various techniques are available to detect and prevent it. Macroscopic and microscopic methods provide initial insights, while phytochemical tests offer a quick way to check for the presence of key compounds. More advanced chromatographic and molecular techniques are essential for precise identification and ensuring the authenticity, purity, and safety of herbal products. Together, these techniques safeguard consumers from the risks associated with adulterated herbal materials and help maintain the therapeutic efficacy of herbal medicines.

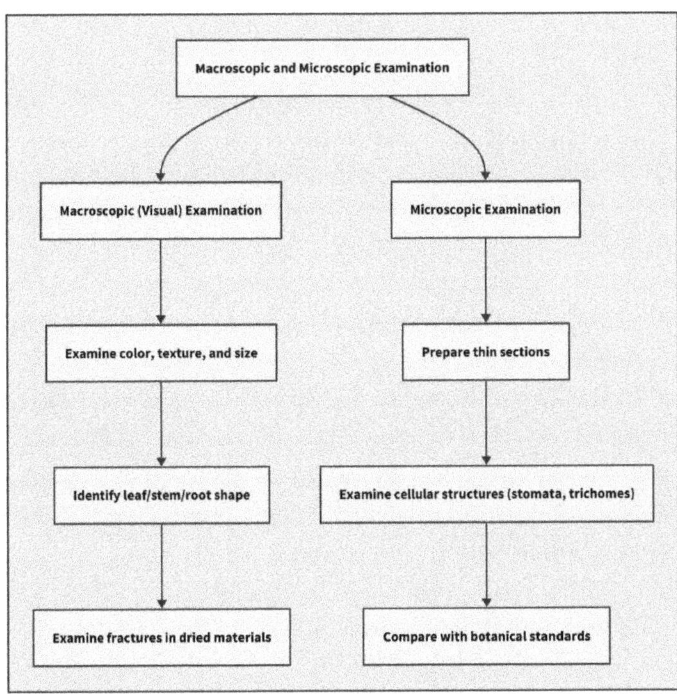

Flowchart: Macroscopic and Microscopic Examination

1.4 Processing of Herbal Raw Materials

Proper **processing of herbal raw materials** is essential for preserving the **medicinal properties** of herbs. The way herbs are processed after harvesting has a significant impact on the **quality, potency,** and **shelf life** of the final herbal product. One of the most important steps in processing herbs is **drying,** which helps reduce the moisture content of the plant material to prevent **microbial growth** and **spoilage.** Different drying methods are used depending on the type of herb and the specific compounds that need to be preserved. These methods include **air drying, shade drying,** and **oven drying,** each with its advantages and disadvantages.

1.4.1 Drying Methods (Air Drying, Shade Drying, Oven Drying)

The drying of herbal raw materials is a crucial step in ensuring that the herbs retain their **active compounds** and are protected from **degradation** due to excess moisture. Proper drying techniques help maintain the **color, aroma,** and **therapeutic properties** of the herbs. The choice of drying method depends on the type of herb being processed, its **moisture content,** and the **sensitivity** of its active compounds to **heat** and **light.**

Air Drying

Air drying, also known as **natural drying,** is one of the simplest and most traditional methods of drying herbs. In this method, herbs are spread out in **well-ventilated areas** where natural airflow helps to evaporate the moisture from the plant material. This method is ideal for herbs that are not too sensitive to heat or light exposure and that have **moderate moisture content.**

To air dry herbs, the plant material is typically **spread out in thin layers** on clean surfaces such as **drying racks, sheets,** or **paper towels.** The herbs are placed in areas with **good air circulation** but protected from direct sunlight to prevent the degradation of **volatile oils** and **sensitive compounds.** The drying time can vary from **several days to a few weeks,** depending on the size of the herb and environmental factors like **temperature** and **humidity.**

Air drying is particularly useful for **leaves, flowers,** and **stems** that are delicate and do not require intense heat for preservation. For instance, **basil** (Ocimum basilicum), **peppermint** (Mentha piperita), and **chamomile** (Matricaria chamomilla) are often air-dried to retain their essential oils and therapeutic properties.

However, this method can be slow and may not be suitable for herbs with high moisture content or for situations where rapid drying is needed to prevent **mold growth.** The success of air drying also depends heavily on

weather conditions; high humidity can hinder the drying process, making the herbs more susceptible to spoilage.

Shade Drying

Shade drying is a variation of air drying, where the herbs are dried in a **shaded area** to protect them from **direct sunlight**. This method is particularly important for herbs that contain **light-sensitive compounds** or **volatile oils** that can degrade when exposed to UV rays.

In shade drying, the herbs are spread out in a similar manner to air drying, but they are placed in areas that are shielded from the sun. The herbs may be dried in **open-air rooms, barns,** or **covered porches.** This method ensures that the herbs dry slowly at **ambient temperatures**, which helps preserve their **color, flavor,** and **medicinal properties.**

Shade drying is commonly used for herbs like **Turmeric** (Curcuma longa) and **Ashwagandha** (Withania somnifera) root, which contain bioactive compounds such as **curcumin** and **withanolides** that are sensitive to heat and light. Additionally, shade drying is the preferred method for drying **delicate flowers** such as **rose petals** and **calendula**, where preserving the natural pigments and essential oils is critical for their medicinal and cosmetic uses.

While shade drying helps preserve the quality of herbs, it can be slower than other methods, especially in humid environments. As with air drying, proper ventilation is necessary to prevent mold formation, and drying times can vary depending on the herb and environmental factors.

Oven Drying

Oven drying is a more controlled method that uses a **low-temperature oven** to remove moisture from herbs. This method is particularly useful when a faster drying process is required or when environmental conditions (such as high humidity) are not suitable for air or shade drying. Oven drying provides the advantage of consistent and **controlled heat**, which allows for more **uniform drying** of the herbs.

To oven dry herbs, they are spread out in a single layer on **baking trays** or **racks** and placed in an oven set to a low temperature, typically between **30-50°C (86-122°F)**. The oven door is often left slightly open to allow moisture to escape, and the herbs are checked periodically to ensure they do not become too dry or lose their potency due to excessive heat.

This method is commonly used for herbs with **higher moisture content** or **thicker plant parts**, such as **roots, barks,** and **seeds.** For example, **Ginger** (Zingiber officinale) and **Licorice** (Glycyrrhiza glabra) roots are often dried using this method to preserve their active constituents, such as **gingerol** and **glycyrrhizin**, while preventing microbial growth.

Oven drying offers the advantage of faster drying times, usually completed within **a few hours** to **a day**, depending on the herb. However, care must be taken to use low temperatures, as high heat can degrade sensitive compounds, reducing the herb's therapeutic value. For instance, excessive heat can cause the **volatile oils** in **lavender** (Lavandula angustifolia) to evaporate, diminishing its medicinal effects.

The choice of drying method is crucial for maintaining the **quality, potency,** and **efficacy** of herbal raw materials. **Air drying** and **shade drying** are preferred for more delicate herbs and those sensitive to heat or light, while **oven drying** is suited for herbs with higher moisture content that require faster drying. Each method has its own benefits and limitations, and the selection of the appropriate method depends on the type of herb, the environmental conditions, and the desired outcome in terms of **herbal quality.** By using the right drying method, herbal practitioners can ensure that the herbs retain their medicinal properties and are suitable for further processing into **herbal formulations.**

1.4.2 Grinding, Pulverization, and Extraction Techniques

The **processing of herbal raw materials** involves several critical steps to ensure that the **medicinal compounds** in herbs are efficiently extracted and preserved. Among these steps, **grinding, pulverization,** and **extraction** play a pivotal role in preparing the herbs for various formulations, such as **powders, capsules, tinctures,** and **extracts.** These processes aim to increase the surface area of the herbs, allowing for better extraction of their active compounds and enhancing the **bioavailability** of these compounds in the final product. Each method is chosen based on the type of herb, the desired formulation, and the target compounds.

Grinding

Grinding is one of the fundamental processes used in herbal medicine preparation, where raw plant materials are reduced into smaller particles or powders. This step is essential for improving the **efficiency** of subsequent extraction processes, as it increases the surface area of the herb, allowing solvents to penetrate more effectively. Grinding is particularly important for preparing **herbal powders** used in **capsules, teas,** and **topical applications.**

To achieve the desired particle size, herbal materials such as **roots, stems, barks,** or **seeds** are typically dried first and then ground using equipment such as **mortar and pestle, mechanical grinders,** or **mills.** The choice of equipment depends on the hardness of the material and the desired fineness of the final product.

- For instance, **ginger** (Zingiber officinale) is often ground into a fine powder after drying, which is used in various herbal formulations for its **anti-inflammatory** and **digestive** properties.
- **Turmeric** (Curcuma longa) is another herb commonly ground into a fine powder to be used in both dietary and medicinal products, where the particle size of the powder can affect the **bioavailability** of **curcumin,** its primary active compound.

The grinding process must be carried out carefully to prevent **overheating,** which can degrade heat-sensitive compounds, such as **volatile oils** in herbs like **peppermint** (Mentha piperita). The heat generated during grinding can lead to a loss of efficacy, so low-speed or **cold grinding** techniques are sometimes used to preserve these delicate compounds.

Pulverization

Pulverization is the next level of grinding, where herbs are reduced to an even finer consistency than regular grinding. This technique is used when very fine powders are required for specialized formulations. Pulverization often involves the use of **high-speed grinders** or **pulverizers** that can break down the herbal material into **micro-particles** or **nano-particles.**

Pulverization is particularly useful when preparing **standardized herbal formulations** that require precise control over particle size, ensuring uniformity and **homogeneity** in the final product. The fine powder produced by pulverization has enhanced **solubility** and **bioavailability,** making it suitable for formulations such as **herbal capsules, tablets,** and **topical creams.**

- **Ashwagandha** (Withania somnifera) root powder, for example, may be pulverized to produce a fine powder used in **capsule formulations** that support **stress relief** and **immune function.**
- Similarly, **licorice** (Glycyrrhiza glabra) root is often pulverized into a very fine powder to ensure that its **glycyrrhizin** content is consistent across formulations used for **digestive health** and **respiratory support.**

The main advantage of pulverization is the increased **surface area** and **improved dispersion** of the herb, which allows for more efficient extraction of active compounds during the **extraction** process.

Extraction Techniques

Extraction is the process of removing **bioactive compounds** from herbal raw materials using various solvents or mechanical methods. The purpose of extraction is to isolate the active constituents of the plant, which can then be concentrated and used in medicinal formulations. Several extraction techniques are employed depending on the nature of the herb, the target compounds, and the desired end product.

1. Maceration

Maceration is one of the oldest and simplest extraction techniques, where the herbal material is soaked in a solvent (typically **water, alcohol, or oil**) for an extended period, allowing the **soluble compounds** to diffuse into the solvent. This method is commonly used for herbs that contain compounds that are sensitive to heat, such as **volatile oils** or **flavonoids**.

To macerate, about **100 grams** of dried herb is placed in **1 liter** of solvent, and the mixture is allowed to sit for **several days** or even weeks, depending on the desired strength of the extract. Periodic stirring ensures that the active compounds are thoroughly extracted. After the extraction period, the liquid is strained, and the herb is discarded.

- **Echinacea** tinctures, commonly used to support the **immune system**, are prepared using maceration, where the herb is soaked in alcohol to extract the active **alkamides** and **polysaccharides**.

Maceration is simple but time-consuming, and the resulting extract may not be as concentrated as those obtained through more advanced techniques.

2. Percolation

Percolation is a more efficient extraction method than maceration. In percolation, the herbal material is packed into a **percolator**, and the solvent is allowed to drip through the herb continuously. This process ensures that fresh solvent is constantly in contact with the herb, resulting in faster and more complete extraction of active compounds.

Percolation is often used for making **fluid extracts**, where the herb-to-solvent ratio is tightly controlled to produce a highly concentrated extract. The process is usually completed within **hours to days**, depending on the herb and solvent used.

- **Ginseng** (Panax ginseng) and **goldenseal** (Hydrastis canadensis) are often extracted using percolation to ensure maximum extraction of **ginsenosides** and **alkaloids**, respectively.

3. Decoction

Decoction is an extraction method used for **hard plant materials,** such as **roots, barks,** or **seeds,** where boiling is required to break down the fibrous structures and release the active compounds. In decoction, the herb is simmered in water for an extended period, usually **20-30 minutes,** to extract the medicinal properties.

Decoctions are commonly used in **traditional herbal medicine,** especially in the preparation of **herbal teas** and **tonics.** For example, **astragalus** (Astragalus membranaceus) root is often decocted to create an immune-boosting tea, and **ginger** root is boiled to extract its **anti-inflammatory** and **digestive** compounds.

Decoction is particularly effective for extracting **water-soluble compounds,** but it may not be suitable for herbs with **heat-sensitive** components, as prolonged boiling can degrade these compounds.

4. Soxhlet Extraction

Soxhlet extraction is an advanced technique used for **continuous extraction** of compounds from herbs using a solvent that is continuously cycled through the herb material. In this method, the solvent is heated to its boiling point and condenses onto the herbal material, dissolving the active compounds, which are then collected in a separate chamber. This process is repeated multiple times, resulting in a highly concentrated extract.

Soxhlet extraction is particularly useful for **lipophilic compounds** (fat-soluble) found in herbs like **St. John's wort** (Hypericum perforatum), where the active **hypericin** is extracted into an alcohol-based solvent.

5. Supercritical Fluid Extraction

Supercritical fluid extraction (SFE) is a modern technique that uses **supercritical carbon dioxide (CO_2)** as the extraction solvent. This method is highly efficient for extracting **thermally sensitive compounds** because it does not require high temperatures. CO_2 is maintained at a temperature and pressure where it acts as both a gas and a liquid, allowing it to penetrate the herbal material and dissolve active compounds.

SFE is used to extract **essential oils** and other volatile compounds from herbs, such as **lavender** and **peppermint**. This technique is favored for its ability to produce **high-purity extracts** without the use of harsh chemicals.

The processes of **grinding, pulverization, and extraction** are essential in ensuring that the **medicinal properties** of herbal raw materials are maximized. **Grinding** and **pulverization** allow for increased surface area, which enhances the efficiency of **extraction** methods such as **maceration, percolation, decoction,** and **advanced techniques** like **Soxhlet extraction** and **supercritical fluid extraction.** By choosing the appropriate techniques based on the properties of the herb and the desired outcome, practitioners can ensure that the herbal preparations are **potent, pure,** and **therapeutically effective.**

1.4.3 Influence of Processing on Herbal Efficacy

The **efficacy** of herbal medicines is significantly influenced by the methods used to process the raw materials. Processing plays a crucial role in preserving the **bioactive compounds**, enhancing their **bioavailability**, and reducing **toxicity** or undesirable effects. However, improper processing can lead to the degradation of key **phytochemicals**, resulting in reduced therapeutic value or even potential harm. Various stages of processing, including **drying, grinding, pulverization,** and **extraction**, can either preserve or diminish the herb's medicinal properties depending on how they are applied. Understanding the **impact** of each stage of processing is vital to ensuring that herbs retain their potency and efficacy.

1. Drying

The drying process plays a pivotal role in maintaining the **stability** and **potency** of herbs by removing excess moisture, which can lead to microbial growth and spoilage. However, the **method of drying** can greatly affect the **active constituents** of the herb. For example, herbs rich in **volatile oils,** such as **peppermint** (Mentha piperita), can lose a significant portion of their medicinal properties if exposed to excessive heat or direct sunlight during drying.

- **Air drying** and **shade drying** help preserve **heat-sensitive compounds** such as essential oils and flavonoids. For example, **chamomile** (Matricaria chamomilla) retains its **anti-inflammatory** and **calming properties** when dried in the shade, as exposure to direct sunlight can degrade its volatile components like **bisabolol.**

- **Oven drying** or **high-heat drying** methods, on the other hand, can lead to the loss of delicate compounds and may also cause **oxidation** of certain phytochemicals, reducing the overall efficacy of the herb. **Curcumin**, the active component in **turmeric** (Curcuma longa), is sensitive to high heat, and improper drying methods can lower its anti-inflammatory and antioxidant potential.

Properly dried herbs maintain their **therapeutic properties** and have a **longer shelf life**, but the drying method must be chosen carefully depending on the type of herb and its specific compounds.

2. Grinding and Pulverization

The processes of **grinding** and **pulverization** are essential for converting herbal raw materials into powders or smaller particles, increasing their **surface area** for better extraction and absorption. However, the mechanical friction involved in these processes can generate **heat**, potentially causing the loss of **volatile compounds** and the degradation of sensitive phytochemicals.

- In **cold grinding** or using **low-speed grinders**, the medicinal properties of heat-sensitive herbs, such as **ginger** (Zingiber officinale), are preserved. The anti-inflammatory compound **gingerol** can be degraded if the grinding process generates excessive heat, thereby reducing its **therapeutic effects** in herbal formulations.
- **Pulverization**, which results in ultra-fine powders, improves the **bioavailability** of active compounds by allowing for better dissolution and absorption in the body. For example, finely pulverized **Ashwagandha** (Withania somnifera) root powder has been shown to increase the **bioavailability** of **withanolides**, which are responsible for the herb's **adaptogenic** and **stress-relieving** effects.

However, care must be taken to control the heat generated during grinding or pulverization to avoid losing efficacy, especially in herbs with volatile constituents.

3. Extraction

Extraction methods are among the most critical processes that influence the efficacy of herbal medicines, as they determine the concentration and quality of the **bioactive compounds** that are drawn out from the raw plant material. Different extraction techniques can yield different **potency levels** and chemical profiles, directly affecting the herbal formulation's ability to deliver therapeutic benefits.

- **Maceration** and **infusion** processes are gentle methods that are suitable for herbs with delicate compounds, such as **flavonoids** or **tannins**. These methods are commonly used for herbs like **elderflower** (Sambucus nigra) to extract its anti-inflammatory properties without degrading its active ingredients. However, these methods may not always result in the highest concentration of compounds.
- **Decoction**, which involves boiling the herbs, is more effective for **tough plant parts** like **roots**, **bark**, and **seeds**, as it helps break down cell walls and release **water-soluble** compounds such as **polysaccharides** and **saponins**. This method is frequently used for **Astragalus** (Astragalus membranaceus) and **licorice** (Glycyrrhiza glabra) roots, enhancing their immune-boosting and anti-inflammatory efficacy.
- More advanced extraction techniques, such as **Soxhlet extraction** and **supercritical fluid extraction (SFE)**, provide more efficient extraction of bioactive compounds with minimal degradation. **SFE using carbon dioxide (CO_2)** is particularly effective for preserving the **thermally sensitive** and **volatile compounds** in herbs like **lavender** (Lavandula angustifolia) and **peppermint** (Mentha piperita). These methods yield **high-purity extracts**, ensuring that the final product is rich in active compounds without contamination or degradation.

4. Stability and Storage After Processing

Processing not only affects the immediate efficacy of herbal materials but also influences their **stability** during storage. Improperly processed herbs are more prone to **oxidation, microbial growth**, or **moisture retention**, which can degrade their medicinal properties over time.

- Herbs like **green tea** (Camellia sinensis), rich in **polyphenols** and **antioxidants**, are highly susceptible to oxidation. Proper drying and storage techniques, such as **vacuum sealing** or **cool storage**, are necessary to maintain their **antioxidant potential** and **health benefits**.
- The use of preservatives and **standardized extracts** can help extend the **shelf life** of herbal products, ensuring that their efficacy remains intact until consumption. **Encapsulation** of sensitive compounds, such as **curcumin** in turmeric, helps prevent exposure to air and moisture,

preserving its potency for longer periods.

5. Potential Loss of Active Compounds

In addition to enhancing efficacy, processing can also lead to the **loss of certain bioactive compounds**, depending on the herb and the method used. For example, prolonged exposure to **heat** or **light** during drying can cause the breakdown of **essential oils** and **antioxidants**, significantly reducing the herb's therapeutic potential.

- **Anthocyanins**, which are powerful antioxidants found in berries like **bilberry** (Vaccinium myrtillus), are sensitive to heat. If processed improperly, their levels can significantly drop, reducing the herb's efficacy in treating **eye health** or **vascular disorders.**
- Similarly, **chlorophyll**-rich herbs such as **spirulina** (Arthrospira platensis) require low-temperature drying methods to preserve their **detoxifying** and **nutritional benefits.**

The **efficacy** of herbal medicines is deeply influenced by the way herbs are processed, as each method can either enhance or diminish the potency of the herb's active compounds. Proper **drying, grinding,** and **extraction** techniques help maintain the therapeutic value of herbs, ensuring that they retain their **medicinal properties** and **bioavailability.** Conversely, improper processing can lead to the **degradation** of essential compounds, resulting in reduced **effectiveness.** Therefore, understanding and applying the right techniques for each herb and compound is essential for producing **high-quality** and **efficacious herbal medicines.**

1.5 Biodynamic Agriculture

Biodynamic agriculture is a holistic, **ecologically balanced** approach to farming that integrates organic agricultural practices with the **spiritual and cosmic principles** first articulated by Austrian philosopher **Rudolf Steiner** in the early 20th century. It is considered one of the earliest forms of organic farming, placing emphasis on the **interconnectedness of soil, plants, animals, and cosmic forces** to maintain and enhance the health and fertility of the farm ecosystem. In **herbal cultivation,** biodynamic agriculture is particularly valued for promoting the growth of **medicinal plants** that are rich in **bioactive compounds** and free from harmful chemicals or synthetic additives.

1.5.1 Principles of Biodynamic Farming

Biodynamic farming operates on a set of core principles that go beyond the traditional organic approach, encompassing the use of **biodynamic preparations**, attention to **astronomical rhythms**, and the creation of a **self-sustaining farm ecosystem**. These principles are believed to promote soil health, improve plant vitality, and enhance the quality of the crops produced, including herbs used in **medicinal** and **nutraceutical** applications.

1. **Biodynamic Preparations**: Biodynamic farming relies on a series of **special preparations** made from fermented plant materials, animal manure, and minerals. These preparations are applied to the soil or used as compost enhancers to improve soil fertility and promote plant health. Examples of these preparations include:

   - **Preparation 500 (horn manure)**: Cow manure is buried in a cow horn over the winter and then applied to the soil to enhance **soil structure** and stimulate **microbial activity**.
   - **Preparation 501 (horn silica)**: Ground quartz is buried in a cow horn and later sprayed onto crops to enhance **photosynthesis** and promote healthy plant growth.

2. **Cosmic and Astronomical Rhythms**: A key aspect of biodynamic farming is the synchronization of farming activities with the **cosmic cycles**, particularly the movements of the **moon, planets,** and **stars**. Farmers follow a **biodynamic calendar** that suggests optimal times for planting, cultivating, and harvesting based on lunar and celestial phases. It is believed that these rhythms influence the growth and vitality of plants, with certain times being more favorable for specific agricultural tasks.

3. **Closed Farm Ecosystem**: Biodynamic farms strive to be **self-sustaining ecosystems**, where inputs such as fertilizers and pest control agents are produced within the farm itself. This is achieved through a **closed-loop system**, where the natural cycles of the farm are harmonized, including **crop rotation, cover cropping,** and the integration of **livestock** to manage fertility and pest control. The farm functions as a **living organism**, where each component (soil, plants, animals, and people) plays a vital role in maintaining overall health and productivity.

4. **Focus on Soil Health**: In biodynamic farming, the soil is regarded as a **living entity**, and maintaining its health is paramount. Biodynamic practices emphasize **composting, mulching,** and the use of **green manure** to enrich the soil with organic matter, encouraging a healthy population of **microorganisms**. This results in improved **nutrient cycling**, enhanced **soil structure**, and increased **biodiversity** in the soil, which all contribute to the long-term sustainability of the farm.

1.5.2 Impact of Biodynamic Agriculture on Medicinal Plant Quality

Biodynamic agriculture is known to enhance the **quality** and **potency** of medicinal plants, making it particularly relevant for the cultivation of **herbal medicines** and **nutraceuticals**. The principles of biodynamic farming are believed to yield herbs with higher concentrations of **bioactive compounds**, such as **alkaloids, flavonoids, tannins,** and **terpenoids**, which are responsible for the therapeutic properties of medicinal plants.

1. **Enhanced Bioactivity**: Biodynamically grown medicinal plants are often found to have higher levels of **secondary metabolites**, which are crucial for the plant's medicinal properties. These secondary metabolites play roles in the plant's defense mechanisms and contribute to the herb's ability to address **inflammation, oxidative stress,** and **immune modulation** in humans. For example, **biodynamically grown turmeric** (Curcuma longa) may have higher levels of **curcumin**, enhancing its **anti-inflammatory** and **antioxidant** properties.

2. **Improved Soil-Plant Interaction**: The focus on **soil health** in biodynamic farming leads to plants growing in nutrient-rich, biologically active soils. This **enhanced soil-plant interaction** results in the plants absorbing a broader range of **micronutrients** and **trace elements**, which are crucial for their medicinal properties. **Ashwagandha** (Withania somnifera), a key herb in Ayurveda, is an example of a plant that thrives in biodynamically managed soils, resulting in higher concentrations of **withanolides**—compounds that support **stress relief** and **immune health**.

3. **Sustainability and Purity**: One of the key advantages of biodynamic farming is the **purity** of the herbs produced. Biodynamic practices avoid the use of **synthetic pesticides, herbicides,** or **chemical fertilizers,** resulting in plants that are free from **toxic residues**. This is particularly important for the production of **medicinal herbs**, where contamination

can reduce the efficacy of the medicine or introduce harmful substances to consumers. The **closed-loop ecosystem** of biodynamic farms also minimizes the risk of contamination from external sources, ensuring that the medicinal plants maintain their natural purity.

4. **Energy and Vitality of Plants**: Biodynamic practitioners believe that the use of cosmic rhythms and biodynamic preparations enhances the **vitality** of the plants, making them more **resilient** to pests, diseases, and environmental stress. Medicinal plants grown under these conditions are thought to have greater **healing potential**, as they are nurtured in harmony with nature's cycles. This increased vitality may result in herbs that are more effective in supporting **human health**.

5. **Consumer Demand for Holistic Products**: There is growing consumer interest in **holistic**, **sustainable**, and **natural products**, which has led to an increased demand for biodynamically grown herbs in the **natural health** and **organic markets**. Consumers often perceive biodynamic products as being of higher quality and more aligned with **ecological principles**, making them an attractive choice for **herbal supplements** and **medicinal formulations**.

Biodynamic agriculture offers a holistic approach to farming that not only respects the natural environment but also promotes the cultivation of **high-quality medicinal plants**. By emphasizing **soil health**, the use of **biodynamic preparations**, and the alignment of farming activities with **cosmic rhythms**, biodynamic practices yield plants with enhanced **bioactive compounds**, improved **potency**, and **sustainability**. For medicinal herb cultivation, biodynamic farming ensures that herbs are not only **pure** and **chemical-free** but also retain their full **therapeutic potential**, making them a valuable resource in modern **herbal medicine** and **nutraceuticals**.

1.5.1 Principles of Biodynamic Farming

Biodynamic farming is a holistic, ecological, and ethical approach to agriculture that treats the farm as a **self-sustaining organism**. It integrates spiritual, cosmic, and environmental principles with traditional agricultural practices to enhance the health and vitality of the **soil, plants, and animals** on the farm. Developed by **Rudolf Steiner** in the 1920s, biodynamic farming goes beyond organic farming by incorporating **cosmic rhythms** and **biodynamic preparations** to support a balanced and regenerative agricultural system. The key principles of biodynamic farming include the use of **biodynamic preparations**, synchronization with **cosmic rhythms**, the creation of a **closed farm ecosystem**, and a focus on **soil health**.

1. Biodynamic Preparations

A fundamental aspect of biodynamic farming is the use of **biodynamic preparations**, which are specialized natural substances that are applied to the soil or compost to enhance its fertility, structure, and biological activity. These preparations are made from a combination of **plant materials, animal manures**, and **minerals**, and are carefully prepared using specific techniques such as **fermentation** and **burial in animal organs**. The biodynamic preparations are numbered from **500 to 508**, each serving a distinct purpose in enriching the farm ecosystem.

- **Preparation 500 (Horn Manure)**: Made from cow manure that is buried in a cow horn during the winter months, this preparation is sprayed on the soil to improve **soil fertility**, stimulate **root growth**, and increase **microbial activity**. It is used to enhance the overall health and vitality of the soil.
- **Preparation 501 (Horn Silica)**: This preparation is made from finely ground quartz (silica) that is buried in a cow horn during the summer months. When applied to plants, it enhances **photosynthesis**, strengthens plant structures, and helps plants absorb **light energy** more effectively, promoting growth and vitality.
- **Compost Preparations**: Biodynamic farming also uses a set of six compost preparations (502-507) made from herbs such as **yarrow, chamomile, nettle**, and **dandelion**. These are added to compost piles to accelerate decomposition and improve the **nutrient content** of the compost, which is then applied to the fields to nourish crops.

The use of these preparations is intended to support the farm's natural processes, promoting soil regeneration and enhancing the quality of the crops produced.

2. Cosmic and Astronomical Rhythms

A unique aspect of biodynamic farming is the attention paid to **cosmic rhythms** and **astronomical cycles**. Biodynamic farmers believe that the movements of the **moon, planets**, and **stars** affect the growth and development of plants, much like how the moon influences ocean tides. To harness these forces, farming activities such as **planting, cultivating, fertilizing,** and **harvesting** are scheduled according to a **biodynamic calendar** that aligns with lunar and planetary rhythms.

- **Lunar Phases**: The moon's phases, such as the **waxing** and **waning moon**, are believed to influence **water movement** within plants. For example, planting during the waxing moon, when the moon is increasing in size, is thought to promote upward growth and the development of leaves and flowers, while the waning moon favors root development.
- **Zodiac Influence**: The biodynamic calendar also considers the position of the moon in the **zodiac constellations**, which are grouped into four elements: **earth, water, air,** and **fire**. Each element is believed to correspond to different parts of the plant (roots, leaves, flowers, and fruits), and farmers use this knowledge to time their activities to enhance specific plant qualities.

By working in harmony with these cosmic rhythms, biodynamic farmers aim to create **balanced and resilient crops** that are in tune with natural forces, resulting in **healthier plants** with improved nutritional and medicinal qualities.

3. Closed Farm Ecosystem

In biodynamic farming, the farm is viewed as a **self-sustaining organism**, where all inputs needed for crop production are generated within the farm itself. This concept promotes a **closed-loop system**, where the cycles of **fertility, waste management,** and **animal husbandry** are integrated and balanced. The farm produces its own **fertilizers, feeds,** and **pest control measures**, minimizing the need for external inputs and reducing reliance on synthetic chemicals or fertilizers.

- **Livestock Integration**: Livestock play a crucial role in biodynamic farming by contributing **manure** for composting and helping to manage the fertility of the soil. The animals are considered an integral part of the ecosystem, and their care and well-being are prioritized. For example, **cow manure** is an essential component in biodynamic preparations and composting processes.
- **Crop Rotation and Diversity**: Biodynamic farms practice **crop rotation** and maintain a diverse array of plants to promote **soil health**, prevent **pest outbreaks**, and encourage **biodiversity**. Diverse crop systems improve **nutrient cycling** and reduce the risk of soil depletion, making the farm more resilient and sustainable.

By creating a balanced and self-sustaining ecosystem, biodynamic farms reduce their environmental impact and contribute to the overall health of the **soil, plants**, and **animals**, resulting in higher-quality crops and more nutritious food.

4. Focus on Soil Health

A central tenet of biodynamic farming is the belief that the **soil is a living entity** and that maintaining its health is fundamental to producing nutritious and high-quality crops. Biodynamic practices focus on **building soil fertility** through the use of organic matter, compost, and **biodynamic preparations**.

- **Composting**: Composting is an essential practice in biodynamic farming. Farmers use organic waste materials such as **manure, crop residues**, and **kitchen waste** to create rich, nutrient-dense compost that enhances **soil structure**, improves **nutrient availability**, and supports a healthy **microbial community**. The application of biodynamic preparations to compost piles accelerates the decomposition process and improves the compost's ability to nourish plants.

- **Mulching and Green Manure**: Biodynamic farmers also use **mulching** and **green manure** crops to protect the soil from erosion, retain moisture, and add organic matter to the soil. Cover crops such as **legumes** are grown between planting seasons to fix nitrogen in the soil, enriching it for the next crop cycle.

The emphasis on soil health ensures that biodynamic farms produce **nutrient-rich plants** that are free from harmful chemicals and pesticides. This results in crops that are not only more nutritious but also possess higher levels of **bioactive compounds** beneficial for **human health**.

The principles of **biodynamic farming** are centered around the idea of creating a **self-sustaining, regenerative farm ecosystem** that works in harmony with the natural world. Through the use of **biodynamic preparations**, attention to **cosmic rhythms**, and a focus on **soil health** and **biodiversity**, biodynamic farmers are able to produce crops that are not only environmentally sustainable but also of the highest quality in terms of **nutritional** and **medicinal value**. Biodynamic farming represents a **holistic approach** to agriculture that seeks to enhance the **health** and **vitality** of the entire farm organism, ensuring long-term sustainability and productivity.

1.5.2 Impact of Biodynamic Agriculture on Medicinal Plant Quality

Biodynamic agriculture has a profound impact on the **quality** of medicinal plants, primarily through its focus on **holistic farm management, soil health,** and the use of **biodynamic preparations**. This farming method not only promotes sustainable agricultural practices but also enhances the **bioactive compounds, potency,** and **purity** of medicinal plants, making them more effective for therapeutic use. Biodynamic agriculture is becoming increasingly important in the cultivation of medicinal plants due to the growing demand for **natural, chemical-free,** and **nutrient-rich herbs** used in traditional and modern medicine.

1. Enhanced Concentration of Bioactive Compounds

One of the key benefits of biodynamic agriculture is the improvement in the **concentration of bioactive compounds** in medicinal plants. Biodynamically grown plants often have higher levels of **secondary metabolites,** such as **alkaloids, flavonoids, terpenoids,** and **polyphenols,** which are responsible for the medicinal properties of the plants. These compounds serve as the active ingredients in herbal medicines and play critical roles in treating various health conditions, including **inflammation, oxidative stress,** and **immune disorders.**

- For instance, **curcumin,** the primary bioactive compound in **turmeric** (Curcuma longa), is found in higher concentrations in biodynamically cultivated plants. This results in more potent anti-inflammatory and antioxidant effects, enhancing the therapeutic efficacy of turmeric in treating conditions like **arthritis** and **digestive disorders.**
- Similarly, **Ashwagandha** (Withania somnifera), a widely used herb in Ayurveda for its adaptogenic properties, tends to have increased levels of **withanolides** when grown under biodynamic practices. This enhances the herb's ability to combat **stress, anxiety,** and **immune dysfunction,** making it more effective in traditional formulations.

2. Improved Soil-Plant Interaction and Nutrient Density

Biodynamic agriculture places a strong emphasis on **soil health,** which directly impacts the nutrient content of medicinal plants. The use of **biodynamic preparations,** composting, and cover cropping enhances the **biological activity** of the soil, leading to better **nutrient cycling** and more **micronutrient-rich plants.** Plants that grow in healthy, biologically active soils are better able to absorb essential nutrients and minerals, which are crucial for their **therapeutic potential.**

- For example, **biodynamically grown ginger** (Zingiber officinale) shows higher levels of **gingerol**, a compound known for its anti-inflammatory and digestive benefits. The increased availability of **nutrients** and **minerals** in biodynamic soils supports the production of such compounds, making the plant more potent and effective in treating ailments.
- **Ginseng** (Panax ginseng), known for its adaptogenic and immune-boosting properties, also benefits from the nutrient-rich soils of biodynamic farms. Ginsenosides, the active compounds in ginseng, are found in higher concentrations in plants cultivated biodynamically due to the enhanced **soil-plant interaction.**

3. Higher Plant Vitality and Resistance

Plants grown under biodynamic principles exhibit higher **vitality** and **resistance** to pests, diseases, and environmental stressors. This is because biodynamic agriculture nurtures the plant's natural defense mechanisms by promoting **balanced growth** and a harmonious relationship between the plant and its environment. The use of **compost preparations** and the alignment of farming practices with **cosmic rhythms** are believed to enhance the plant's resilience, resulting in stronger, healthier plants with **greater medicinal potential.**

- For medicinal plants such as **Echinacea** (Echinacea purpurea), which is known for its immune-boosting properties, biodynamic cultivation leads to stronger plants with increased levels of **caffeic acid derivatives**—compounds that are key to its immune-modulating effects. These plants are more resilient to environmental stress and pest attacks, ensuring a higher-quality yield of medicinal herbs.
- **Lavender** (Lavandula angustifolia), a herb prized for its calming and anti-anxiety properties, benefits from biodynamic cultivation through improved **essential oil content** and overall plant vigor. The enhanced vitality of the plant contributes to its **potent therapeutic properties,** making it more effective in **aromatherapy** and **herbal remedies.**

4. Purity and Absence of Chemical Residues

One of the most significant advantages of biodynamic agriculture is the **absence of chemical residues** in the final plant material. Biodynamic farming strictly avoids the use of **synthetic pesticides, herbicides,** and

chemical fertilizers, ensuring that the medicinal plants produced are **pure** and free from harmful contaminants. This is particularly important in the production of medicinal plants, as the presence of chemical residues can compromise the efficacy and safety of the herbal medicines derived from them.

- **Chamomile** (Matricaria chamomilla), which is widely used for its calming and anti-inflammatory properties, retains its natural purity when grown biodynamically. The avoidance of chemical treatments ensures that the essential oils and flavonoids in chamomile are not contaminated, making it safer and more effective for use in teas, tinctures, and topical preparations.
- In the case of **Neem** (Azadirachta indica), a medicinal plant known for its antimicrobial and skin-healing properties, biodynamic farming enhances the quality of the herb by ensuring it is free from pesticide residues. This increases its efficacy in treating skin conditions and infections while minimizing the risk of side effects from chemical exposure.

5. Sustainability and Long-Term Soil Fertility

Biodynamic agriculture promotes the **sustainability** of medicinal plant cultivation by focusing on long-term soil fertility and ecological balance. The use of **composting, crop rotation**, and **cover cropping** ensures that the soil remains fertile and biologically active, supporting the continued growth of high-quality medicinal plants over time. The emphasis on sustainability also aligns with the growing demand for **ethical** and **environmentally responsible** sourcing of medicinal herbs in the global market.

- The sustainable cultivation of **St. John's Wort** (Hypericum perforatum), a herb used for its antidepressant and mood-regulating effects, is supported by biodynamic practices that maintain soil fertility and biodiversity. This allows for continuous cultivation without depleting soil resources, ensuring a steady supply of high-quality plant material for medicinal use.
- **Rosemary** (Rosmarinus officinalis), a herb used for its cognitive-enhancing and anti-inflammatory properties, benefits from biodynamic practices that enhance soil fertility and plant resilience. The sustainable nature of biodynamic farming ensures that rosemary and other

medicinal plants can be cultivated year after year without compromising soil health or plant quality.

Biodynamic agriculture has a significant positive impact on the **quality** of medicinal plants by enhancing their **bioactive compound content, nutrient density, vitality,** and **resistance** to environmental stress. The emphasis on **soil health, purity,** and **sustainability** ensures that biodynamically grown medicinal plants are free from harmful chemicals and rich in the compounds that give them their therapeutic value. As a result, biodynamic farming is becoming an increasingly important method for cultivating high-quality medicinal plants, providing consumers with **safe, effective,** and **ethically sourced** herbal medicines

1.6 Good Agricultural Practices (GAP) in Cultivation of Medicinal Plants

Good Agricultural Practices (GAP) are a set of guidelines and standards aimed at ensuring the **quality, safety,** and **sustainability** of agricultural products, including medicinal plants. In the context of medicinal plant cultivation, GAP provides a framework for cultivating plants in a way that preserves their **therapeutic properties**, protects the environment, and ensures that the final products are safe for consumers. GAP focuses on all aspects of farming, from **site selection** and **soil management** to **harvesting, processing,** and **record-keeping**. By adhering to GAP standards, farmers and producers can ensure that their medicinal plants are of high quality and free from **contaminants, pesticide residues,** and **adulterants.**

1.6.1 Principles of GAP

The **principles of GAP** in the cultivation of medicinal plants revolve around maintaining **quality control** throughout the production process, ensuring **traceability**, promoting **environmental sustainability**, and guaranteeing the safety and purity of medicinal plant products. The key principles include:

1. Site Selection and Management

The selection of a suitable site for the cultivation of medicinal plants is crucial for ensuring their quality and therapeutic efficacy. GAP recommends that the cultivation site be chosen based on factors such as **climatic conditions, soil quality,** and **proximity to pollution sources** (e.g., industrial areas or highways). The site must be free from contamination by **heavy metals, pesticides,** and other pollutants, as these can affect the purity and safety of the medicinal plants.

- **Soil testing** is essential to ensure that the soil is rich in nutrients and free from harmful substances. Soil with the right balance of nutrients helps the plants develop a strong **phytochemical profile**, enhancing their medicinal properties.
- Proper **water management** is also critical, and GAP emphasizes the use of clean, uncontaminated water sources for **irrigation** to avoid introducing pollutants or pathogens to the plants.

2. Seed and Planting Material Selection

The selection of high-quality **seeds** or **planting materials** is a foundational principle of GAP. Medicinal plants should be propagated from **certified seeds** or **plant parts** that are genetically true to their species, free from diseases, and of high **germination capacity**.

- **Certified seeds** ensure that the plants are true to their **botanical identity**, avoiding issues of **misidentification** or **adulteration**. For example, using certified seeds for plants like **Echinacea** or **Ginseng** ensures that the final product will have the desired therapeutic effects associated with these species.
- **Proper storage** of seeds and planting materials is also critical to maintaining their viability and ensuring successful cultivation.

3. Sustainable Soil and Crop Management

Maintaining **soil health** and practicing sustainable **crop management** techniques are fundamental to GAP. The long-term fertility of the soil must be preserved to ensure the continuous cultivation of medicinal plants with high therapeutic value.

- **Organic farming techniques** are encouraged under GAP to avoid the use of synthetic fertilizers and pesticides. Instead, natural fertilizers such as **compost, manure,** and **green manure** are used to enrich the soil.
- **Crop rotation** and **intercropping** are important practices that help maintain soil fertility and reduce pest pressure. For instance, planting **leguminous crops** between medicinal plant cycles can help fix nitrogen in the soil, benefiting crops such as **turmeric** (Curcuma longa) or **ginger** (Zingiber officinale).
- GAP also emphasizes the control of **pests, diseases,** and **weeds** through environmentally friendly methods, such as the use of **biopesticides** and

biological control agents, rather than relying on harmful chemical pesticides that can leave residues in the plants.

4. Harvesting Practices

Harvesting medicinal plants at the right stage of maturity is critical to ensuring that their **bioactive compounds** are at peak concentration. GAP sets clear guidelines on **timing, methods,** and **tools** for harvesting to preserve the quality of the plants and minimize contamination.

- Medicinal plants should be harvested during their **optimal growth phase**, when the concentration of therapeutic compounds is highest. For example, **lavender** (Lavandula angustifolia) is typically harvested when its essential oil content is at its peak, ensuring maximum potency for medicinal use.
- Tools used for harvesting must be **clean** and **well-maintained** to prevent contamination. Farmers are advised to use stainless steel tools and avoid using tools that could rust or contaminate the plant material.
- **Post-harvest handling** is equally important, with a focus on **cleaning, drying,** and **storing** the harvested material in a controlled environment to prevent degradation of the active compounds.

5. Environmental Sustainability

One of the core principles of GAP is ensuring that medicinal plant cultivation is done in an **environmentally sustainable** manner. This involves minimizing the impact of farming practices on the surrounding ecosystem and ensuring the **long-term viability** of the land.

- **Water conservation** practices, such as the use of **drip irrigation** or **rainwater harvesting**, are encouraged to reduce water usage and prevent water contamination.
- The use of **cover crops** and **mulching** helps reduce soil erosion and maintain soil moisture levels, while also contributing to the overall health of the ecosystem.
- GAP also promotes the conservation of **biodiversity**, encouraging farmers to cultivate a range of medicinal plant species to prevent monoculture and to support a diverse, resilient ecosystem.

6. Traceability and Record-Keeping

GAP emphasizes the importance of **traceability** throughout the entire production process. From planting to harvesting and processing, detailed records must be kept to ensure that the origins and handling of the medicinal plants can be traced back to the source. This is crucial for **quality control**, ensuring that any potential issues with contamination or adulteration can be identified and addressed.

- Farmers are required to maintain records of all **inputs** (e.g., seeds, fertilizers, water sources) and **practices** (e.g., pest control, harvesting) used during cultivation.
- **Batch labeling** is essential to link each harvested batch of medicinal plants to its corresponding cultivation records, providing transparency in the supply chain.

7. Worker Safety and Hygiene

Ensuring the **safety** and **hygiene** of workers is another key principle of GAP. Workers involved in the cultivation, harvesting, and processing of medicinal plants must be provided with appropriate **protective gear** and trained in **hygienic practices** to prevent contamination of the plants.

- Personal hygiene, including the washing of hands and the use of clean clothing, is important when handling medicinal plants, especially during harvesting and post-harvest processing.
- Adequate facilities for **clean water, sanitation**, and **hygiene** must be provided on the farm to prevent contamination of the medicinal plants by human pathogens.

8. Quality Assurance and Testing

GAP places a strong emphasis on **quality assurance**, with guidelines for conducting **routine testing** of medicinal plant products to ensure they meet **purity, potency**, and **safety** standards. This includes testing for **pesticide residues, heavy metals**, and **microbial contamination** to ensure that the medicinal plants are safe for use in herbal medicines.

- Regular **chemical analysis** of soil and plant materials helps ensure that the plants meet the required standards for active compounds, such as **alkaloids, flavonoids**, or **essential oils**.

- **Microbial testing** is conducted to ensure that the plants are free from harmful bacteria or fungi that could affect their safety and efficacy.

The **principles of Good Agricultural Practices (GAP)** in the cultivation of medicinal plants ensure that the entire production process, from seed selection to harvesting and processing, is carried out in a manner that preserves the **quality, safety,** and **therapeutic efficacy** of the plants. By adhering to GAP, farmers can produce high-quality medicinal plants that are free from contaminants, sustainably grown, and rich in bioactive compounds, providing consumers with safe and effective herbal products.

1.6.2 Organic Farming in Medicinal Plants

Organic farming of medicinal plants is a farming system that focuses on cultivating herbs and plants without the use of **synthetic chemicals,** such as pesticides, herbicides, and fertilizers. Instead, organic farming relies on **natural processes, biological pest control,** and **organic inputs** like compost and manure to maintain **soil fertility** and promote **healthy plant growth.** Organic farming is particularly significant in the cultivation of medicinal plants as it ensures that the final product is free from **toxic residues,** which can compromise the **therapeutic efficacy** and **safety** of the medicinal plants used in **herbal formulations.** The core philosophy of organic farming is to work in harmony with nature, fostering **biodiversity,** protecting the **environment,** and producing **sustainable,** high-quality medicinal plants that are rich in **bioactive compounds.**

1. Sustainability and Soil Health

One of the key components of organic farming is the emphasis on **sustainable farming practices** that prioritize long-term soil health and environmental conservation. Medicinal plants grown organically benefit from healthy, nutrient-rich soil, which supports the development of **bioactive compounds** critical for the plant's medicinal properties.

- **Soil fertility** is maintained using **natural fertilizers** like compost, **green manure,** and **animal manure.** These organic inputs enrich the soil with essential nutrients, improve **soil structure,** and encourage beneficial microbial activity. This, in turn, enhances the plant's ability to absorb **minerals** and **micronutrients,** leading to stronger plants with higher concentrations of therapeutic compounds.
- **Crop rotation** and **cover cropping** are integral practices in organic farming that help maintain soil fertility and prevent soil depletion. For

instance, legumes are often grown in rotation with medicinal plants like **ginger** (Zingiber officinale) or **turmeric** (Curcuma longa) to fix nitrogen in the soil, boosting plant growth and enhancing the potency of these herbs.

2. Elimination of Chemical Residues

A major advantage of organic farming is the complete avoidance of **synthetic pesticides** and **chemical fertilizers**, which can leave harmful residues on medicinal plants. These residues not only reduce the **purity** of the plants but also pose potential health risks to consumers when used in herbal medicines. In organic farming, **natural pest control methods** are used to manage diseases and pests without compromising the quality or safety of the medicinal plants.

- **Biological pest control** techniques are employed, such as introducing **beneficial insects** (e.g., ladybugs or predatory wasps) that feed on harmful pests. **Neem oil**, an extract from the **Neem tree** (Azadirachta indica), is another organic alternative commonly used to control pests without introducing toxic chemicals into the ecosystem.
- The use of **biopesticides**, derived from natural sources like plants, bacteria, and minerals, further protects the crops from pests and diseases while keeping the plant material free from synthetic contaminants. For example, **pyrethrin**, a natural insecticide derived from chrysanthemums, is often used in organic farming to protect medicinal herbs from pests without the use of synthetic chemicals.

By eliminating chemical inputs, organic farming ensures that the medicinal plants produced are **pure**, making them suitable for therapeutic use in **tinctures, powders, capsules**, and other herbal formulations.

3. Higher Quality of Bioactive Compounds

Organic farming practices promote the growth of medicinal plants with higher concentrations of **bioactive compounds** such as **alkaloids, flavonoids, terpenoids**, and **glycosides**. These compounds are essential for the therapeutic effects of medicinal plants, and their levels can be influenced by the **farming techniques** used.

- Studies have shown that organically grown medicinal plants often contain higher levels of these **secondary metabolites** compared to conventionally grown plants. For instance, organically cultivated **Echinacea** (Echinacea purpurea), known for its immune-boosting properties, has been found to contain higher concentrations of **phenolic compounds**, which are responsible for its medicinal effects.

- **Peppermint** (Mentha piperita), when grown organically, retains more of its **essential oils**—which include **menthol** and **menthone**—making it more effective for treating digestive disorders and respiratory conditions.

The absence of synthetic chemicals and the use of **organic fertilizers** and **natural pest control** methods enhance the plant's natural defense mechanisms, leading to increased production of these valuable compounds. This results in medicinal plants that are more potent and effective in treating health conditions.

4. Environmental Benefits

Organic farming practices align with the principles of **environmental sustainability**, protecting **biodiversity**, and reducing the **carbon footprint** of agriculture. By avoiding synthetic chemicals and focusing on **natural inputs**, organic farming helps maintain the health of the ecosystem surrounding the farm and contributes to the long-term sustainability of medicinal plant cultivation.

- **Biodiversity** is promoted through the use of **crop diversification** and the cultivation of a variety of medicinal plants alongside other crops. This not only supports the health of the ecosystem but also reduces the risk of **pest outbreaks** and **disease**, which are more common in monoculture systems.
- **Water conservation** is another key aspect of organic farming. Techniques such as **drip irrigation** and **rainwater harvesting** reduce water usage and help prevent soil erosion, while ensuring that medicinal plants have adequate moisture for optimal growth.
- Organic farming also minimizes **soil degradation** and promotes **carbon sequestration** by maintaining **healthy soil** rich in organic matter. This helps reduce the overall environmental impact of farming and supports the long-term viability of medicinal plant cultivation.

5. Consumer Demand and Certification

As consumer awareness of the benefits of organic products grows, there is increasing demand for **organic medicinal plants** that are free from harmful chemicals and sustainably sourced. Organic farming offers a way for producers to meet this demand while also adhering to high standards of **quality** and **safety**.

- **Organic certification** is an important aspect of organic farming in medicinal plants, as it ensures that the farm adheres to the standards set by regulatory bodies, such as **USDA Organic** or **European Organic**. This certification provides consumers with confidence that the medicinal plants they purchase are produced using organic methods and are free from synthetic additives.
- Organic certification also supports **traceability**, allowing consumers to know the origin of the plants and the farming practices used. This transparency is particularly important in the **herbal medicine** market, where the purity and quality of the plants directly impact the effectiveness of the products.

6. Organic Processing and Post-Harvest Handling

In addition to cultivation, organic farming includes standards for **post-harvest handling** and **processing** of medicinal plants. Proper handling ensures that the **bioactive compounds** in the plants are preserved and that contamination is avoided during **drying**, **grinding**, and **extraction** processes.

- **Drying methods** in organic farming often use **solar drying** or **air drying**, which are gentle methods that help retain the active constituents of the plant. Care is taken to avoid the use of high temperatures or synthetic additives during processing, ensuring that the medicinal properties of the plants remain intact.
- During **processing**, organic farmers must ensure that there is no contamination with non-organic materials, and only certified organic inputs are used. This ensures that the final products meet the criteria for organic certification and provide consumers with high-quality, effective herbal remedies.

Organic farming of medicinal plants offers numerous benefits, including the production of **high-quality, chemical-free herbs**, the enhancement of **bioactive compounds,** and the protection of the **environment** through sustainable farming practices. By eliminating synthetic inputs and focusing on natural farming methods, organic farming ensures that medicinal plants are not only safer for consumers but also more potent and effective for therapeutic use. The growing demand for organic medicinal plants underscores the importance of adopting **organic farming** techniques to meet consumer expectations while promoting the **sustainability** and **biodiversity** of medicinal plant cultivation.

1.6.3 Certification and Standards for GAP

Good Agricultural Practices (GAP) certification and standards are essential for ensuring the **quality, safety,** and **sustainability** of medicinal plants throughout the cultivation process. These certifications provide a framework for farmers to follow, ensuring that the cultivation of medicinal plants meets strict guidelines related to **environmental sustainability, worker safety, traceability,** and **product quality.** GAP certification allows producers to demonstrate their commitment to producing high-quality medicinal plants that are safe for use in **herbal medicines** and **nutraceuticals,** while also complying with **international regulations** and **consumer expectations.**

1. GAP Certification

GAP certification is awarded to farms that meet specific criteria laid out by national or international regulatory bodies. This certification ensures that the entire process of cultivating medicinal plants, from **planting** to **harvesting** and **post-harvest handling,** follows **sustainable agricultural practices** and meets the necessary safety and quality standards. Various organizations offer GAP certification, including national agricultural bodies, **WHO** guidelines, and **GlobalGAP,** a widely recognized global standard.

- **GlobalGAP:** One of the most recognized certification schemes for agricultural products, including medicinal plants, is **GlobalGAP.** GlobalGAP focuses on **food safety, environmental sustainability, worker welfare,** and **traceability.** It covers various aspects of agricultural production, including the responsible use of pesticides, water management, and the ethical treatment of workers.

- **WHO GAP Guidelines:** The **World Health Organization (WHO)** has established guidelines for the cultivation and collection of medicinal plants. These guidelines provide a framework for ensuring that medicinal plants are grown in conditions that safeguard their **quality,**

purity, and **safety**. WHO's GAP guidelines cover aspects such as **seed selection**, **cultivation techniques**, **harvesting methods**, and **post-harvest handling** to preserve the **active ingredients** in medicinal plants.

- **USDA Organic and Other National Standards**: While GAP certification focuses on general agricultural practices, many medicinal plants are also grown under **organic standards** set by national organizations such as the **USDA** or **European Union Organic Farming** regulations. These standards may complement GAP certifications, ensuring that medicinal plants are free from synthetic pesticides, herbicides, and fertilizers.

2. Standards Covered by GAP Certification

To receive GAP certification, farmers must adhere to a comprehensive set of standards that ensure the safety and quality of their medicinal plants. These standards cover various aspects of farming, including **soil management, water use, pest control, worker safety**, and **traceability**.

- **Soil and Water Management**: GAP standards emphasize the responsible management of **soil** and **water** to prevent contamination and degradation. This includes practices such as regular **soil testing** to monitor fertility and avoid heavy metal contamination, and the use of **sustainable irrigation** techniques to prevent overuse of water resources.
- **Pesticide Use and Residue Limits**: One of the critical aspects of GAP is the strict regulation of **pesticide use**. Farmers must follow guidelines that limit the type and quantity of **pesticides, herbicides**, and **fertilizers** used in the cultivation of medicinal plants to avoid harmful chemical residues. GAP standards often require the use of **biopesticides** or other natural methods for controlling pests and diseases.
- **Worker Safety and Welfare**: GAP certification includes guidelines for the **safety** and **welfare** of farm workers. This involves providing proper training on the safe use of agricultural chemicals, protective gear, and hygiene practices to ensure that workers do not inadvertently contaminate medicinal plants during the cultivation or harvesting process.
- **Harvesting and Post-Harvest Handling**: GAP standards regulate how medicinal plants are harvested and handled after harvesting. This includes specifications on the optimal time for harvesting to preserve the active compounds, as well as guidelines for **drying, processing**, and **storage** to maintain the **potency** and **purity** of the plants. Proper

sanitation and **hygiene** practices are also enforced to prevent microbial contamination during the post-harvest process.

- **Record Keeping and Traceability**: One of the key components of GAP certification is **traceability**. Farmers must maintain detailed records of all activities, including **seed sourcing, planting dates, fertilizer and pesticide applications**, and **harvesting times**. These records allow the entire production process to be traced back in case of any quality issues or contamination, ensuring transparency in the supply chain.

3. Benefits of GAP Certification for Medicinal Plants

Obtaining GAP certification offers multiple benefits to farmers, producers, and consumers of medicinal plants. It not only ensures that the plants are grown under **safe and sustainable conditions**, but it also enhances **marketability** and **consumer confidence** in the final product.

- **Quality Assurance**: GAP-certified medicinal plants are grown following strict quality standards, ensuring that they meet the necessary **purity, safety**, and **therapeutic efficacy** requirements. Consumers can trust that the herbal products they use are of the highest quality, free from contaminants, and rich in the bioactive compounds essential for their medicinal properties.
- **Increased Market Access**: Many international markets, particularly in the **European Union, United States**, and **Asia**, require GAP certification for the import of medicinal plants and herbal products. Farmers and producers who obtain GAP certification can access these lucrative markets and meet the growing global demand for **safe** and **sustainable** medicinal plants.
- **Environmental Protection**: By adhering to GAP standards, farmers contribute to the **conservation of natural resources**, including soil, water, and biodiversity. The sustainable practices encouraged by GAP help protect the environment and promote **long-term agricultural productivity**, ensuring that medicinal plants can continue to be grown without depleting the ecosystem.

4. Challenges and Implementation of GAP

While GAP certification offers many benefits, its implementation can present challenges, particularly for **small-scale farmers** in developing countries. The costs associated with meeting certification standards, such as investing in infrastructure, equipment, and record-keeping systems, can be prohibitive for some farmers.

- **Training and Education**: To achieve and maintain GAP certification, farmers must undergo **training** to understand the specific guidelines and practices required. This may include training on the safe use of pesticides, proper sanitation practices, and how to implement **traceability systems**. Access to these training programs is essential for the successful adoption of GAP.
- **Cost of Certification**: Obtaining GAP certification can be expensive due to the fees associated with audits, inspections, and compliance with infrastructure requirements. However, governments and non-governmental organizations (NGOs) often provide **subsidies** or **support programs** to help small-scale farmers achieve certification.
- **Record-Keeping Requirements**: GAP requires detailed record-keeping, which can be difficult for farmers who are not familiar with such practices. This can include documentation of pesticide use, water sources, and harvest times, all of which need to be accurately maintained to ensure compliance with certification standards.

Certification and standards for Good Agricultural Practices (GAP) are critical for ensuring that medicinal plants are cultivated in a way that meets **quality**, **safety**, and **sustainability** requirements. GAP certification helps ensure that medicinal plants are free from harmful residues, grown in environmentally sustainable ways, and handled under hygienic conditions to maintain their **therapeutic efficacy**. While there are challenges associated with obtaining GAP certification, the benefits—including increased market access, consumer trust, and environmental protection—make it an essential practice for producers of high-quality medicinal plants.

1.7 Pest and Pest Management in Medicinal Plants

The cultivation of **medicinal plants** requires careful management of **pests** and **diseases** to ensure the health and quality of the plants without compromising their therapeutic efficacy. Unlike conventional crops, medicinal plants are highly valued for their **bioactive compounds**, and any contamination with **chemical pesticides** can lower their medicinal properties or pose risks to consumers. Therefore, **pest management** in medicinal plants focuses on using **eco-friendly, sustainable,** and **biological**

control methods to minimize damage while preserving the quality and purity of the plants. Effective pest management also ensures higher yields and prevents economic losses for farmers.

1.7.1 Importance of Pest Management

Pest management in medicinal plants is critical for several reasons:

- **Preservation of Active Compounds**: Medicinal plants are prized for their **phytochemicals**, such as **alkaloids, flavonoids,** and **terpenoids,** which are sensitive to environmental stress caused by pest attacks. Damage caused by pests can alter the plant's metabolic processes, reducing the concentration of these compounds and diminishing their medicinal value.
- **Protection Against Economic Losses**: Pests and diseases can lead to significant **yield losses**, affecting the supply of high-quality medicinal plants. Unchecked pest infestations may result in substantial damage to crops, making them unsuitable for processing into herbal medicines.
- **Consumer Safety**: In pest-infested plants, growers may resort to synthetic pesticides, which can leave **chemical residues** on the plant material. For medicinal plants used in **herbal formulations**, this is especially concerning, as such residues could pose health risks to consumers. Proper pest management ensures that plants are grown in ways that minimize the use of harmful chemicals, maintaining the safety of the herbal products.

1.7.2 Biopesticides and Bioinsecticides in Herbal Cultivation

In the context of medicinal plants, using **biopesticides** and **bioinsecticides** is a preferred method for managing pests. These biological control agents are derived from natural sources such as **plants, bacteria, fungi,** and **minerals,** and they offer an environmentally friendly alternative to synthetic pesticides. Their use helps maintain the **organic integrity** of medicinal plants while minimizing the risk of contamination.

- **Neem Oil**: Extracted from the **Neem tree** (Azadirachta indica), neem oil is one of the most effective biopesticides in medicinal plant cultivation. It contains **azadirachtin**, which disrupts the growth and reproduction of many insect pests, including **aphids, whiteflies,** and **leafhoppers,** without harming beneficial insects like pollinators. Neem oil is used in the cultivation of medicinal plants such as **turmeric** (Curcuma longa) and **ginger** (Zingiber officinale) to prevent pest infestations without leaving harmful residues.

- **Bacillus thuringiensis (Bt)**: This bacterium produces toxins that target the larvae of various pests, particularly **caterpillars** and **moths**, which are common in medicinal plant fields. Bt is widely used in organic farming and is safe for humans and non-target organisms. It is particularly effective in controlling pests that attack medicinal plants like **Echinacea** and **peppermint** (Mentha piperita).

- **Pyrethrin**: Derived from **chrysanthemum flowers**, pyrethrin is a natural insecticide that affects the nervous system of insects, making it effective against a wide range of pests, including **mites, aphids**, and **beetles**. It is used in the cultivation of medicinal plants such as **ginseng** (Panax ginseng) and **lavender** (Lavandula angustifolia).

Using biopesticides ensures that medicinal plants remain free from toxic pesticide residues, preserving their therapeutic efficacy and maintaining their **organic certification**.

1.7.3 Common Pests and Diseases in Medicinal Plants

Medicinal plants are susceptible to a wide range of **pests** and **diseases** that can negatively affect their growth, yield, and medicinal quality. The following are some of the most common pests and diseases encountered in medicinal plant cultivation:

- **Aphids**: Aphids are tiny, sap-sucking insects that infest the leaves and stems of medicinal plants, causing **distortion, yellowing**, and **wilting** of plant tissues. They can also transmit viruses that further damage the plants. Aphids are commonly found on medicinal herbs like **basil** (Ocimum basilicum) and **peppermint**.

  - **Management**: Neem oil and insecticidal soaps are commonly used to control aphid populations, while beneficial insects such as **ladybugs** and **lacewings** can help reduce infestations naturally.

- **Spider Mites**: These pests are small arachnids that feed on plant sap, causing **stippling** and **yellowing** of the leaves. They are particularly problematic in dry, hot conditions and can weaken medicinal plants such as **echinacea, lavender**, and **rosemary** (Rosmarinus officinalis).

- **Management**: Spraying with a **water jet** or using **sulfur-based sprays** can help control spider mite populations. Additionally, maintaining adequate humidity levels can deter mite infestations.

- **Leafhoppers**: Leafhoppers are insects that feed on plant sap, resulting in **stunted growth** and **distorted leaves**. They are known to transmit plant diseases, including viruses that can significantly reduce the medicinal value of crops like **ginger, basil**, and **ashwagandha** (Withania somnifera).

  - **Management**: Floating row covers can protect plants from leafhoppers, and neem oil can be applied as a natural deterrent.

- **Fungal Diseases (Powdery Mildew)**: Powdery mildew is a fungal disease that appears as white, powdery spots on the leaves and stems of plants, particularly in warm, humid conditions. It affects medicinal plants such as **peppermint, oregano** (Origanum vulgare), and **chamomile** (Matricaria chamomilla).

  - **Management**: Using **sulfur-based fungicides** and ensuring proper **air circulation** around plants can help prevent and control powdery mildew. Additionally, pruning infected plant parts and avoiding overhead watering can reduce the spread of the disease.

- **Root Rot (Phytophthora)**: Root rot is caused by soil-borne pathogens such as **Phytophthora**, which thrive in poorly drained, waterlogged soils. This disease affects the roots of medicinal plants like **turmeric** and **ginseng**, leading to yellowing of leaves, stunted growth, and eventual plant death.

  - **Management**: Proper soil drainage is essential for preventing root rot. Treating the soil with **biological fungicides** like **Trichoderma** and using raised beds can also reduce the risk of infection.

- **Caterpillars and Moths**: Caterpillars and moth larvae feed on the leaves and stems of many medicinal plants, causing significant defoliation and plant stress. **Ginseng, echinacea,** and **lavender** are particularly vulnerable to caterpillar infestations.

- ◦ **Management: Bacillus thuringiensis (Bt)** is an effective biological control method for caterpillars. Handpicking caterpillars and using pheromone traps to monitor moth populations are also common practices.

Integrated Pest Management (IPM)

The most effective approach to managing pests and diseases in medicinal plants is through **Integrated Pest Management (IPM)**, which combines a variety of control strategies to minimize pest damage while reducing the reliance on chemical pesticides. IPM emphasizes **prevention, monitoring,** and the use of **biological** and **cultural controls** before resorting to chemical treatments.

- **Cultural Controls:** Cultural practices, such as **crop rotation, intercropping,** and maintaining proper **spacing** between plants, can reduce the risk of pest infestations. Using resistant plant varieties and practicing good **sanitation** (e.g., removing plant debris) also helps prevent the spread of diseases.
- **Biological Controls:** Encouraging the presence of **natural predators,** such as ladybugs, lacewings, and parasitoid wasps, can help keep pest populations in check. Farmers can also introduce beneficial organisms like **Trichogramma** wasps or **nematodes** to control specific pests.
- **Mechanical Controls:** Techniques like **handpicking** pests, using **sticky traps,** and installing **barrier crops** or **row covers** can physically prevent pests from damaging the medicinal plants.
- **Chemical Controls (as a Last Resort):** If pest populations become unmanageable, the use of **organic-approved insecticides** or biopesticides is preferred under IPM. Chemical controls should be used sparingly and only when necessary to minimize the risk of contaminating medicinal plants with harmful residues.

Pest management is crucial for ensuring the health, quality, and **therapeutic efficacy** of medicinal plants. The use of **biopesticides, biological control methods,** and Integrated Pest Management **(IPM)** practices helps to protect medicinal plants from pests while maintaining their organic integrity and avoiding the use of harmful chemicals. By carefully managing pests, growers can ensure that their medicinal plants are safe, pure, and effective for use in herbal formulations, contributing to the production of high-quality herbal medicines.

1.8 Indian Systems of Medicine

India has a rich and diverse tradition of medicine, which has evolved over thousands of years and continues to play a crucial role in the healthcare system. The **Indian Systems of Medicine** include **Ayurveda, Siddha, Unani, and Homeopathy**—each with unique philosophies, practices, and treatments aimed at promoting health and curing diseases. These systems are deeply rooted in holistic principles, viewing the body, mind, and spirit as interconnected entities, and emphasize the importance of **natural healing, herbal remedies, diet**, and **lifestyle adjustments** for maintaining health and well-being.

1.8.1 Introduction to Ayurveda, Siddha, Unani, and Homeopathy

Each of these traditional systems of medicine offers a different perspective on health and healing, yet all share the common goal of restoring balance and harmony within the body.

Ayurveda

Ayurveda, meaning "science of life" in Sanskrit, is one of the oldest systems of medicine in the world, originating over **5,000 years ago** in India. It is based on the belief that health is a state of balance between three fundamental biological energies or **doshas—Vata** (air and space), **Pitta** (fire and water), and **Kapha** (earth and water). These doshas govern all physiological and psychological functions in the body.

- **Core Principles**: Ayurveda emphasizes the concept of **personalized medicine**, where treatments are tailored to the individual's dosha constitution, current imbalance, and lifestyle. The balance of the doshas is affected by factors such as diet, weather, emotions, and physical activities.
- **Treatments**: Ayurveda utilizes a wide range of **herbal remedies, dietary adjustments, detoxification therapies** (such as **Panchakarma**), and **yoga** and **meditation** to restore balance and promote longevity. Commonly used herbs in Ayurveda include **Ashwagandha** (Withania somnifera), **Turmeric** (Curcuma longa), and **Triphala**.
- **Preventive Care**: Ayurveda places a strong emphasis on **preventive healthcare**, advising seasonal detoxes, daily routines, and dietary regimens based on one's dosha type to maintain health.

Siddha

The **Siddha system of medicine** is an ancient Indian medical tradition that originated in South India, particularly in the Tamil-speaking region. The word "Siddha" refers to **Siddhars**, spiritual masters who are believed to have developed this system by acquiring **knowledge of nature, herbs**, and **alchemy** through meditation and yogic practices.

- **Core Principles**: Siddha medicine, like Ayurveda, is based on the theory of **three humors** or **Doshas—Vatham**, **Pitham**, and **Kapham**—which correspond to the Ayurvedic doshas but have slight variations in interpretation. Siddha places a greater emphasis on **spiritual healing, alchemy**, and the use of **metals** and **minerals** in treatments.
- **Treatments**: Siddha uses a wide range of **herbal, mineral**, and **metal-based formulations** to treat diseases. Notable remedies include **Kayakalpa**, a form of rejuvenation therapy aimed at prolonging life and preventing aging, as well as herbs like **Nilavembu** (Andrographis paniculata) for treating fever and infections.
- **Holistic Approach**: Siddha is holistic in nature, addressing not only the physical body but also the mind and soul. **Yoga, meditation**, and **detoxification therapies** are key components of Siddha treatments.

Unani

The **Unani system of medicine** originated in Greece and was later developed and enriched by Arab and Persian physicians. Unani medicine was introduced to India during the **Medieval period**, where it merged with local traditions and became a prominent system of healthcare.

- **Core Principles**: Unani medicine is based on the **four humors** theory—**Dam (blood)**, **Balgham (phlegm)**, **Safra (yellow bile)**, and **Sauda (black bile)**—which are considered essential for maintaining the body's balance and health. According to Unani philosophy, disease occurs when there is an imbalance in these humors.
- **Treatments**: Unani treatments focus on restoring humor balance using **herbal remedies, dietary management, cupping therapy (Hijama), massage**, and **detoxification techniques**. Herbs like **Ajwain** (Carom seeds), **Kalunji** (Black seed), and **Zafran** (Saffron) are frequently used in Unani medicine.
- **Preventive Care**: Unani places a significant emphasis on **preventive care**, stressing the importance of maintaining a healthy lifestyle,

balanced diet, and regular detoxification to prevent disease.

Homeopathy

Homeopathy is a more recent system of medicine that was founded by **Samuel Hahnemann** in **Germany** in the late 18th century. It was introduced to India in the early 19th century and quickly gained popularity due to its gentle, holistic approach and effectiveness in treating both acute and chronic conditions.

- **Core Principles:** Homeopathy operates on the principle of **"like cures like"**, meaning that a substance that causes symptoms in a healthy person can be used in small, diluted amounts to treat those same symptoms in a sick person. This system uses **highly diluted substances**, called remedies, derived from plants, minerals, or animal sources to stimulate the body's natural healing processes.
- **Treatments:** Homeopathy is highly individualized, where remedies are chosen based on the patient's specific symptoms and constitutional makeup. Remedies are administered in very small doses, aiming to trigger the body's own defense mechanisms. Common remedies include **Arnica** for trauma and bruising, **Belladonna** for fever, and **Nux Vomica** for digestive disorders.
- **Holistic Care:** Homeopathy is holistic, considering the emotional, mental, and physical aspects of a patient in the treatment process. Homeopaths believe that addressing the root cause of the illness rather than just the symptoms leads to long-lasting health improvements.

The **Indian Systems of Medicine—Ayurveda, Siddha, Unani,** and **Homeopathy**—offer diverse and complementary approaches to healthcare. Each system is grounded in holistic healing principles, focusing on the balance of physical, mental, and spiritual health. These traditional systems continue to thrive in India and around the world, offering valuable contributions to **natural healing** and **preventive healthcare** through the use of **herbal remedies, diet, lifestyle modifications,** and **therapies** aimed at restoring balance and promoting well-being.

1.8.2 Basic Principles and Theories of Ayurveda

Ayurveda, the ancient Indian system of medicine, is based on a holistic approach to health, emphasizing the balance between body, mind, and spirit. The term "Ayurveda" comes from the Sanskrit words **"Ayur"** (life) and **"Veda"** (science or knowledge), meaning "the science of life." Rooted in **5,000 years** of Indian tradition, Ayurveda focuses on maintaining health through the balance of fundamental biological elements, called **doshas**, as well as through proper diet, lifestyle, and natural treatments such as **herbal medicines, detoxification**, and **spiritual practices**. The core principles of Ayurveda are based on the belief that individual health is determined by the dynamic balance of natural elements and energies in the body.

1. Dosha Theory (Tridosha)

The central theory in Ayurveda revolves around the concept of **Tridosha**, or the three vital energies (doshas) that govern all physiological and psychological functions in the human body. These three doshas—**Vata, Pitta**, and **Kapha**—are derived from the five elements of nature: **ether, air, fire, water**, and **earth**. Each dosha represents a combination of these elements and plays a unique role in maintaining health.

- **Vata (Air and Ether)**: Vata governs all movement in the body, including **circulation, breathing**, and **nerve impulses**. It is responsible for physical and mental agility and is associated with qualities such as **lightness, dryness**, and **coldness**. When balanced, Vata promotes creativity and vitality, but when out of balance, it can lead to anxiety, dryness, and digestive disorders.

- **Pitta (Fire and Water)**: Pitta is responsible for **metabolism, digestion**, and the transformation of food into energy. It is associated with qualities like **heat, sharpness**, and **intensity**. A balanced Pitta maintains clear thinking, strong digestion, and a healthy complexion. Imbalances can cause inflammation, ulcers, anger, and skin problems.

- **Kapha (Water and Earth)**: Kapha governs **structure, stability**, and **lubrication** in the body. It provides the body with **strength, immunity**, and **resilience**. Kapha has qualities such as **heaviness, coolness**, and **steadiness**. When balanced, it promotes calmness, strong immunity, and endurance. Imbalances in Kapha can result in lethargy, weight gain, congestion, and depression.

Each individual has a unique combination of these three doshas, known as their **Prakriti**, which determines their physical and psychological characteristics. The goal of Ayurveda is to maintain or restore the balance of these doshas, as any imbalance leads to disease.

2. The Panchamahabhuta Theory (Five Elements)

Ayurveda posits that all living beings, including humans, are composed of the **Panchamahabhutas** or the five basic elements: **ether (space)**, **air, fire, water**, and **earth**. These elements are present in varying proportions in different doshas and contribute to the formation of tissues, organs, and physiological functions.

- **Ether (Akasha)**: Represents space and is associated with openness, expansion, and emptiness.
- **Air (Vayu)**: The principle of movement and is related to mobility and circulation.
- **Fire (Agni)**: Represents transformation, heat, and metabolism.
- **Water (Jala)**: Governs liquidity, cohesion, and fluidity within the body.
- **Earth (Prithvi)**: Symbolizes stability, solidity, and structure.

Together, the **five elements** and the **doshas** form the basis of Ayurveda's understanding of the body and its connection to the universe.

3. The Dhatus (Body Tissues)

In Ayurveda, the body is supported and nourished by seven types of tissues called **Dhatus**. These Dhatus are responsible for the body's **growth, strength, immunity**, and overall health. They are sequentially formed in the body through the process of digestion and metabolism.

- **Rasa (Plasma/Lymph)**: Nourishes the body and carries essential nutrients.
- **Rakta (Blood)**: Responsible for oxygenating the body and supporting vitality.
- **Mamsa (Muscle Tissue)**: Provides structure and movement to the body.
- **Meda (Fat/Adipose Tissue)**: Lubricates the body and provides stored energy.
- **Asthi (Bone)**: Supports the body and provides structure.
- **Majja (Bone Marrow/Nervous Tissue)**: Nourishes the nervous system and bones.
- **Shukra (Reproductive Tissue)**: Responsible for reproduction and vitality.

When the Dhatus are balanced, they maintain overall health, but when there is an imbalance or depletion, disease arises.

4. Agni (Digestive Fire)

In Ayurveda, **Agni**, or the digestive fire, is central to maintaining health. It is believed that all illnesses originate from the improper functioning of Agni. **Agni** is responsible for **digesting food, assimilating nutrients**, and eliminating waste products. There are four types of Agni:

- **Sama Agni** (Balanced Digestion): When Agni is balanced, digestion is strong and proper, leading to optimal health.
- **Vishama Agni** (Irregular Digestion): Affected by Vata dosha, leading to irregular digestion, bloating, and gas.
- **Tikshna Agni** (Intense Digestion): Governed by Pitta, resulting in rapid digestion, acidity, and heartburn.
- **Manda Agni** (Slow Digestion): Influenced by Kapha, causing sluggish digestion, weight gain, and indigestion.

Proper digestion is considered the cornerstone of health in Ayurveda, and balancing **Agni** is essential for preventing disease.

5. The Malas (Waste Products)

The efficient elimination of waste products, known as **Malas**, is another critical principle in Ayurveda. The three main Malas are:

- **Purisha (Feces)**: Solid waste eliminated from the digestive tract.
- **Mutra (Urine)**: Liquid waste filtered by the kidneys.
- **Sweda (Sweat)**: Waste excreted through the skin.

Proper elimination of waste ensures the body is free from toxins (Ama), which, if accumulated, can lead to illness.

6. Srotas (Body Channels)

Srotas are the **channels** or pathways through which **nutrients, waste, air**, and **fluids** flow within the body. There are numerous Srotas in the body, each responsible for transporting specific substances such as food, water, and air. Proper functioning of these channels is vital for maintaining health. Any blockages or obstructions in the Srotas can cause diseases, and Ayurveda focuses on keeping these channels open through detoxification and purification therapies.

7. Prakriti (Constitution)

Ayurveda emphasizes the importance of an individual's **Prakriti**, or unique constitution, which is the inherent balance of the three doshas that defines a person's physical and mental characteristics. Each person's

Prakriti is unique, and Ayurveda tailors its treatments based on this constitution. **Personalized medicine** is a key concept in Ayurveda, with treatments such as **herbal remedies, dietary adjustments**, and **lifestyle modifications** being customized according to a person's dosha balance and constitution.

The **basic principles and theories of Ayurveda** revolve around achieving and maintaining the balance of the **doshas, Dhatus, Agni**, and **Srotas** to promote health and prevent disease. Ayurveda's holistic approach to health, which considers physical, emotional, and spiritual well-being, has made it a timeless system of medicine that remains relevant today. Through the regulation of diet, lifestyle, and natural treatments, Ayurveda offers personalized care to restore balance and promote long-lasting health.

1.8.3 Basic Principles and Theories of Siddha

The **Siddha system of medicine** is one of the oldest traditional healing systems, believed to have originated in South India, particularly in the **Tamil-speaking region**. The word "Siddha" comes from **Siddhars**, who were ancient sages and spiritual masters with profound knowledge of **nature, medicine, alchemy**, and **yoga**. The Siddha system is rooted in the idea that the balance of the body, mind, and spirit is essential for maintaining health, and it combines **natural remedies, spiritual practices**, and **alchemy** to treat various ailments. Siddha focuses on **individualized medicine**, tailoring treatments according to the specific needs and constitution of the individual.

1. The Three Humors (Tridosham)

Similar to Ayurveda, Siddha medicine revolves around the concept of the **three humors** or **Tridosham**, which govern all physiological processes in the human body. The three humors in Siddha are:

- **Vatham (Air and Ether)**: Vatham is associated with **movement** and governs functions like **breathing, circulation**, and **nerve impulses**. It also controls the **flexibility** of the body and **mental clarity**. When Vatham is in balance, a person experiences **vitality, quick thinking**, and **creativity**. An imbalance, however, can lead to conditions such as **arthritis, constipation**, and **anxiety**.

- **Pitham (Fire and Water)**: Pitham controls **digestion, metabolism**, and **body temperature**. It is responsible for the transformation of food into energy and the regulation of emotions such as anger and frustration. When Pitham is balanced, the person exhibits **intelligence, good**

digestion, and a healthy complexion. An excess of Pitham can result in **inflammation, ulcers, fever**, and emotional irritability.

- **Kapham (Water and Earth)**: Kapham represents **structure** and **stability**. It governs **strength, endurance**, and the body's lubrication. Kapham also plays a role in **immunity** and **hydration**. When balanced, Kapham promotes **calmness, stability, and strength**. An imbalance in Kapham can lead to issues like **obesity, congestion,** and **lethargy**.

The balance of these three humors is vital for health, and disease is believed to occur when one or more humors become imbalanced. Siddha treatments aim to restore harmony between Vatham, Pitham, and Kapham through **herbal medicines, diet,** and **spiritual practices**.

2. Panchabhootham (Five Elements)

Siddha medicine believes that the **universe** and all living beings, including humans, are made up of **five elements** known as **Panchabhootham: earth, water, fire, air,** and **ether (space)**. These elements combine in different proportions to form the three humors (Vatham, Pitham, and Kapham), which regulate all bodily functions.

- **Earth (Prithvi)**: Provides structure and stability.
- **Water (Apas)**: Governs fluid balance and lubrication.
- **Fire (Agni)**: Responsible for digestion, metabolism, and transformation.
- **Air (Vayu)**: Controls movement and circulation.
- **Ether (Akasha)**: Represents space and is linked to mental clarity and openness.

The **balance** of these elements within the body is crucial for maintaining health. Any disturbance in the harmony of the five elements can result in disease, and Siddha treatments are designed to bring these elements back into equilibrium.

3. Kayakalpa Therapy (Rejuvenation and Longevity)

One of the most unique and defining aspects of Siddha medicine is **Kayakalpa therapy**, a system of **rejuvenation** and **longevity** aimed at delaying the aging process, detoxifying the body, and enhancing **vitality**. Kayakalpa is based on the idea that the body can be regenerated through a combination of **herbs, dietary regulation, yoga,** and **meditation**. This therapy focuses on:

- **Detoxification:** Cleansing the body of toxins that accumulate due to improper diet, lifestyle, or disease.
- **Rejuvenation:** Rebuilding and restoring the tissues, improving **energy levels**, and promoting **longevity**.
- **Spiritual and Mental Well-being:** Siddha emphasizes that rejuvenation is not only physical but also mental and spiritual. Kayakalpa therapy encourages **meditation, yogic practices,** and ethical living to achieve mental clarity and spiritual growth.

Kayakalpa formulations often use potent herbal and **mineral-based preparations,** such as **Mandoor bhasma** (purified iron oxide), **mercurial compounds,** and rare herbs like **Amukkara** (Ashwagandha) and **Nannari** (Indian Sarsaparilla).

4. Importance of Diet and Lifestyle (Pathyam)

Siddha places great emphasis on **diet (Pathyam)** and **lifestyle** as key components of treatment. The belief is that the body is **nourished** by what we consume, and the wrong foods can lead to an imbalance in the humors, thus causing illness.

- **Dietary Regulations:** Siddha prescribes specific foods based on an individual's body constitution (Prakriti) and the dominant humor. Certain foods are recommended to **balance** the humors, while others are restricted based on the **nature of the disease.** For example, to balance an aggravated **Pitham, cooling foods** like cucumber and coconut are encouraged, while **spicy** and **acidic** foods are avoided.
- **Fasting:** Periodic **fasting** or **detoxification** is encouraged to allow the digestive system to rest and help eliminate toxins from the body. Siddha emphasizes that fasting can help regulate metabolism and restore the balance of the humors.
- **Lifestyle and Conduct: Yoga, meditation,** and **breathing exercises** are integral to maintaining physical, mental, and spiritual health. The **Siddhars** believed that a disciplined lifestyle, including regular sleep, ethical conduct, and mental calmness, is essential for maintaining balance in the body.

5. Siddha Medicine and Alchemy (Rasa Shastra)

Alchemy, or **Rasa Shastra,** plays an important role in Siddha medicine, where **metals** and **minerals** are used in therapeutic formulations. The

Siddhars believed that metals and minerals could be purified and processed to become medicinally beneficial.

- **Metals and Minerals**: Siddha uses a variety of metals such as **gold, silver, copper, mercury,** and **iron** in its medicines. These metals are carefully purified through processes like **calcination** (burning to ash) to create safe and effective formulations known as **Bhasmas** (calcinated metal powders).
- **Rasa Parpam**: One of the famous formulations in Siddha is **Rasa Parpam**, a medicine made from purified mercury that is believed to **strengthen immunity, increase longevity,** and cure chronic illnesses when used in small, regulated doses.

Alchemy in Siddha is regarded as a spiritual science where **herbal** and **mineral** medicines are combined to heal the body and extend life. However, it is practiced with caution to ensure the safety of patients.

6. Vital Life Energy (Prana)

In Siddha philosophy, **Prana** (vital life energy) is considered crucial for sustaining life. This concept is closely linked to the **nervous system** and the flow of **energy** within the body's channels. **Pranayama** (breathing exercises), **meditation,** and **yoga** are practices used to regulate and enhance Prana, thereby promoting **mental clarity, vitality,** and **spiritual well-being**.

The Siddhars believed that by controlling Prana, one could control the body's internal functions, boost immunity, and slow down the aging process. Thus, Siddha treatments often incorporate breathing exercises and spiritual practices alongside herbal medicines.

7. Pulse Diagnosis (Nadi)

In Siddha medicine, **pulse diagnosis** (Nadi) is a key diagnostic tool used to assess the balance of the three humors and determine the root cause of disease. Practitioners examine the patient's pulse to detect imbalances in **Vatham, Pitham,** and **Kapham,** as well as to gain insight into the patient's **mental** and **emotional** state. Nadi diagnosis provides a comprehensive picture of the patient's overall health and helps tailor individualized treatment plans.

The **basic principles and theories of Siddha** medicine emphasize the balance of the **three humors,** the **five elements,** and **vital life energy** (Prana) in maintaining health and preventing disease. Through the use of **herbal remedies, mineral-based medicines, dietary regulations,** and

spiritual practices, Siddha offers a holistic approach to healing that addresses both the physical and spiritual aspects of health. With its focus on **personalized treatments, Kayakalpa therapy** for rejuvenation, and the incorporation of **alchemy**, Siddha remains a unique and ancient system of medicine that continues to contribute to **natural healing** and **well-being**.

1.8.4 Basic Principles and Theories of Unani

Unani medicine, also known as **Unani Tibb** or **Greek-Arabic medicine**, is a traditional healing system that traces its roots to **Hippocrates** and **Galen** of ancient Greece and was later developed by **Arab** and **Persian** physicians, notably **Avicenna** (Ibn Sina). The term "Unani" is derived from "**Ionian,**" a region in ancient Greece. This system of medicine was introduced to India during the **medieval period** and became an integral part of the Indian traditional healthcare system. Unani medicine is based on the theory of **humoral balance**, where health is seen as the equilibrium between four essential body fluids, and disease results from an imbalance in these humors.

1. The Four Humors (Akhlat)

The foundation of Unani medicine rests on the theory of **four humors**, known as **Akhlat**, which regulate the body's physiological functions. The four humors are:

1. **Dam (Blood)**: Represents warmth and moisture, associated with vitality, strength, and nourishment. Blood supports growth, health, and the warmth of the body.
2. **Balgham (Phlegm)**: Cold and moist in nature, phlegm is responsible for maintaining the body's moisture balance and helps lubricate joints, support digestion, and cool the body.
3. **Safra (Yellow Bile)**: Warm and dry, yellow bile is associated with metabolism and digestion, particularly the breakdown of food and production of heat.
4. **Sauda (Black Bile)**: Cold and dry, black bile is linked to the function of the spleen and supports solid structures like bones, helping in strength and stability.

In Unani medicine, health is maintained by a proper balance of these humors, and disease occurs when one or more humors become imbalanced or corrupted. The physician's role is to identify which humor is out of balance and to restore it through natural remedies, diet, and lifestyle adjustments.

2. Mizaj (Temperament)

A key concept in Unani medicine is the notion of **Mizaj** or temperament. Every individual is believed to have a unique temperament that is influenced by the balance of the four humors. Mizaj is considered fundamental in diagnosing illness and prescribing treatments. There are four basic temperaments corresponding to the dominance of each humor:

1. **Sanguine (Dammi)**: Predominantly blood, characterized by warmth and moisture. Sanguine individuals are energetic, optimistic, and active but may become restless and overly emotional when out of balance.
2. **Phlegmatic (Balghami)**: Linked to phlegm, these individuals are cold and moist. They tend to be calm, patient, and slow-moving but may suffer from lethargy and respiratory issues if phlegm accumulates.
3. **Choleric (Safrawi)**: Governed by yellow bile, this temperament is warm and dry. Choleric individuals are ambitious, passionate, and decisive, though they may experience irritability, anger, and digestive problems when yellow bile increases.
4. **Melancholic (Saudawi)**: Associated with black bile, melancholic individuals are cold and dry, often introspective, serious, and thoughtful. However, they may experience issues such as anxiety, depression, and constipation if black bile becomes excessive.

Understanding an individual's temperament is essential for Unani practitioners as it helps in **customizing treatments** based on the person's natural tendencies and humor imbalance.

3. Asbab-e-Sitta Zarooriya (Six Essential Factors)

Unani medicine emphasizes the importance of six essential factors, known as **Asbab-e-Sitta Zarooriya**, which play a crucial role in maintaining health and preventing illness. These six factors are considered the pillars of health management and must be regulated to maintain humoral balance:

1. **Hawa (Air)**: Refers to the quality of the environment, particularly air. The temperature, humidity, and quality of the air you breathe significantly impact the balance of the humors.
2. **Makool wa Mashroob (Food and Drink)**: Nutrition is a cornerstone of Unani medicine. The quality, quantity, and type of food and drink consumed can affect the balance of humors. A proper diet is tailored to

an individual's temperament and season.

3. **Harkat wa Sukoon-e-Badani (Physical Activity and Rest):** Unani emphasizes the need for a balance between **physical activity** and **rest** to ensure the proper circulation of humors. Overexertion or inactivity can disturb humoral balance.

4. **Harkat wa Sukoon-e-Nafsani (Mental Activity and Rest):** Mental well-being is as important as physical health. Emotional disturbances, stress, and mental fatigue can disrupt the balance of humors, leading to mental and physical illnesses.

5. **Naum wa Yaqza (Sleep and Wakefulness):** Sleep plays a vital role in the healing and rejuvenation process. Proper sleep patterns support the body's natural balance, while sleep deprivation or excessive sleep can lead to health problems.

6. **Ihtibas wa Istifragh (Retention and Elimination):** This refers to the retention of essential bodily substances and the elimination of waste products (such as urine, feces, and sweat). Proper elimination is necessary to prevent the buildup of toxins (Fasad-e-Akhlat) and to maintain health.

Regulating these six essential factors is critical for the prevention of diseases and the promotion of overall well-being in Unani medicine.

4. Tabiat (The Body's Natural Healing Power)

A fundamental belief in Unani medicine is that the body possesses an innate ability to heal itself, known as **Tabiat.** Tabiat is considered the **natural intelligence** or **vital force** within the body that strives to maintain balance and health. The role of the Unani physician is to support Tabiat by providing the body with the necessary tools—such as the right diet, remedies, and lifestyle adjustments—so it can restore balance and recover from illness.

- **Tabiat** works by adjusting the levels of humors, facilitating the elimination of harmful substances, and promoting the natural repair of tissues. It is believed that the body, when supported appropriately, can self-regulate and overcome disease.

5. Ilaj bil Ghiza (Dietotherapy)

Dietotherapy (Ilaj bil Ghiza) is an essential aspect of Unani medicine, which emphasizes that food and nutrition are the first lines of treatment for any disease. Food is seen as both a cause of disease and a cure, and specific dietary recommendations are made based on the individual's temperament and humor imbalance.

- Unani practitioners use diet to **correct imbalances** in the humors. For example, if there is an excess of Safra (yellow bile), cooling foods such as cucumbers, yogurt, and barley water may be prescribed to restore balance. Similarly, warming and nourishing foods like meat broth and lentils may be recommended for someone with an excess of Balgham (phlegm).
- Dietary restrictions are also emphasized, with certain foods being avoided during illnesses to prevent further aggravation of the humors.

6. Ilaj bil Dawa (Pharmacotherapy)

When diet alone is insufficient to restore balance, **herbal remedies and natural medicines** are prescribed under **Ilaj bil Dawa**. Unani pharmacotherapy is based on the use of natural substances such as herbs, minerals, and animal products, each of which has specific effects on the humors and temperaments.

- **Herbs**: Unani medicine uses a wide array of herbs, such as **Ajwain** (Carom seeds) for digestion, **Kalunji** (Black seed) for immune enhancement, and **Zafran** (Saffron) for mental clarity and mood enhancement.
- **Safiqat** (compound formulations) are complex mixtures of herbs and minerals prepared according to traditional methods. These formulations are designed to target specific humor imbalances and are personalized to the patient's temperament.
- Medicines are often classified by their **temperamental qualities** (hot, cold, dry, moist) and are prescribed accordingly to counteract the humor imbalance.

7. Ilaj bil Tadbeer (Regimenal Therapy)

Regimenal therapy (Ilaj bil Tadbeer) includes techniques aimed at **detoxification** and **balance restoration**. These therapeutic interventions help cleanse the body of impurities and enhance the healing process. Key techniques include:

- **Hijama (Cupping therapy)**: This involves creating suction on the skin to draw out excess humors, especially Safra (yellow bile) and Sauda (black bile).
- **Massage**: Used to improve blood circulation, reduce muscle tension, and balance the humors.
- **Dalk (Rubbing)**: The application of oils and ointments on the body to stimulate circulation and balance moisture levels.
- **Hammam (Bathing therapy)**: Unani practitioners often recommend therapeutic baths to cleanse the body, soothe the nerves, and regulate humoral imbalances.

The **basic principles and theories of Unani medicine** focus on maintaining the balance of the **four humors** through an individualized approach to treatment, which includes **diet therapy**, **herbal medicines**, and **lifestyle adjustments**. By balancing **temperament** and supporting the body's **natural healing power (Tabiat)**, Unani medicine promotes both preventive health and effective treatment of diseases. With its holistic approach, Unani continues to be a vital component of traditional medicine, offering natural and time-tested remedies for a variety of health conditions.

1.8.5 Basic Principles and Theories of Homeopathy

Homeopathy, a system of alternative medicine developed by **Samuel Hahnemann** in the late **18th** century, is based on the principle of **"like cures like"** (also known as the **Law of Similars**). This means that a substance that causes symptoms in a healthy person can be used in a highly diluted form to treat similar symptoms in a sick person. Homeopathy emphasizes stimulating the body's natural healing processes by using extremely diluted substances derived from plants, minerals, or animals. The key principles of homeopathy focus on individualized treatment, minimal doses, and the holistic approach of treating the patient as a whole, including physical, emotional, and mental aspects.

1. Law of Similars (Similia Similibus Curentur)

The cornerstone of homeopathic medicine is the **Law of Similars**, which posits that diseases can be cured by substances that produce similar symptoms in a healthy person. This principle is based on the idea that the body has an inherent capacity to heal itself, and a small dose of a substance that mimics the disease symptoms will stimulate this self-healing process.

- For example, **Arnica montana**, a plant that can cause bruising and soreness when taken in large doses, is used in homeopathic remedies to treat bruises, muscle soreness, and injuries.
- Similarly, **Allium cepa** (onion), which causes watery eyes and a runny nose in healthy individuals, is used as a remedy for cold symptoms that involve watery eyes and nasal discharge.

This concept is similar to the principle of **vaccination** in conventional medicine, where a small dose of a virus or bacterium is introduced to stimulate the immune system.

2. Law of Infinitesimal Dose (Potentization)

Another key principle in homeopathy is the **Law of Infinitesimal Dose**, which states that the effectiveness of a remedy increases as it is diluted and potentized (shaken or succussed). Homeopathic remedies are prepared through a process known as **potentization**, which involves serial dilution and vigorous shaking (succussion) of the substance at each step of dilution. This process is believed to **enhance** the healing properties of the remedy while minimizing toxicity.

- Homeopathic remedies are prepared in **decimal (X), centesimal (C),** and **millesimal (M)** potencies, where each step involves diluting the original substance by 1:10, 1:100, or 1:1000, respectively.
- Despite the extreme dilution (sometimes to the point where no molecules of the original substance remain), homeopaths believe that the remedy retains an energetic imprint of the substance, which stimulates the body's healing mechanisms.

For example, **Nux vomica**, derived from the strychnine tree, is toxic in large doses, but when diluted to a high potency in homeopathy, it is used to treat symptoms such as indigestion, headaches, and irritability.

3. Individualized Treatment

Homeopathy is highly **individualized**, meaning that treatment is tailored to the specific symptoms and characteristics of the patient rather than to the disease itself. Two people with the same condition might receive different homeopathic remedies based on their unique physical, emotional, and mental symptoms.

- Homeopaths take a detailed case history of the patient, including not only their physical symptoms but also their **emotional state**, **personality**, **lifestyle**, and **environmental factors**. This comprehensive approach allows for the selection of a remedy that best matches the patient's overall symptom profile.
- For example, two patients with migraines may receive different remedies—one might be prescribed **Belladonna** if their migraines are characterized by throbbing pain and sensitivity to light, while another might be given **Pulsatilla** if their headaches are accompanied by emotional sensitivity and weepiness.

The **holistic approach** ensures that the patient's overall constitution and life situation are taken into account, leading to a more personalized and targeted treatment.

4. Minimum Dose

Homeopathy operates on the principle of using the **minimum dose** necessary to trigger the body's healing response. This is in line with the **Law of Infinitesimal Dose**, where highly diluted remedies are believed to be more effective and less harmful than larger doses of the active substance.

- The rationale behind this principle is that small doses avoid **side effects** and toxic reactions while still stimulating the body's innate healing ability. Homeopaths believe that the body needs only a subtle signal to initiate healing and that higher doses could potentially overwhelm or suppress the natural healing process.
- This principle makes homeopathy particularly appealing for treating sensitive individuals, such as children, pregnant women, and the elderly, as it minimizes the risk of adverse reactions.

5. Vital Force (Life Energy)

Homeopathy is based on the concept of **Vital Force**, a life energy or vital principle that sustains the body and maintains health. According to homeopathic theory, disease arises when there is a disturbance or imbalance in the Vital Force. The purpose of homeopathic treatment is to **restore balance** to the Vital Force, thereby allowing the body to heal itself.

- In homeopathy, the Vital Force is seen as the governing energy that regulates bodily functions and defends against illness. When the Vital

Force is weakened or disturbed, symptoms of illness arise.

- Homeopathic remedies act as catalysts to stimulate the Vital Force, restoring harmony and balance to the patient's physical, emotional, and mental well-being.

This concept of Vital Force is similar to the **Qi** in **Traditional Chinese Medicine** and **Prana** in **Ayurveda**, both of which are seen as essential life energies that support health and vitality.

6. Holistic Approach

Homeopathy treats the patient as a **whole person**, addressing not only the physical symptoms but also the **mental**, **emotional**, and **spiritual** aspects of health. This holistic approach is based on the idea that the body, mind, and spirit are interconnected, and that imbalances in one area can affect the others.

- Homeopathy recognizes the importance of **mental and emotional health** in the healing process. Conditions like **stress, anxiety, depression**, and **emotional trauma** are taken into account when prescribing remedies.
- For instance, a homeopath treating a patient with asthma might look beyond the physical symptoms and consider emotional factors like stress, anxiety, or fear, which could be contributing to the condition. Remedies such as **Ignatia** or **Aconite** may be prescribed depending on the patient's emotional state in addition to their physical symptoms.

7. Constitutional Treatment

In homeopathy, **constitutional treatment** refers to the long-term management of an individual's overall health by addressing their constitution or natural predispositions. This is not limited to the treatment of acute conditions but aims to maintain **long-term well-being** by strengthening the person's overall vitality.

- A person's constitution is determined by their **temperament, genetic makeup, lifestyle**, and past medical history. Homeopathic remedies are selected based on the person's overall constitution to prevent future illnesses and support a healthy balance of mind, body, and spirit.
- For example, someone with a **constitutional predisposition** to digestive disorders might receive **Sulphur** or **Calcarea carbonica** as a long-term

remedy to enhance their overall health and reduce the frequency or severity of digestive complaints.

8. Chronic and Acute Treatment

Homeopathy is effective in treating both **acute** and **chronic** conditions. Acute treatments are aimed at addressing **short-term illnesses**, such as the flu, headaches, or injuries, by matching the symptoms with an appropriate remedy. On the other hand, chronic treatment focuses on **long-term health issues**, such as arthritis, skin conditions, or autoimmune diseases, by addressing the underlying imbalance in the Vital Force.

- **Acute conditions** are usually treated with remedies that match the symptoms of the illness in a rapid manner, such as **Aconite** for sudden-onset fever or **Apis mellifica** for allergic reactions and swelling.
- **Chronic conditions** require a more in-depth understanding of the patient's overall constitution, temperament, and life history, with remedies such as **Lycopodium** or **Silicea** being used to restore long-term balance.

The **basic principles and theories of homeopathy** revolve around the ideas of **like cures like, minimal doses, individualized treatment**, and **stimulating the body's innate healing powers**. Homeopathy is a holistic system that takes into account the patient's physical, emotional, and mental state, treating the person as a whole. Through the use of highly diluted remedies and a personalized approach, homeopathy aims to **restore balance** and promote long-lasting health by strengthening the **Vital Force** and addressing both acute and chronic illnesses.

1.9.1 Aristas and Asawas – Fermented Formulations

Aristas and **Asawas** are traditional **Ayurvedic fermented formulations** widely used for their therapeutic benefits. These preparations are unique in that they involve **natural fermentation**, which not only preserves the active ingredients but also enhances their efficacy and shelf life. Both Aristas and Asawas are liquid formulations, but the key difference between them lies in the method of preparation: **Aristas** are made by boiling the herbs, while **Asawas** are prepared without boiling. These formulations are primarily used to promote digestion, improve metabolism, and treat various disorders, including respiratory, digestive, and immune system ailments.

Preparation of Aristas

Aristas are prepared by boiling medicinal herbs in water to extract the active ingredients, followed by **fermentation** with sugar, jaggery, or honey. The preparation process involves the following steps:

1. **Herbal Decoction**: In the preparation of Aristas, the selected medicinal herbs are boiled in water to form a **decoction**. The amount of water used is typically four to sixteen times the weight of the herbs, depending on the formulation. The decoction is boiled until the water is reduced to one-fourth or one-eighth of its original volume, ensuring the concentration of the active constituents.

2. **Addition of Fermenting Agents**: After the decoction has cooled, **fermenting agents** such as sugar, jaggery, or honey are added. These agents provide the necessary sugars to facilitate fermentation. In some formulations, medicinal substances like **Dhataki flowers** (Woodfordia fruticosa) are also added to enhance the fermentation process.

3. **Fermentation**: The mixture is transferred to fermentation vats or vessels, which are sealed and kept in a warm environment for **30 to 60 days**, depending on the formulation. During this period, natural fermentation takes place, converting the sugars into **alcohol**. The alcohol produced acts as a self-preservative and also facilitates the absorption of the medicinal compounds.

4. **Filtration and Storage**: After the fermentation process is complete, the liquid is filtered to remove solid residues and impurities. The final product is stored in airtight containers. Aristas can be stored for long periods, and their efficacy improves with aging.

Examples of commonly used Aristas include:

- **Dashmoolarishta**: Used to treat weakness, respiratory conditions, and joint pain.
- **Ashwagandharishta**: Known for its adaptogenic properties, it helps reduce stress and anxiety while promoting vitality.
- **Balarishta**: Primarily used to improve strength and treat neuromuscular disorders.

Preparation of Asawas

Unlike Aristas, **Asawas** are prepared without boiling the herbs. Instead, the raw herbs are soaked directly in water along with the fermenting agents.

The key steps in preparing Asawas are:

1. **Mixing of Ingredients**: In the preparation of Asawas, the medicinal herbs are soaked in water, along with sugar, jaggery, or honey. Unlike Aristas, there is no decoction or boiling process, which helps preserve heat-sensitive compounds in the herbs.
2. **Fermentation**: The mixture is allowed to ferment naturally in a sealed container for a period of **30 to 60 days**. The fermentation process is driven by the natural sugars present in the ingredients, which are converted into alcohol. The alcohol not only preserves the formulation but also aids in the extraction of the active compounds from the herbs.
3. **Filtration and Storage**: After the fermentation process, the liquid is filtered to remove solid particles. The final Asawa product is stored in sealed containers, and, like Aristas, Asawas can also be aged to enhance their therapeutic properties.

Examples of popular Asawas include:

- **Lohasava**: Used to treat iron deficiency anemia and improve overall vitality.
- **Kumaryasava**: Beneficial for liver disorders, digestive issues, and menstrual problems.
- **Chandanasava**: Known for its cooling properties, it is used to treat urinary tract infections and heat-related conditions.

Therapeutic Benefits of Aristas and Asawas

1. **Improved Digestion and Absorption**: The **fermentation process** involved in the preparation of Aristas and Asawas produces small amounts of alcohol, which acts as a natural preservative and a medium that enhances the bioavailability of the active ingredients. This makes it easier for the body to absorb the medicinal compounds, leading to better therapeutic outcomes.
2. **Preservation of Medicinal Properties**: Both Aristas and Asawas have a long shelf life due to the alcohol produced during fermentation. This ensures that the **therapeutic potency** of the herbs is maintained over time, and in some cases, the efficacy of these formulations increases as they age.

3. **Adaptogenic and Immunomodulatory Effects**: Many Aristas and Asawas, such as **Ashwagandharishta** and **Balarishta**, are known for their **adaptogenic properties**, helping the body cope with stress and promoting overall vitality. These formulations are also used to **strengthen the immune system** and improve resilience to diseases.

4. **Detoxification and Rejuvenation**: Aristas and Asawas are often prescribed for detoxification and rejuvenation purposes. They help remove **toxins (Ama)** from the body, improve metabolic function, and promote the **rejuvenation** of tissues and organs.

Standardization of Aristas and Asawas

Standardization is crucial to ensure the **quality**, **safety**, and **efficacy** of Aristas and Asawas. The standardization process includes:

1. **Raw Material Quality**: The quality of the raw herbs used in the preparation is crucial for the effectiveness of the final product. Proper **identification** and **authentication** of herbs are necessary to avoid adulteration and ensure that the correct species are used.

2. **Fermentation Process Control**: The fermentation process must be carefully monitored to ensure the optimal conversion of sugars into alcohol and the proper extraction of active ingredients. Parameters such as **temperature, pH**, and **fermentation duration** are standardized to achieve consistency across batches.

3. **Alcohol Content**: The **alcohol content** in the final product is measured and standardized to ensure that it falls within safe and effective limits, typically ranging between **5-10%** in most formulations.

4. **Chemical and Microbial Testing**: The final product is subjected to **chemical analysis** to confirm the presence and concentration of key active compounds. Additionally, microbial testing is performed to ensure that the product is free from harmful microorganisms.

Aristas and Asawas are integral parts of **Ayurvedic pharmacology**, offering numerous therapeutic benefits through the natural fermentation process. These formulations are highly effective in treating a wide range of health conditions, from **digestive disorders** to **immune deficiencies**. Their long shelf life, improved bioavailability, and minimal side effects make them popular choices in Ayurvedic medicine. The standardization of Aristas and Asawas ensures the consistent quality and safety of these traditional remedies, allowing them to continue playing a vital role in modern Ayurvedic healthcare.

1.9.2 Ghutika – Pills and Tablets in Ayurveda

Ghutika refers to **Ayurvedic pills** or **tablets** that are widely used in traditional medicine for their ease of administration, long shelf life, and ability to deliver concentrated doses of medicinal herbs and minerals. The term "Ghutika" is derived from Sanskrit, meaning a **small round pill**, and it represents one of the most convenient forms of Ayurvedic medicine. These pills are made by **processing herbal powders** or **extracts**, often combined with natural binders and liquids like **honey, ghee,** or **herbal decoctions,** which are then shaped into pills or tablets. Ghutikas are used to treat a wide range of health conditions, including digestive disorders, respiratory problems, and chronic diseases, and they allow for precise dosage control of potent medicinal substances.

Preparation of Ghutika

The preparation of Ghutika involves a step-by-step process to ensure that the active ingredients are effectively concentrated and stabilized for therapeutic use. The basic steps in preparing Ghutikas are as follows:

1. **Selection of Ingredients**: The first step in the preparation of Ghutika is the careful selection of **medicinal herbs, minerals,** or **metals** (in the case of **Bhasmas,** or calcined metals) that are known to have therapeutic effects. The herbs used can be single or a combination of multiple ingredients, depending on the formulation and intended use.

2. **Powdering (Churna)**: The selected herbs are then dried and ground into a **fine powder (Churna).** In many formulations, the powder is passed through a fine sieve to ensure a uniform consistency. This powder may sometimes be roasted with **ghee** or **oil** to enhance its therapeutic efficacy, as in the case of **Vatsanabha Ghutika,** which uses purified **aconite** for stimulating digestive function.

3. **Binding Agents:** To bind the powdered ingredients into pill form, natural agents such as **honey, ghee, sugar,** or **herbal decoctions** (like **Kashaya**) are used. These agents not only help in shaping the pills but also enhance the **bioavailability** and **therapeutic effects** of the ingredients.

4. **Formation of Pills:** The herbal powder is mixed with the binding agent to form a paste, which is then rolled into small round pills (typically the size of a chickpea). In modern practice, this paste can be compressed into tablet form using machinery.

5. **Drying**: Once the pills are formed, they are dried naturally in a shaded area to prevent the loss of volatile oils or other sensitive compounds. The drying process ensures that the Ghutika is **preserved** and can be stored for long periods without spoilage.

6. **Storage**: After drying, the pills are stored in **airtight containers** to protect them from moisture, air, and contamination. Ghutikas can last for several months to years if stored properly, making them a convenient form of medication for both patients and practitioners.

Types of Ghutika

There are various types of Ghutikas, each designed for specific health concerns. Some well-known examples include:

- **Lavangadi Vati**: A common Ghutika used to treat **cough, sore throat,** and **respiratory infections**. It contains ingredients like **lavanga (clove), cinnamon,** and **cardamom,** which have expectorant and soothing properties.

- **Vatsanabha Ghutika**: This formulation contains **Vatsanabha (aconite)** and is primarily used to treat **digestive disorders, rheumatism,** and **fevers**. Aconite is a potent herb that is detoxified and processed carefully before use.

- **Sutshekhar Ras**: This Ghutika is used for **gastric disorders, acid reflux,** and **indigestion**. It combines herbs like **ginger, pepper,** and **cardamom** with mineral ingredients such as **sodium carbonate** to balance digestive function.

- **Chandraprabha Vati**: Known for its **rejuvenating** and **detoxifying** properties, Chandraprabha Vati is used to treat a range of conditions including **urinary disorders, diabetes,** and **joint pain**. It contains herbs like **Haritaki, Guggulu,** and **Shilajit,** which promote overall vitality and well-being.

Therapeutic Uses of Ghutika

Ghutika formulations are versatile and can be used to treat a wide range of ailments. Some of their primary therapeutic applications include:

1. **Digestive Health**: Many Ghutikas are formulated to improve **digestion, reduce bloating, stimulate appetite,** and treat **constipation**. Ingredients like **ginger, black pepper,** and **cardamom** are common in digestive

formulations as they stimulate digestive enzymes and reduce gas.

2. **Respiratory Disorders**: Ghutikas like **Lavangadi Vati** are used to treat **cough, asthma, bronchitis**, and **respiratory infections**. The combination of anti-inflammatory and expectorant herbs helps soothe the respiratory tract and expel phlegm.

3. **Pain and Inflammation**: Formulations such as **Brihat Vata Chintamani Ras** are used for **joint pain, rheumatoid arthritis**, and **muscle aches**. These Ghutikas often contain anti-inflammatory herbs like **Guggulu** and **Shallaki** (Boswellia).

4. **Chronic Conditions**: Many Ghutikas, such as **Chandraprabha Vati**, are used for chronic health issues like **diabetes, urinary disorders**, and **reproductive health**. These formulations contain a blend of **rejuvenating herbs** that help restore normal function and maintain long-term health.

5. **Stress and Mental Health**: Some Ghutikas are used for improving mental clarity, reducing stress, and promoting emotional balance. For instance, **Ashwagandha Ghutika** is known for its **adaptogenic** properties, helping individuals cope with stress and anxiety.

Standardization of Ghutika

Standardization is critical to ensure the **quality**, **purity**, and **efficacy** of Ghutika formulations. The process includes:

1. **Raw Material Quality**: Ensuring the use of authentic, pure, and well-processed herbs is essential for the effectiveness of Ghutika. Herbs should be collected during their optimal season, and their active compounds must be preserved.

2. **Consistency in Formulation**: Every batch of Ghutika should be prepared with consistent ratios of ingredients and undergo strict quality control to maintain uniformity. Modern technology helps in achieving this consistency by using standardized manufacturing techniques.

3. **Chemical Analysis**: The final product undergoes **chemical testing** to check the concentration of active compounds, ensuring that the Ghutika meets the required therapeutic standards.

4. **Microbial Testing**: Microbial contamination is a concern for all Ayurvedic formulations, and Ghutikas are no exception. Rigorous **microbial testing** ensures that the product is free from harmful bacteria, fungi, or other contaminants.

5. **Stability Testing**: Stability tests are conducted to check how long the product retains its efficacy. This helps in determining the shelf life and ensuring the product's safety and effectiveness over time.

Ghutika, or **Ayurvedic pills and tablets**, are an integral part of **Ayurvedic medicine**, offering a convenient and effective way to deliver the therapeutic benefits of herbs and minerals. Through careful preparation and standardization, these formulations provide targeted treatment for a wide range of health conditions, from digestive disorders to respiratory ailments, pain, and chronic diseases. The combination of traditional knowledge and modern standardization techniques ensures that Ghutikas remain a reliable and effective form of Ayurvedic medicine, enhancing patient compliance and offering a practical solution for long-term healthcare.

1.9.3 Churna – Herbal Powders

Churna refers to finely powdered herbal formulations used in **Ayurvedic medicine**. The word "Churna" in Sanskrit means powder, and it represents a traditional and popular dosage form in Ayurveda, where the medicinal herbs are **dried, ground**, and **sifted** into fine powders for therapeutic use. Churnas are commonly prescribed for a wide range of health conditions due to their versatility, ease of preparation, and quick absorption in the body. These powdered formulations can be used internally (orally) or externally (as pastes or poultices) to treat various ailments ranging from **digestive disorders** to **respiratory issues, skin diseases**, and more. Some well-known examples of Churnas include **Triphala Churna, Hingvastak Churna**, and **Sitopaladi Churna**.

Preparation of Churna

The preparation of Churna involves a series of systematic steps to ensure the uniformity, potency, and efficacy of the final product. These steps include:

1. **Selection of Ingredients**: The first step in preparing Churna is the **selection of medicinal herbs** based on their therapeutic properties. Each herb is chosen for its specific effect on the doshas (Vata, Pitta, Kapha), the tissues, or organs. In multi-herb formulations, herbs are combined to enhance or balance their effects. For example, in **Triphala Churna**, three fruits—**Haritaki (Terminalia chebula), Bibhitaki (Terminalia bellirica)**, and **Amalaki (Emblica officinalis)**—are used in equal

proportions to form a balanced formula.

2. **Drying:** The selected herbs are dried in the shade to preserve their **volatile oils** and **active compounds**. Shade drying is preferred over sun drying to protect the herbs from losing their potency and from potential photochemical degradation.

3. **Powdering:** Once dried, the herbs are ground into a **fine powder** using a mortar and pestle or, in modern practice, using mechanical grinders. The grinding process is carefully controlled to achieve the right consistency, as overly coarse or too fine a powder can affect the formulation's absorption and effectiveness.

4. **Sieving:** The powdered herbs are then passed through a **fine sieve** to remove any larger particles or impurities and to ensure a uniform texture. The sieved Churna is usually of a fine consistency, allowing for better absorption and easier ingestion.

5. **Storage:** After sieving, the powder is stored in **airtight containers** to prevent exposure to moisture, air, or light, which can degrade the potency of the herbs. Proper storage also helps in maintaining the shelf life of the Churna, which can typically last for several months to years when stored correctly.

Types of Churna

There are various types of Churnas used in Ayurveda, each serving a unique therapeutic purpose. Some of the most widely used Churnas include:

- **Triphala Churna:** A combination of three fruits—Haritaki, Bibhitaki, and Amalaki—Triphala Churna is a powerful detoxifier and rejuvenator. It is commonly used to improve **digestion**, relieve **constipation**, and support **liver function**. Triphala is also known for its **antioxidant properties** and is used to promote longevity and vitality.

- **Hingvastak Churna:** This Churna is primarily used for digestive issues such as **indigestion, gas,** and **bloating.** It contains **Hing (Asafoetida)** along with other spices like **black pepper, ginger,** and **cumin** that stimulate digestion and reduce Vata-related digestive disorders.

- **Sitopaladi Churna:** Known for its ability to treat **respiratory ailments** like colds, coughs, and bronchitis, Sitopaladi Churna contains ingredients like **long pepper (Pippali), cinnamon, cardamom,** and **bamboo shoots.** It is commonly used to relieve congestion, expel mucus, and boost the immune system.

- **Avipattikar Churna**: This Churna is used to treat **acid reflux, gastritis,** and other Pitta-related digestive issues. It contains a blend of herbs like **Amla, Haritaki, Vibhitaki, ginger,** and **cloves** that help balance excess Pitta and improve digestion.
- **Chandraprabha Churna**: Used for **urinary disorders, kidney stones,** and **reproductive health,** this formulation contains a variety of herbs including **Guggulu, Triphala,** and **Shilajit,** which have detoxifying and rejuvenating effects.

Therapeutic Uses of Churna

Churnas are versatile and used to address a wide range of health concerns. Some of their key therapeutic applications include:

1. **Digestive Disorders**: Many Churnas are formulated to improve **digestion,** reduce **bloating,** relieve **constipation,** and support healthy metabolism. Ingredients like **ginger, asafoetida,** and **pepper** are commonly included in digestive Churnas to stimulate the production of digestive enzymes and relieve indigestion.
2. **Detoxification and Rejuvenation**: Formulations like **Triphala Churna** are used for gentle detoxification of the body. Triphala, in particular, is prized for its ability to remove **toxins (Ama),** promote regular bowel movements, and support liver health.
3. **Respiratory Health**: Churnas like **Sitopaladi Churna** are beneficial for treating **respiratory issues** such as cough, cold, bronchitis, and asthma. The warming and expectorant herbs used in these formulations help expel mucus and ease congestion.
4. **Skin and Hair Health**: Some Churnas, such as **Manjishtha Churna,** are used externally and internally to treat **skin conditions** like acne, eczema, and pigmentation. Manjishtha is known for its **blood-purifying properties,** which help clear skin issues from within. Similarly, **Bhringraj Churna** is used for **hair health,** promoting hair growth and preventing dandruff and premature graying.
5. **Metabolic and Weight Management**: Churnas like **Trikatu Churna,** a blend of **black pepper, long pepper,** and **ginger,** are known to stimulate metabolism and enhance the bioavailability of nutrients. They are often used to support **weight management** and improve overall digestion.
6. **Immunity and Strength**: Some Churnas are designed to boost **immunity** and **energy levels.** For example, **Ashwagandha Churna** is used as a **tonic**

to enhance physical strength, endurance, and resilience to stress, making it a popular adaptogen in Ayurveda.

Standardization of Churna

Standardization is essential to ensure the quality and potency of Churnas, especially as they are widely used in modern Ayurvedic practice. The key aspects of standardization include:

1. **Raw Material Quality**: The herbs used in the preparation of Churnas must be of high quality and properly identified and authenticated to avoid adulteration or substitution. The herbs should be collected during their optimal season and processed immediately to preserve their active compounds.
2. **Powder Fineness**: The particle size of the Churna must be consistent to ensure optimal absorption and ease of consumption. The fineness is checked through sieving to maintain uniformity.
3. **Chemical Testing**: The Churna is subjected to **chemical analysis** to ensure that it contains the correct concentration of **active ingredients**. This is particularly important for formulations with specific therapeutic purposes.
4. **Microbial Testing**: Since Churnas are powdered and consumed orally, they must be tested for microbial contamination, including bacteria, fungi, and yeast, to ensure safety.
5. **Shelf Life and Storage**: Proper storage conditions are essential for maintaining the efficacy of Churnas. Standardization includes testing the stability and shelf life of the product to ensure it remains effective over time.

Churna, as a traditional Ayurvedic formulation, remains one of the most widely used and versatile forms of medicine in Ayurveda. Its ease of preparation, quick absorption, and the wide variety of conditions it can address make it a valuable tool in Ayurvedic treatments. From digestive health and detoxification to respiratory and metabolic support, Churnas offer a practical and effective means of harnessing the healing power of herbs. Standardization ensures that Churnas maintain their quality, safety, and potency, allowing them to continue playing a key role in both traditional and modern Ayurvedic medicine.

1.9.4 Lehya – Herbal Jams

Lehya, also known as **herbal jams**, are a unique and highly effective form of **Ayurvedic medicine** used for their nourishing and rejuvenating properties. These semisolid preparations are made by cooking **medicinal herbs, sugar**, and sometimes **ghee** or **honey** into a thick jam-like consistency. Lehya formulations are known for their ability to improve **digestion, strength**, and **immunity**, while also providing long-lasting therapeutic effects. Due to their rich composition, Lehyas are widely used in Ayurveda for treating chronic ailments, enhancing vitality, and promoting overall health and longevity.

Preparation of Lehya

The process of preparing Lehya is elaborate and involves careful selection of ingredients and precise cooking methods to ensure the efficacy of the final product. The preparation process includes the following steps:

1. **Decoction Preparation (Kwatha)**: The preparation of Lehya begins with creating a **decoction** of the medicinal herbs. The herbs are boiled in water until the liquid reduces to about one-fourth or one-eighth of the original volume. This concentrated decoction extracts the active principles of the herbs.

2. **Addition of Sweetening Agents**: Once the herbal decoction is prepared, **sugar, jaggery**, or **honey** is added to the mixture. The sweetening agent acts as a preservative and improves the taste, making the formulation more palatable, especially for long-term consumption. In some formulations, **ghee** or **oil** is also added to enhance absorption and nourish body tissues.

3. **Cooking to Thick Consistency**: The decoction and sweetening agent mixture is cooked over a low flame until it reaches a **thick, jam-like consistency**. The cooking process must be carefully controlled to avoid burning or overcooking the herbs. The goal is to evaporate excess moisture while preserving the medicinal properties of the herbs.

4. **Addition of Potentiators (Prakshepa Dravyas)**: After the mixture reaches the desired consistency, **potentiating substances** (known as **Prakshepa Dravyas**) like **spices, mineral powders**, or **herbal extracts** may be added. These ingredients enhance the therapeutic effects of the Lehya. For instance, in **Chyawanprash**, ingredients like **Pippali** (long pepper), **cinnamon**, and **cardamom** are added to improve digestion and immunity.

5. **Cooling and Storage**: Once the Lehya is cooked to the correct consistency, it is allowed to cool before being stored in airtight containers. Lehyas can have a long shelf life if stored in a cool, dry place.

Types of Lehyas

Several well-known Lehyas are used in Ayurvedic practice, each offering different health benefits depending on the herbs and ingredients used. Some of the popular Lehyas include:

- **Chyawanprash**: Perhaps the most famous Lehya, Chyawanprash is a **rejuvenative tonic** made from **Amla** (Indian gooseberry) as the primary ingredient, along with dozens of other herbs like **Ashwagandha, Shatavari,** and **Pippali.** It is widely used to boost **immunity,** enhance **digestion,** and improve **vitality.** Chyawanprash is particularly rich in **antioxidants** and is used to prevent aging and promote overall health.
- **Agastya Rasayana**: This Lehya is commonly used for **respiratory ailments** such as **asthma, bronchitis,** and **chronic cough.** It contains ingredients like **Dashamoola, Pippali,** and **Amla,** which have anti-inflammatory and expectorant properties.
- **Ashwagandhadi Lehya**: Made with **Ashwagandha** (Withania somnifera) as the main ingredient, this Lehya is used to promote **strength, endurance,** and **sexual vitality.** It is often prescribed for individuals suffering from stress, fatigue, or muscle weakness.
- **Drakshavaleha**: This formulation is based on **Draksha** (grapes) and is used to treat **anemia, indigestion,** and **respiratory conditions.** It is known for its **cooling** and **nourishing** properties.
- **Kushmanda Lehya**: Made from **Kushmanda (Ash gourd),** this Lehya is used for **respiratory disorders, digestive issues,** and to promote **weight gain** in individuals who are undernourished or weak.

Therapeutic Benefits of Lehya

Lehyas are highly versatile and are used in the treatment of a wide range of health conditions. Some of their primary therapeutic benefits include:

1. **Immunity Boosting**: Many Lehyas, such as **Chyawanprash,** are rich in **antioxidants, vitamins,** and **minerals** that help boost the immune system. These formulations are particularly beneficial for individuals who are prone to **colds, infections,** or **seasonal illnesses.** Regular

consumption of immunity-boosting Lehyas helps protect the body from pathogens and strengthens the body's natural defense mechanisms.

2. **Rejuvenation and Anti-aging**: Lehyas are often used in **Rasayana therapy** for rejuvenation and longevity. They help nourish the body's tissues, improve **energy levels**, and prevent the signs of aging. **Chyawanprash**, for instance, is traditionally consumed to enhance vitality and promote **healthy aging**.

3. **Digestive Health**: Lehyas like **Agastya Rasayana** and **Drakshavaleha** are used to treat digestive disorders such as **indigestion**, **gas**, and **constipation**. The herbs used in these formulations help stimulate digestion, regulate bowel movements, and relieve digestive discomfort.

4. **Respiratory Support**: Many Lehyas are formulated to support **respiratory health** by acting as expectorants, bronchodilators, and anti-inflammatories. Lehyas like **Agastya Rasayana** are commonly prescribed for **asthma, chronic bronchitis,** and **cough**. The herbs in these formulations help expel mucus, reduce inflammation, and clear the respiratory pathways.

5. **Energy and Strength**: Lehyas like **Ashwagandhadi Lehya** are used to promote **physical strength, endurance,** and **muscle growth**. These formulations are especially useful for individuals recovering from illness, surgery, or periods of intense physical or mental stress.

6. **Sexual Vitality and Reproductive Health**: Certain Lehyas, such as **Ashwagandhadi Lehya** and **Kushmanda Lehya**, are used to enhance **sexual vitality** and **reproductive health**. They help boost **libido**, improve **sperm quality**, and address issues related to sexual weakness or fatigue.

Standardization of Lehya

To ensure the **quality**, **safety**, and **efficacy** of Lehyas, proper standardization practices are followed. These include:

1. **Quality of Ingredients**: The herbs and other ingredients used in Lehya must be of high quality, free from **contaminants**, and properly **authenticated**. Ensuring the proper identification of herbs is critical to avoid adulteration.

2. **Consistency in Formulation**: Every batch of Lehya should be prepared with consistent proportions of herbs, sugar, ghee, and other ingredients. Maintaining consistency ensures that the formulation has uniform

therapeutic effects.

3. **Proper Cooking and Processing**: The preparation of Lehya requires precise cooking times and temperatures to ensure the active ingredients are properly extracted and preserved. Overcooking or undercooking can reduce the potency of the formulation.

4. **Microbial Testing**: Since Lehyas contain sweetening agents like sugar and honey, they are prone to microbial contamination. Regular microbial testing ensures that the Lehya is free from harmful microorganisms such as **bacteria, yeast,** and **fungi.**

5. **Shelf Life and Stability**: Lehyas typically have a long shelf life due to their high sugar content and thick consistency, which act as natural preservatives. However, shelf-life testing is important to ensure the product remains effective over time.

Lehya, or **herbal jams,** are a significant part of **Ayurvedic medicine,** offering a potent and long-lasting form of treatment for a wide variety of health issues. Their unique preparation, which combines herbs, sweeteners, and ghee or honey, creates a formulation that is **nourishing, rejuvenating,** and **immune-boosting.** Lehyas like **Chyawanprash, Agastya Rasayana,** and **Ashwagandhadi Lehya** are well-known for their ability to enhance **digestion, immunity, strength,** and **vitality.** The careful **standardization** of Lehyas ensures their quality and effectiveness, making them a valuable addition to modern Ayurvedic practice.

1.9.5 Bhasma – Ayurvedic Metal-Based Formulations

Bhasma refers to **metal-based Ayurvedic formulations** that are created by **calcining metals** or minerals through a meticulous purification and incineration process, resulting in fine, ash-like powders. The term "Bhasma" in Sanskrit means "ash," and these formulations are used in Ayurveda for their **therapeutic and rejuvenating properties. Bhasmas** are known for their **bioavailability,** as the process of calcination transforms metals and minerals into a highly absorbable form, allowing them to deliver their medicinal properties effectively without toxicity. Bhasmas are used to treat a wide range of chronic ailments, including **digestive disorders, respiratory issues, nervous system disorders,** and **anemia,** and they also play a significant role in **Rasayana (rejuvenation) therapy.**

Preparation of Bhasma

The preparation of Bhasma is a sophisticated process that involves multiple stages of purification and calcination to eliminate any toxicity and enhance the medicinal properties of the metals and minerals used. This process is called **Shodhana** (purification) and **Marana** (incineration). The steps are as follows:

1. **Shodhana (Purification):** Before the metal or mineral is incinerated, it must undergo a rigorous purification process called Shodhana to remove impurities and reduce toxicity. This involves **heating** the metal or mineral and **quenching** it in various herbal liquids, such as **cow's urine, milk, butter,** or **herbal decoctions.** Shodhana purifies the material and makes it more suitable for human consumption by reducing its harsh effects on the body.

2. **Bhavana (Trituration):** After purification, the purified metal or mineral is ground into a fine paste using a **mortar and pestle,** often with the addition of herbal juices or decoctions. This process is called **Bhavana,** and it helps in incorporating the medicinal properties of the herbs into the metal or mineral. The paste is then dried and prepared for incineration.

3. **Marana (Incineration):** The dried material is placed in **earthen pots** (Sharavas) and subjected to repeated cycles of heating (Puta) in a closed furnace, a process known as **Marana.** The material is heated at high temperatures (ranging from **500°C to 1,000°C**) in multiple rounds. After each round, the material is ground and triturated with herbal juices, and the process is repeated several times until the metal or mineral is transformed into a **fine ash** or Bhasma. This step is crucial in ensuring that the metal is converted into a bioavailable form that can be safely assimilated by the body.

4. **Sieve and Storage:** The resulting Bhasma is carefully sieved to achieve a fine consistency and is then stored in airtight containers. The final product is a highly purified and potent powder that can be consumed in very small doses.

Types of Bhasmas

Different types of Bhasmas are made from a variety of metals and minerals, each offering unique therapeutic benefits. Some well-known Bhasmas include:

- **Swarna Bhasma (Gold Bhasma):** Made from purified gold, Swarna Bhasma is considered a powerful **rejuvenator** and is used to improve immunity, strength, and **mental clarity**. It is often prescribed for conditions like **tuberculosis, asthma, arthritis**, and **anemia**. Swarna Bhasma is also used as an **anti-aging** and **anti-stress** agent in Rasayana therapy.

- **Rajata Bhasma (Silver Bhasma)**: Rajata Bhasma, made from silver, is used to treat **nervous system disorders**, including **anxiety, depression**, and **insomnia**. It is known for its cooling properties and is often used in Pitta-related disorders like **hyperacidity** and **burning sensations**.

- **Loha Bhasma (Iron Bhasma)**: Loha Bhasma is used to treat **iron deficiency anemia, general debility**, and **liver disorders**. It helps in improving hemoglobin levels and promoting healthy blood circulation. Loha Bhasma is also used in cases of **digestive weakness** and **fatigue**.

- **Tamra Bhasma (Copper Bhasma)**: Tamra Bhasma is prepared from copper and is primarily used to treat **liver disorders, digestive issues**, and **skin diseases**. It is also beneficial in conditions like **jaundice, hepatitis**, and **high cholesterol**.

- **Abhrak Bhasma (Mica Bhasma)**: Abhrak Bhasma, made from purified mica, is used for its **rejuvenating properties** and is beneficial in treating **respiratory disorders, chronic cough**, and **asthma**. It also supports healthy tissue regeneration and enhances vitality.

Therapeutic Benefits of Bhasma

Bhasma formulations are widely used in Ayurveda due to their unique ability to deliver the therapeutic benefits of metals and minerals in a safe and bioavailable form. Some of the key therapeutic benefits of Bhasma include:

1. **Enhanced Bioavailability**: The calcination process makes metals and minerals highly absorbable and bioavailable, allowing the body to effectively utilize their medicinal properties. Bhasmas are finely powdered and thus easily assimilated into the bloodstream, enhancing their therapeutic effects.

2. **Rasayana and Rejuvenation**: Many Bhasmas, such as **Swarna Bhasma** and **Abhrak Bhasma**, are used in **Rasayana therapy** for rejuvenation and to promote longevity. These formulations help **revitalize the body, boost immunity**, and **slow down aging** by enhancing tissue regeneration and improving overall vitality.

3. **Treatment of Chronic Diseases:** Bhasmas are especially effective in treating **chronic ailments** such as **arthritis, asthma, digestive disorders,** and **liver diseases. Tamra Bhasma,** for example, is known for its efficacy in treating liver disorders like **jaundice** and **cirrhosis,** while **Loha Bhasma** is widely used to address iron deficiency and anemia.

4. **Strengthening Immunity and Vitality:** Bhasmas like **Swarna Bhasma** are known for their ability to **enhance immunity** and **mental clarity.** These formulations are often prescribed for individuals recovering from serious illnesses or surgery, as they help **rebuild strength** and improve overall well-being.

5. **Nervous System Support:** Certain Bhasmas, such as **Rajata Bhasma,** are known for their calming effects on the nervous system. These formulations are used to treat conditions like **anxiety, insomnia,** and **depression,** helping to stabilize mood and improve mental health.

6. **Detoxification and Metabolic Support:** Bhasmas like **Tamra Bhasma** and **Loha Bhasma** are used for their detoxifying effects, especially in the liver and digestive tract. They help **remove toxins** (Ama) from the body and support metabolic processes, making them useful in managing conditions related to poor digestion, sluggish metabolism, and toxin buildup.

Standardization of Bhasma

Given the complexity of preparing Bhasma, standardization is critical to ensure its **safety, quality,** and **efficacy.** The standardization process involves several key aspects:

1. **Raw Material Quality:** The metals or minerals used in the preparation of Bhasma must be of high quality and free from impurities. Proper sourcing and **authentication** of the raw materials are essential to ensure the safety and effectiveness of the final product.

2. **Purification and Calcination Standards:** The processes of **Shodhana** (purification) and **Marana** (calcination) must be carried out according to classical Ayurvedic guidelines, and each step must be carefully monitored to ensure the elimination of toxicity and the transformation of the metal or mineral into a bioavailable form.

3. **Particle Size and Consistency:** The final Bhasma should be **ultra-fine,** with particles so small that they can easily penetrate tissues and be absorbed by the body. This is tested by methods such as the **Varitara**

test, where the Bhasma should float on water, indicating its fineness and lightness.

4. **Chemical Composition and Safety Testing**: Bhasmas undergo rigorous **chemical analysis** to ensure that they contain the correct concentrations of active ingredients and are free from harmful impurities such as **heavy metals**. Additionally, **toxicity tests** are performed to confirm the safety of the formulation.

5. **Shelf Life and Stability**: Proper **shelf-life testing** ensures that Bhasmas remain effective and safe for extended periods. The final product is stored in airtight containers to protect it from moisture and contamination.

Bhasma, as a metal-based Ayurvedic formulation, plays a vital role in **traditional Indian medicine** due to its ability to deliver the **therapeutic benefits** of metals and minerals in a safe, bioavailable form. The process of **calcination** and **purification** ensures that the metals used in Bhasma are not only detoxified but also transformed into highly absorbable powders that the body can effectively utilize for healing. From promoting **immunity** and **rejuvenation** to treating **chronic diseases**, Bhasmas offer a potent and time-tested approach to restoring health and balance in the body. The strict standardization practices followed in the preparation of Bhasma ensure that these formulations remain **safe**, **effective**, and **reliable** in Ayurvedic treatment.

CHAPTER II

Nutraceuticals

2.1 General Aspects of Nutraceuticals

The term **nutraceuticals** is derived from the combination of the words "**nutrition**" and "**pharmaceuticals**", highlighting the bridge between food and medicine. Nutraceuticals refer to products derived from food sources that offer **additional health benefits** beyond their basic nutritional value. These products are widely used to **prevent diseases**, improve **health**, and enhance **longevity**. Nutraceuticals have gained global attention due to their ability to promote **well-being**, reduce the risk of **chronic diseases**, and provide **therapeutic effects**. They occupy a space between **conventional food** and **medicinal drugs**, often marketed as **dietary supplements**, **functional foods**, or **fortified foods**. As of 2023, the global nutraceuticals market is valued at approximately **USD 400 billion**, with a projected compound annual growth rate (CAGR) of 7.5% over the next five years. The rising demand for nutraceuticals is driven by an increasing awareness of **preventive healthcare**, a growing aging population, and the shift toward **natural** and **organic** remedies.

2.1.1 Definition and Classification of Nutraceuticals

Nutraceuticals are broadly defined as **food components** or **nutritional products** that provide **health benefits** beyond basic nutrition. They can be natural or **synthetically** derived and come in various forms such as **tablets**, **capsules**, **powders**, and **liquids**. The **U.S. Food and Drug Administration (FDA)** does not formally recognize the term nutraceuticals, and they are instead categorized as **dietary supplements** or **functional foods** depending on their composition and intended use.

Nutraceuticals are classified into several categories based on their **source, purpose,** and **mode of action:**

- **Dietary supplements**: These include vitamins, minerals, amino acids, and other substances taken to **complement** the diet. Common examples are **vitamin C, calcium supplements,** and **omega-3 fatty acids.**
- **Functional foods**: These are foods that are fortified with **bioactive compounds** to enhance their health benefits. For example, **fortified cereals** with added **iron** or **milk** enriched with **calcium** are popular

functional foods.

- **Medical foods**: These are specially formulated for patients who need specific nutrients to manage **chronic diseases**. Medical foods are often used under medical supervision and include products like **high-protein shakes** for patients with **muscle-wasting diseases** or **glucose-free formulas** for managing **diabetes**.
- **Probiotics and prebiotics**: These are specific types of nutraceuticals that focus on improving **gut health**. **Probiotics** contain live beneficial bacteria, like **Lactobacillus** or **Bifidobacterium**, while **prebiotics** are dietary fibers that nourish gut bacteria, such as **inulin** found in **chicory**.
- **Herbals and botanicals**: This group includes **herbal extracts** and **botanical compounds** used for their medicinal properties. Examples include **turmeric**, known for its **anti-inflammatory** properties due to the active compound **curcumin**, and **green tea extracts**, rich in **antioxidants**.

These classifications help consumers and healthcare providers choose the appropriate nutraceutical based on specific health needs, whether for **disease prevention**, **therapeutic purposes**, or general **wellness**. Additionally, nutraceuticals can be used to address specific conditions such as **heart disease**, **arthritis**, **osteoporosis**, and **cognitive decline**. Studies have shown that regular consumption of nutraceuticals like **omega-3 fatty acids** can reduce the risk of cardiovascular diseases by **up to 30%**.

2.1.2 Difference Between Nutraceuticals and Pharmaceuticals

While **nutraceuticals** and **pharmaceuticals** both play significant roles in the promotion of health and the prevention of disease, there are critical differences between the two categories. Nutraceuticals are derived primarily from **natural sources**, often from foods or plants, and are consumed with the intent of **enhancing health**, preventing disease, or **managing symptoms** of certain conditions. Unlike pharmaceuticals, nutraceuticals are not meant to **treat or cure diseases** but to **support bodily functions** and **prevent illness** through **nutrition-based mechanisms**.

One of the major differences lies in their **regulation**. Pharmaceuticals are subject to rigorous testing and approval processes by regulatory bodies such as the **FDA** or **EMA** (European Medicines Agency). Before a pharmaceutical drug is approved, it must undergo **preclinical studies**, **clinical trials**, and extensive evaluations to prove its **safety, efficacy**, and **potential side effects**. Pharmaceuticals must meet strict standards of

dosage, purity, and **quality**, and their **manufacturing processes** are highly controlled. For example, a **hypertension** drug must demonstrate a specific **therapeutic effect** in lowering blood pressure through well-documented clinical evidence.

In contrast, nutraceuticals do not require the same level of stringent testing or clinical trials, particularly in many countries. Although some nutraceuticals have shown **positive health outcomes** in clinical studies, they are typically marketed as **dietary supplements** rather than drugs, which means their **claims** are often less regulated. As long as a nutraceutical does not make direct **medical claims** such as curing a disease, it can be sold without extensive clinical validation. For instance, **probiotics** are commonly sold to support **digestive health**, but they do not require the same evidence as a drug that treats **irritable bowel syndrome (IBS)**.

Another distinction is in the **mechanism of action**. Pharmaceuticals are designed to address specific **pathophysiological processes**, targeting specific **biomolecules** or **cellular pathways** to treat a disease. For example, **statins** lower **cholesterol** by inhibiting the enzyme **HMG-CoA reductase**. Nutraceuticals, on the other hand, work through more **general mechanisms**, often supporting overall **metabolic processes**, **immune functions**, or **cellular health**. For example, **antioxidants** in nutraceuticals like **vitamin E** and **resveratrol** work by neutralizing **free radicals** to reduce **oxidative stress** and inflammation.

In terms of **safety profiles**, nutraceuticals are generally considered **safer** than pharmaceuticals since they are derived from food sources that are often part of the regular diet. However, this does not mean that nutraceuticals are entirely free from side effects or **interactions**. Excessive intake of certain nutraceuticals, like **vitamin A**, can lead to toxicity, and some herbal supplements, such as **St. John's Wort**, can interact with prescription medications, affecting their efficacy. In comparison, pharmaceuticals have well-documented **side effect profiles**, and their interactions with other drugs are closely monitored.

2.2 Market, Growth, and Scope of Nutraceuticals

The **nutraceuticals market** has witnessed significant growth over the past few decades, driven by increasing consumer awareness of **health and wellness**, the rising burden of **chronic diseases**, and the global shift toward **preventive healthcare**. The market, which includes dietary supplements, functional foods, and herbal products, is expanding rapidly as consumers seek natural alternatives to pharmaceuticals to support long-term health.

The increasing demand for **plant-based products, organic supplements, and fortified foods** has further accelerated the market's growth, both globally and in India. The growing emphasis on **fitness, immunity-boosting products**, and **anti-aging solutions** has also contributed to the rising popularity of nutraceuticals.

2.2.1 Global and Indian Market Trends

The **global nutraceuticals market** is currently valued at approximately **USD 400 billion** and is expected to grow at a **CAGR of 7.5%** over the next five years. The rapid growth is driven by increasing health consciousness, particularly in developed countries like the **United States, Japan**, and **Germany**, where consumers are more focused on **preventive health**. In the U.S., the nutraceuticals market is dominated by **dietary supplements**, especially vitamins, minerals, and **protein-based products**, driven by the rising popularity of **sports nutrition** and **weight management**. The **Asia-Pacific** region is expected to witness the fastest growth due to increasing awareness of **natural remedies** and the growing middle class with higher disposable incomes. Countries like **China, India**, and **South Korea** are leading this trend, with China being the largest producer and consumer of nutraceuticals in Asia.

In **India**, the nutraceuticals market is valued at around **USD 10 billion** as of 2023, and it is expected to reach **USD 18 billion** by 2025, growing at a **CAGR of 12-15%**. This growth is fueled by the increasing demand for **Ayurvedic products, herbal supplements**, and **functional foods**, especially after the COVID-19 pandemic, which heightened consumer focus on **immunity** and **preventive healthcare**. The Indian nutraceutical market is unique in that it has a strong reliance on **traditional medicine systems** like **Ayurveda** and **Unani**, with products like **Ashwagandha, Tulsi**, and **Giloy** becoming highly popular in the post-pandemic era. Companies like **Dabur, Patanjali**, and **Himalaya** are leaders in the Indian nutraceutical market, offering a wide range of herbal and Ayurvedic supplements targeting **immunity, energy**, and **general wellness**.

Functional foods are another growing segment in India, with consumers increasingly opting for **fortified products** like **breakfast cereals, yogurt**, and **energy bars** that provide additional health benefits beyond basic nutrition. The market for **protein supplements** is also expanding, driven by the growth of **fitness culture** in urban India. **Sports nutrition** products, especially **whey protein** and **plant-based protein supplements**, have gained popularity among fitness enthusiasts and athletes.

The Indian government has played a key role in supporting the growth of the nutraceutical industry through initiatives such as the **National Health Policy**, which emphasizes **preventive health** and the promotion of natural remedies. The regulatory framework, governed by agencies like the **Food Safety and Standards Authority of India (FSSAI)**, has been evolving to support the growth of the nutraceuticals industry by implementing safety and quality standards for dietary supplements and functional foods.

Additionally, the **export potential** of Indian nutraceutical products is growing, with demand for **Ayurvedic supplements** and **herbal products** rising in countries like the **U.S.**, **Canada**, **Europe**, and parts of **Africa**. The increasing popularity of **organic and plant-based products** in these regions has opened new avenues for Indian nutraceutical companies to expand globally. This is particularly relevant for products like **organic turmeric supplements**, **moringa powder**, and **spirulina**, which are highly sought after in international markets for their medicinal and health-promoting properties.

2.2.2 Future Scope and Innovations in Nutraceuticals

The **future scope of nutraceuticals** is incredibly promising, driven by growing consumer demand for **natural health solutions**, advancements in **biotechnology**, and ongoing research into the **health benefits** of various plant-based and functional foods. As more consumers prioritize **preventive healthcare** over traditional treatments, the nutraceutical market is expected to witness significant innovations in the coming years, ranging from personalized nutrition to the integration of cutting-edge technologies like **nanotechnology** and **genomics**. These advancements will enhance the efficacy, bioavailability, and precision of nutraceutical products, providing more targeted health benefits.

One of the key trends shaping the future of the nutraceutical industry is **personalized nutrition**, where supplements and functional foods are tailored to an individual's **genetic makeup, lifestyle,** and **health status**. By leveraging data from **DNA testing, microbiome analysis,** and **artificial intelligence**, companies can create customized nutraceutical regimens that meet specific health needs, such as enhancing **gut health**, managing **blood sugar levels**, or improving **cognitive function**. This approach offers a more **personalized, data-driven** solution to health management, making nutraceuticals more effective in achieving desired health outcomes.

Another important innovation is the use of **nanotechnology** to improve the **bioavailability** of nutraceutical compounds. Many nutraceuticals, such as **curcumin** from turmeric or **resveratrol** from grapes, have limited absorption in the body due to their **poor solubility** in water. **Nanoencapsulation** techniques can encapsulate these bioactive compounds in **nanoscale carriers**, increasing their stability, absorption, and delivery to target tissues. This technology is expected to revolutionize the nutraceutical industry by enhancing the **efficacy** of existing supplements and functional foods, making them more potent in lower doses.

In addition to nanotechnology, **biotechnology** is playing a crucial role in developing **new functional ingredients**. For example, the use of **fermentation technology** to create **bioactive peptides** or **probiotics** that support **gut health** and **immune function** is gaining popularity. **Synthetic biology** is also being explored to produce **nutraceutical ingredients** like **omega-3 fatty acids** or **antioxidants** in a more sustainable and scalable manner, reducing the reliance on natural sources like fish or certain plants. These biotechnological advancements will expand the range of **functional ingredients** available for use in dietary supplements and functional foods.

The rise of **plant-based nutraceuticals** is another significant trend, driven by the growing consumer preference for **vegan, organic,** and **sustainably sourced** products. Plant-based ingredients such as **moringa, ashwagandha,** and **spirulina** are already popular for their high nutritional value and health benefits, and this trend is expected to continue with the development of more plant-based **protein supplements, antioxidants,** and **adaptogens**. The shift toward **clean-label products**, free from synthetic additives, preservatives, and animal-derived ingredients, is fueling innovation in plant-based nutraceuticals.

Gut health remains a major focus in the nutraceutical industry, with innovations in **prebiotics, probiotics,** and **postbiotics** gaining traction. The growing understanding of the **gut-brain axis** and its influence on mental health and overall well-being is pushing forward the development of **synbiotic** products that combine probiotics and prebiotics for enhanced gut microbiome support. These products are not only beneficial for **digestive health** but also show promise in improving **immune function**, reducing **inflammation**, and supporting **mental clarity**.

The incorporation of **artificial intelligence (AI)** and **machine learning** into **nutraceutical product development** is another exciting area of innovation. AI can be used to analyze large datasets from clinical trials, consumer feedback, and biochemical research to identify trends, predict market demand, and formulate new nutraceutical products that are more aligned with consumer needs. This technology will streamline the **research and development (R&D)** process, making it faster and more efficient to bring new products to market.

In terms of **sustainability**, the nutraceutical industry is seeing innovations in the development of **eco-friendly packaging** and **sustainable sourcing** of raw materials. With increasing concerns over **plastic waste** and environmental impact, companies are exploring **biodegradable** or **recyclable packaging** options for nutraceutical products. Additionally, the use of **sustainably farmed herbs** and **organic ingredients** is becoming a priority for manufacturers looking to appeal to environmentally conscious consumers.

2.3 Types of Nutraceutical Products

Nutraceutical products are categorized based on their **function, form,** and **intended use**, with the primary goal of enhancing **health** and **preventing diseases**. These products often bridge the gap between food and medicine, offering therapeutic benefits beyond basic nutrition. Among the most popular and widely used nutraceutical products are **dietary supplements**, which play a crucial role in supporting **nutrition** and **health management**.

2.3.1 Dietary Supplements

Dietary supplements are one of the most commonly used types of nutraceutical products. They are formulated to provide additional **nutrients** that may not be consumed in sufficient quantities through regular diet alone. Dietary supplements typically come in the form of **tablets, capsules, soft gels, powders,** or **liquids,** and they contain concentrated amounts of **vitamins, minerals, amino acids, enzymes, herbal extracts,** or **other bioactive compounds.**

The global market for dietary supplements was valued at **USD 150 billion** in 2022 and is projected to grow at a **CAGR of 8%** over the next decade. This growth is driven by rising awareness of **preventive health,** increasing interest in **sports nutrition,** and a growing aging population seeking ways to maintain **vitality** and manage **chronic conditions.**

Dietary supplements can be classified into several categories based on the nutrients they provide:

- **Vitamins:** Vitamin supplements are among the most common types, with **vitamin D, vitamin C,** and **vitamin B12** being widely used. For instance, vitamin D supplements are crucial for **bone health,** especially in populations with limited exposure to sunlight. Vitamin C is popular for its role in boosting **immune function** and protecting against **oxidative stress**.

- **Minerals:** Mineral supplements such as **calcium, magnesium,** and **iron** are essential for maintaining various bodily functions. **Calcium** supplements, for example, are critical for **bone density** and are often prescribed to prevent **osteoporosis**, especially in postmenopausal women. Iron supplements are commonly used to treat **anemia**, particularly in women of childbearing age.

- **Amino acids:** These supplements, such as **branched-chain amino acids (BCAAs)** and **L-arginine**, are popular among athletes and individuals focused on **muscle growth** and **recovery**. BCAAs, specifically **leucine, isoleucine,** and **valine**, are known for promoting **muscle protein synthesis** and reducing **exercise-induced muscle damage**.

- **Probiotics and prebiotics:** Probiotic supplements contain beneficial **live bacteria**, such as **Lactobacillus** and **Bifidobacterium**, which help to support a healthy **gut microbiome**. Prebiotics, such as **inulin** and **fructooligosaccharides (FOS)**, serve as food for these beneficial bacteria, promoting their growth. Together, these supplements aid in **digestive health, immune system support**, and the prevention of conditions like **irritable bowel syndrome (IBS)**.

- **Herbal supplements:** Herbal dietary supplements contain extracts from **plants** and **herbs** known for their medicinal properties. Common examples include **ginseng** for energy, **gingko biloba** for cognitive function, and **turmeric** for its potent **anti-inflammatory** effects due to the presence of **curcumin**. Herbal supplements have gained popularity for managing conditions such as **stress, anxiety,** and **inflammation**.

- **Omega-3 fatty acids:** Supplements like **fish oil** or **algal oil** are rich in **EPA** and **DHA**, which are essential for **heart health**. Omega-3 fatty acids have been extensively studied for their role in reducing **triglycerides,** improving **heart function**, and supporting **brain health**.

- **Antioxidants:** These supplements, such as **resveratrol, green tea extract,** and **vitamin E**, are widely used to protect cells from **oxidative stress** caused by free radicals. Antioxidants help reduce the risk of chronic diseases, including **cancer** and **heart disease**.

Dietary supplements are particularly popular among people with specific **nutritional deficiencies**, athletes looking for performance enhancement, and the elderly who may require extra nutritional support. However, the efficacy of dietary supplements can depend on factors such as **bioavailability**, dosage, and the individual's **metabolic state**.

In terms of regulation, dietary supplements fall under **different categories** based on the region. In the **United States**, for example, they are regulated by the **Food and Drug Administration (FDA)** as **foods**, not as drugs, meaning they do not undergo the same rigorous clinical testing as pharmaceuticals. However, manufacturers are required to ensure their products are **safe** and properly labeled. Similarly, in **India**, dietary supplements are regulated by the **Food Safety and Standards Authority of India (FSSAI)**, which sets guidelines for the safe production and marketing of these products.

While dietary supplements offer numerous health benefits, **quality control** remains an important issue. Consumers must be aware of the potential risks of **over-supplementation** or interactions with **medications**. For instance, excess intake of **fat-soluble vitamins** like **vitamin A** or **vitamin D** can lead to toxicity, while supplements like **St. John's Wort** can interact with certain **prescription medications** such as **antidepressants**, affecting their efficacy.

In summary, **dietary supplements** are an essential category within nutraceutical products, offering targeted support for **nutritional deficiencies**, **sports performance**, and **chronic disease management**. As the global demand for **preventive healthcare** grows, the role of dietary supplements in maintaining **health and wellness** is set to expand further, with new innovations and more personalized approaches to supplement use expected in the future.

2.3.2 Functional Foods

Functional foods are a significant category within the nutraceutical industry, offering health benefits beyond basic nutrition. These foods are consumed not only for their **nutritional value** but also for their ability to support specific **physiological functions** or help in the **prevention** and **management** of diseases. Functional foods include both natural foods and **fortified, enhanced, or modified foods** that are formulated to improve **health outcomes**. The global market for functional foods has seen tremendous growth, with a valuation of approximately **USD 250 billion** in 2023, and is expected to grow at a **CAGR of 8-10%** over the next few years. This expansion is driven by rising consumer interest in **wellness, disease prevention**, and **healthy aging**, along with the increasing availability of innovative products in the market.

Functional foods are defined as foods that contain **bioactive compounds, fortified nutrients,** or **naturally occurring substances** that provide benefits beyond basic nutrition. They are often used to address specific health concerns, such as **heart disease, diabetes, obesity,** and **gut health.** These foods may be consumed as part of a regular diet and are not classified as supplements or medications.

There are several key categories of functional foods:

- **Fortified foods:** These are foods that have been enhanced with additional nutrients. For example, **fortified cereals** often contain added **iron, vitamins,** and **fiber** to support overall health. Similarly, **fortified milk** may contain **calcium** and **vitamin D,** both essential for maintaining **bone health** and preventing **osteoporosis,** especially in older adults.
- **Probiotic and prebiotic foods:** Probiotic foods, such as **yogurt, kefir,** and **fermented vegetables,** contain **live beneficial bacteria** that support gut health and boost **immune function.** Prebiotic foods, like **bananas, garlic,** and **onions,** provide **dietary fibers** that nourish these beneficial bacteria in the digestive system, improving overall **digestive health.** These foods are increasingly being recognized for their role in the **gut-brain axis,** highlighting the connection between gut health and **mental well-being.**
- **Functional beverages:** Drinks that are fortified with **vitamins, minerals,** or **herbal extracts** to deliver specific health benefits are becoming increasingly popular. Examples include **green tea,** which is rich in **antioxidants** like **catechins** that help reduce the risk of **cardiovascular diseases,** and **enhanced waters** containing **electrolytes, fiber,** or **probiotics** to support hydration, digestion, and overall health.
- **Omega-3 enriched foods:** Foods fortified with **omega-3 fatty acids,** such as **eggs, bread,** or **margarine,** are designed to support **heart health** and reduce inflammation. Omega-3 fatty acids, especially **EPA** and **DHA,** have been shown to lower **triglyceride levels,** reduce the risk of **heart disease,** and improve **cognitive function.** These functional foods are particularly beneficial for individuals who may not consume enough **fatty fish** in their diets.
- **Whole grains and fiber-rich foods:** Foods such as **oats, barley,** and **whole wheat** are rich in **soluble fiber** like **beta-glucan,** which helps lower **cholesterol levels** and improves **cardiovascular health.** These

grains are also beneficial for managing **blood sugar levels**, making them ideal for individuals with **diabetes** or those at risk of developing **metabolic syndrome.**

- **Phytochemicals and antioxidants**: Certain fruits, vegetables, and beverages contain high levels of **phytochemicals** and **antioxidants**, such as **polyphenols, flavonoids,** and **carotenoids,** which protect cells from oxidative stress and reduce inflammation. Foods like **blueberries, spinach,** and **green tea** are rich in these compounds and are associated with a reduced risk of **chronic diseases,** including **cancer, diabetes,** and **neurodegenerative diseases** like **Alzheimer's.**

The role of functional foods in **preventive health** is growing as consumers become more educated about the link between **diet** and **well-being.** Many people are shifting toward foods that not only meet their nutritional needs but also provide **therapeutic benefits.** For example, **cholesterol-lowering spreads** containing **plant sterols** are marketed specifically to individuals seeking to reduce their **LDL cholesterol** levels naturally, without medication. Similarly, **high-fiber cereals** and **oat-based products** are promoted for their ability to improve **digestive health** and prevent **constipation.**

In India, the demand for functional foods is on the rise, particularly with the increasing awareness of **Ayurvedic principles** and **traditional Indian ingredients.** Products like **turmeric lattes** (which capitalize on turmeric's anti-inflammatory properties due to **curcumin**) and **Amla-based** beverages (rich in **vitamin** C) are gaining popularity both domestically and internationally. Indian consumers are increasingly seeking foods that support **immunity, mental health,** and **digestive wellness,** especially in the wake of the **COVID-19 pandemic.**

The future of functional foods will likely see greater innovation in areas such as **personalized nutrition,** where foods are tailored to an individual's **genetic makeup, lifestyle,** and **health goals.** Advances in **food technology** are enabling the development of **functional ingredients** that offer more precise health benefits, such as **plant-based proteins** and **fermented plant foods,** which are designed to meet the growing demand for **vegan** and **sustainable diets.**

2.3.3 Medical Foods

Medical foods represent a specialized category within the nutraceuticals market, formulated to meet the **nutritional needs** of individuals with specific **health conditions** or **diseases**. Unlike dietary supplements or functional foods, medical foods are designed for the **dietary management** of diseases that require **distinctive nutritional needs** that cannot be met by normal diet alone. These products are typically used under medical supervision and are often prescribed as part of a treatment plan for **chronic conditions**, metabolic disorders, or illnesses that necessitate specialized nutrition.

Medical foods are not considered **drugs**, but they must adhere to stringent guidelines to ensure they meet **safety, quality**, and **effectiveness** standards. In the **United States**, medical foods are regulated by the **Food and Drug Administration (FDA)** under the **Orphan Drug Act**, which defines them as products intended for the dietary management of a disease with medically recognized needs. These foods differ from dietary supplements and functional foods in that they are specifically tailored to address the metabolic and physiological changes associated with certain diseases, requiring a **prescription** or medical guidance for use.

Medical foods are often available in the form of **liquids, powders**, or **bars** and are designed to be easily digestible and absorbed by patients who may have compromised **digestive systems** or other **health issues**. Some of the most common applications of medical foods include their use in managing diseases such as **diabetes, chronic kidney disease, Alzheimer's disease,** and **inborn errors of metabolism** (IEMs) like **phenylketonuria (PKU)**.

Key types of medical foods include:

- **Enteral nutrition products**: These are formulated to provide complete nutrition through a **feeding tube** for individuals who are unable to consume food orally due to conditions such as **stroke, neurological disorders**, or **cancer**. Enteral nutrition solutions are typically rich in essential **vitamins, minerals, proteins**, and **calories** to support overall health and recovery.
- **Low-protein or amino acid-modified foods**: These are crucial for individuals with **inborn errors of metabolism**, such as **PKU**, where the body cannot process certain proteins or amino acids. Patients with PKU, for example, must avoid foods containing **phenylalanine**, and medical foods provide specially formulated low-protein or amino-acid-modified products to meet their nutritional needs without causing harm.
- **Diabetes-specific medical foods**: These products are designed to help manage **blood sugar levels** in patients with **type 2 diabetes**. These foods

often contain **slow-digesting carbohydrates** and ingredients that support **glycemic control**, such as **fiber** and **healthy fats**. Products like **Glucerna**, a popular diabetes medical food, provide nutrition while helping to minimize **blood sugar spikes** after meals.

- **Neurodegenerative disease-specific foods**: Medical foods are increasingly being formulated for patients with conditions like **Alzheimer's disease** and **Parkinson's disease**. For instance, products containing **ketone bodies** or **MCT (medium-chain triglyceride) oil** are being used to support brain function and energy metabolism in Alzheimer's patients, based on research showing that **ketone metabolism** can improve **cognitive function** in these individuals.

- **Renal-specific medical foods**: Patients with **chronic kidney disease (CKD)** have unique nutritional requirements, particularly regarding **protein, phosphorus**, and **electrolyte** intake. Medical foods for CKD patients are formulated to provide balanced nutrition while managing **electrolyte imbalances** and **metabolic waste** buildup that can result from impaired kidney function. These products are essential in preventing **malnutrition** while supporting overall **renal health**.

The market for medical foods has been growing steadily due to the increasing prevalence of **chronic diseases** and the aging population. As of 2023, the global medical foods market is valued at approximately **USD 20 billion**, with a projected **CAGR of 6.7%** over the next five years. This growth is driven by rising demand for personalized nutrition solutions that cater to the specific needs of patients with complex medical conditions.

One of the major areas of innovation in medical foods is the development of products for **neurological diseases**, particularly **Alzheimer's** and **mild cognitive impairment**. As research into the connection between **nutrition** and **brain health** advances, new medical foods are being designed to support **neuroprotection** and **cognitive function**. Products like **Axona**, which is formulated for Alzheimer's patients, contain ingredients that support **ketone body production** as an alternative fuel for the brain, which is thought to improve cognitive performance in individuals with **dementia**.

Medical foods also play an essential role in the management of **autoimmune diseases**, such as **Crohn's disease** and **ulcerative colitis**, where patients may require specialized nutrition to reduce inflammation and support **intestinal healing**. Formulations rich in **omega-3 fatty acids**,

glutamine, and **anti-inflammatory compounds** are often used to alleviate symptoms and support remission in patients with these conditions.

In India, the demand for medical foods is growing as more healthcare providers recognize the importance of **nutritional therapy** in managing chronic diseases. The Indian market is still developing, but companies are increasingly offering **diabetes-specific products** and **renal nutrition solutions** to meet the needs of patients. With India's large diabetic population, there is significant potential for growth in medical foods tailored to glycemic control and metabolic health.

2.4 Health Benefits of Nutraceuticals

Nutraceuticals offer a wide range of **health benefits**, particularly in the prevention and management of **chronic diseases**. By providing **bioactive compounds, vitamins, minerals**, and other essential nutrients, nutraceuticals help improve **overall health** and **well-being** while playing a vital role in the **management** of conditions such as **diabetes, cardiovascular diseases, cancer**, and **neurodegenerative disorders**. With the growing focus on **preventive healthcare**, nutraceuticals have gained popularity for their ability to enhance **immune function**, support **metabolic health**, and reduce the risk of developing **chronic diseases**. Among the various health conditions, **diabetes** management through nutraceuticals is a key area of focus, given the increasing prevalence of **type 2 diabetes** worldwide.

2.4.1 Role in Managing Chronic Diseases

Chronic diseases, such as **diabetes**, are among the leading causes of **morbidity** and **mortality** globally. Nutraceuticals play a significant role in managing these conditions by providing targeted nutrients that help modulate **metabolic pathways**, reduce **inflammation**, and improve **insulin sensitivity**. The integration of nutraceuticals in managing chronic diseases is seen as an effective complementary approach to **conventional therapies** and **lifestyle modifications**.

2.4.1.1 Diabetes

Diabetes, particularly **type 2 diabetes**, is a chronic metabolic disorder characterized by elevated **blood glucose levels** due to **insulin resistance** or insufficient **insulin production**. The role of nutraceuticals in managing diabetes has become increasingly important, as these products offer natural solutions to help **regulate blood sugar levels**, enhance **insulin sensitivity**, and prevent complications associated with diabetes, such as **cardiovascular disease, kidney damage**, and **nerve damage**.

Several nutraceuticals have demonstrated significant benefits in **blood glucose control** and improving overall **metabolic health**. These include:

- **Cinnamon extract**: Cinnamon is one of the most studied nutraceuticals for diabetes management. It contains **polyphenols** and **antioxidants** that help improve **insulin sensitivity** and lower **fasting blood sugar levels**. Studies have shown that consuming **1 to 6 grams** of cinnamon per day can reduce **hemoglobin A1C** levels (a marker of long-term blood glucose control) by **0.83%** in people with type 2 diabetes.

- **Alpha-lipoic acid (ALA)**: ALA is a powerful **antioxidant** that plays a critical role in improving **insulin sensitivity** and reducing **oxidative stress**, which is a contributing factor in diabetes complications. ALA has been shown to lower **fasting glucose levels** and improve **peripheral nerve function** in individuals with diabetic **neuropathy**.

- **Chromium picolinate**: Chromium is an essential **trace mineral** that enhances the action of **insulin** by improving **glucose uptake** in the body's cells. Studies have indicated that chromium supplementation (typically **200-1,000 mcg** per day) can help reduce **fasting blood sugar** and **insulin resistance** in individuals with type 2 diabetes.

- **Fenugreek**: Fenugreek seeds contain high levels of **soluble fiber** and compounds like **4-hydroxyisoleucine**, which have been shown to lower **postprandial glucose levels** by slowing carbohydrate absorption and improving **insulin secretion**. Clinical studies have shown that consuming **10-15 grams** of fenugreek daily can significantly reduce fasting blood sugar and improve **glycemic control**.

- **Omega-3 fatty acids**: Found in **fish oil** and **flaxseed**, omega-3 fatty acids are known for their **anti-inflammatory** properties and are beneficial in managing **diabetic complications**, particularly **cardiovascular diseases**. Omega-3 fatty acids can improve **lipid profiles**, reduce **triglycerides**, and enhance **vascular health**, all of which are crucial for individuals with diabetes, as they are at a higher risk of developing heart disease.

- **Bitter melon (Momordica charantia)**: Bitter melon is a traditional medicinal plant known for its **hypoglycemic effects**. Its active compounds, such as **charantin** and **polypeptide-p**, mimic insulin's action, helping to lower blood sugar levels. Studies have shown that consuming **50-100 ml** of bitter melon juice daily can significantly reduce **fasting blood glucose** and HbA1c levels in type 2 diabetic patients.

- **Berberine**: Berberine, a bioactive compound found in plants like **goldenseal** and **barberry**, has demonstrated remarkable efficacy in lowering **blood glucose levels**. Berberine works by activating **AMPK (adenosine monophosphate-activated protein kinase)**, an enzyme that helps regulate **glucose metabolism** and increases **insulin sensitivity**. Research has shown that berberine can reduce **fasting blood sugar** by up to **20%** and has similar effects to **metformin**, a commonly prescribed diabetes medication.
- **Psyllium husk**: Psyllium is a soluble fiber that helps regulate **postprandial blood sugar levels** by slowing the absorption of carbohydrates in the gut. Regular consumption of psyllium (typically **5-10 grams** per day) has been shown to improve **glycemic control** and lower cholesterol levels in individuals with type 2 diabetes.

Nutraceuticals not only aid in **glycemic management** but also help address **inflammation, oxidative stress,** and **lipid abnormalities** commonly associated with diabetes. The combination of nutraceuticals with lifestyle interventions like **diet, exercise,** and **weight management** can significantly enhance diabetes care and reduce dependence on medications.

In India, where the incidence of diabetes is high, traditional nutraceuticals like **turmeric, amla** (Indian gooseberry), and **neem** have been widely used to manage blood sugar levels and improve overall health. The Indian market for **diabetes-specific nutraceuticals** is expanding rapidly, with many products incorporating **Ayurvedic herbs** and **plant-based extracts**.

2.4.1.2 Cardiovascular Diseases

Cardiovascular diseases (CVDs), including **heart disease, hypertension, stroke,** and **atherosclerosis**, are among the leading causes of **morbidity** and **mortality** globally. Nutraceuticals have emerged as a significant tool in the management and prevention of CVDs due to their ability to **improve heart health**, reduce **inflammation**, and regulate **lipid levels**. By providing **bioactive compounds, antioxidants**, and essential **fatty acids**, nutraceuticals can play a crucial role in reducing risk factors associated with cardiovascular diseases, such as high **cholesterol, high blood pressure**, and **inflammation**.

Several nutraceuticals have been extensively studied for their positive impact on **cardiovascular health**, and they are often used as a **complementary approach** alongside lifestyle changes and conventional medical treatments.

- **Omega-3 fatty acids**: One of the most well-known nutraceuticals for cardiovascular health is **omega-3 fatty acids**, which are found in **fish oil, flaxseed oil**, and **algal oil**. Omega-3 fatty acids, particularly **EPA (eicosapentaenoic acid)** and **DHA (docosahexaenoic acid)**, help lower **triglyceride levels**, reduce **blood pressure**, and improve **arterial function**. Clinical studies show that regular intake of **1 to 4 grams** of omega-3 fatty acids per day can reduce triglyceride levels by up to **30%**, lower the risk of heart attacks, and reduce **inflammation** associated with atherosclerosis.
- **Coenzyme Q10 (CoQ10)**: CoQ10 is a naturally occurring antioxidant found in the heart, liver, and kidneys, and it plays a crucial role in **energy production** within cells. CoQ10 is beneficial for cardiovascular health, especially for individuals taking **statins**, which can deplete the body's natural CoQ10 levels. Supplementation with **100 to 200 mg** of CoQ10 daily can improve **heart function**, reduce **oxidative stress**, and improve **blood vessel health**, particularly in patients with **heart failure** or **hypertension**.
- **Plant sterols and stanols**: These naturally occurring compounds, found in small amounts in **vegetables, fruits, nuts**, and **seeds**, have been shown to reduce **LDL (low-density lipoprotein) cholesterol** levels by blocking cholesterol absorption in the intestines. Consuming **2 to 3 grams** of plant sterols or stanols daily can lower LDL cholesterol by **5-15%**, significantly reducing the risk of developing coronary heart disease. Functional foods such as **fortified margarines, yogurts**, and **juices** often contain added plant sterols to support heart health.
- **Fiber**: Soluble fibers, such as **psyllium, beta-glucan** (found in oats and barley), and **pectin** (found in fruits like apples and citrus), help reduce blood cholesterol levels and improve cardiovascular health by reducing the absorption of dietary cholesterol in the intestine. Regular consumption of **7 to 10 grams** of soluble fiber per day has been shown to lower **total cholesterol** and **LDL cholesterol** levels by **5-10%**. These fibers also help regulate blood sugar levels and promote healthy weight management, both of which are important factors in reducing CVD risk.
- **Polyphenols**: Polyphenols, such as **flavonoids, resveratrol**, and **quercetin**, are powerful antioxidants found in fruits, vegetables, tea, and wine. They are known for their ability to improve **vascular function**,

reduce **inflammation**, and protect against **oxidative stress**, all of which contribute to heart health. **Resveratrol**, commonly found in **red grapes** and **wine**, has been shown to promote **vasodilation** and prevent the formation of **blood clots**, thus reducing the risk of **atherosclerosis** and heart disease. Daily intake of **150 to 500 mg** of resveratrol has been associated with improved **arterial flexibility** and reduced oxidative damage.

- **Garlic (Allium sativum)**: Garlic has been used for centuries for its heart-protective properties. It contains **allicin**, a compound that has been shown to lower **blood pressure**, reduce **cholesterol levels**, and improve **blood circulation**. Research suggests that consuming **600 to 1,200 mg** of garlic extract daily can reduce **LDL cholesterol** by **10-12%** and lower **systolic blood pressure** by up to **10 mmHg**, making it an effective nutraceutical for hypertension management.

- **L-carnitine**: This amino acid derivative is essential for **energy production** in the heart and skeletal muscles, as it helps transport **fatty acids** into the mitochondria for **energy metabolism**. L-carnitine supplementation (typically **1 to 3 grams** per day) has been shown to improve **exercise capacity** and reduce **mortality** in patients with **chronic heart failure** by enhancing heart function and reducing the risk of **ischemic heart disease**.

- **Magnesium**: Magnesium is a vital mineral involved in over **300 enzymatic reactions** in the body, including the regulation of **blood pressure**, **muscle contraction**, and **vascular tone**. Magnesium supplementation (typically **300 to 400 mg** per day) can help reduce **hypertension**, improve **arterial health**, and prevent **arrhythmias**, making it an important nutraceutical for individuals at risk of cardiovascular disease.

In addition to these specific nutraceuticals, **antioxidants** like **vitamin E, vitamin C**, and **selenium** are also commonly used to prevent oxidative damage to the heart and blood vessels, reducing the risk of plaque buildup and atherosclerosis.

The use of nutraceuticals in cardiovascular disease management offers a **natural, non-invasive**, and **preventive approach** to heart health. When combined with **lifestyle changes**, such as a **healthy diet**, regular **physical activity**, and **smoking cessation**, nutraceuticals can significantly reduce the risk factors associated with CVDs and improve overall **cardiovascular**

function. Given the growing burden of cardiovascular diseases worldwide, nutraceuticals present an important **adjunct therapy** in modern medicine. In countries like **India**, where heart disease rates are rising, the use of traditional nutraceuticals such as **turmeric, ginger**, and **amla** is increasingly integrated with modern nutraceuticals to manage heart health.

2.4.1.3 Cancer

Cancer is one of the most challenging diseases globally, characterized by the uncontrolled growth and spread of **abnormal cells** in the body. It can affect various organs and tissues and has a significant impact on **morbidity** and **mortality** worldwide. While conventional treatments such as **chemotherapy, radiation**, and **surgery** remain central in managing cancer, **nutraceuticals** are gaining attention for their role in **cancer prevention, supporting treatment**, and **reducing side effects** associated with conventional therapies. Nutraceuticals contain **bioactive compounds** such as **antioxidants, phytochemicals, polyphenols**, and **anti-inflammatory agents** that help protect cells from **DNA damage**, reduce **tumor growth**, and support the body's natural **immune defenses**.

Several nutraceuticals have been studied extensively for their potential to combat cancer through **multiple mechanisms**—from **inhibiting cancer cell proliferation** to inducing **apoptosis** (programmed cell death) and preventing **metastasis**.

- **Curcumin (Turmeric):** Curcumin, the active compound in **turmeric (Curcuma longa)**, is one of the most researched nutraceuticals for its **anti-cancer** properties. Curcumin exerts its effects by inhibiting various signaling pathways involved in **cancer cell growth**, such as **NF-kB, STAT3**, and **AP-1**, while also reducing **chronic inflammation**—a major contributing factor in cancer development. Studies have shown that curcumin can suppress the growth of a wide range of cancers, including **breast, colon, lung**, and **prostate cancers**. In clinical trials, doses ranging from **500 mg to 8,000 mg** of curcumin per day have demonstrated a reduction in tumor progression, especially when combined with chemotherapy or radiation therapy.

- **Green tea extract (EGCG):** Epigallocatechin gallate (EGCG), the primary polyphenol in **green tea**, has strong **antioxidant** and **anti-cancer** effects. EGCG inhibits **tumor angiogenesis** (the formation of new blood vessels that tumors need to grow), blocks **cancer cell signaling pathways**, and promotes **apoptosis**. Numerous studies suggest that regular consumption of **green tea** or EGCG supplements (approximately **200-400 mg/day**) can reduce the risk of cancers such as **breast, esophageal**, and **prostate cancer.**

- **Resveratrol:** Found in **grapes, red wine**, and certain berries, resveratrol is a powerful **polyphenol** known for its **anti-inflammatory** and **anti-carcinogenic** effects. Resveratrol acts by blocking several stages of cancer development, including **initiation, promotion,** and **progression.** It also inhibits **cancer cell metastasis** and enhances the effectiveness of chemotherapy by sensitizing cancer cells to treatment. Studies have indicated that daily doses of **100 to 1,000 mg** of resveratrol can help inhibit tumor growth in cancers such as **breast, colon,** and **lung cancer.**

- **Sulforaphane:** Sulforaphane, a compound found in **cruciferous vegetables** like **broccoli, kale,** and **Brussels sprouts**, is known for its ability to enhance **detoxification** processes in the body, protecting cells from **carcinogens.** It also induces **apoptosis** in cancer cells and inhibits the growth of **tumors.** Sulforaphane supplementation (often **10-20 mg** daily) has been associated with reduced risk of cancers, particularly **colon** and **prostate cancer**, due to its ability to modulate **gene expression** and reduce oxidative stress.

- **Quercetin:** Quercetin is a **flavonoid** found in fruits and vegetables, such as **apples, onions,** and **citrus fruits**, and it has strong **anti-inflammatory** and **anti-cancer** properties. Quercetin inhibits cancer cell growth by targeting the **PI3K/Akt** pathway, which is crucial for cell survival and proliferation. It also promotes **apoptosis** and enhances the body's immune response to cancer. Studies suggest that doses of **500 to 1,000 mg** of quercetin daily can help in managing various types of cancers, including **leukemia, lung cancer,** and **breast cancer.**

- **Lycopene:** Lycopene, a **carotenoid** found in **tomatoes** and other red-colored fruits, has demonstrated significant **anti-cancer** potential. Lycopene is a potent antioxidant that helps neutralize **free radicals** and prevents **DNA damage** that can lead to cancer. It has been particularly effective in reducing the risk of **prostate cancer**, as shown in studies where men consuming **10 mg or more** of lycopene daily experienced a significant reduction in **prostate cancer incidence.** Lycopene also helps lower the risk of **lung, breast,** and **stomach cancers.**

- **Omega-3 fatty acids:** **EPA** and **DHA**, the primary omega-3 fatty acids found in **fish oil**, have shown promising effects in reducing inflammation, which is closely linked to cancer progression. Omega-3 fatty acids also inhibit cancer cell growth by suppressing inflammatory pathways and **modulating immune function**. Regular consumption of omega-3s (between **1 to 4 grams** daily) has been associated with a lower risk of cancers such as **breast, colon**, and **prostate cancer**.

- **Probiotics**: The balance of **gut microbiota** plays a critical role in immune function and cancer prevention. **Probiotics**, such as **Lactobacillus** and **Bifidobacterium**, help maintain a healthy gut environment, which is essential for reducing systemic inflammation and enhancing the body's defense against carcinogens. Probiotics can also improve the **efficacy of cancer therapies** and reduce side effects like **chemotherapy-induced diarrhea**. Regular consumption of probiotic-rich foods like **yogurt, kefir**, or supplements with doses of **10-20 billion CFUs** can support overall **immune health** and cancer prevention.

The use of nutraceuticals in cancer management focuses not only on **prevention** but also on enhancing **quality of life** for patients undergoing **conventional treatments**. Many nutraceuticals can help mitigate the **side effects** of chemotherapy and radiation, such as **nausea, fatigue**, and **inflammation**, thereby improving patient outcomes and well-being. For example, **ginger** supplements are effective in reducing **chemotherapy-induced nausea**, while **glutamine** can help reduce **oral mucositis** in cancer patients.

2.4.1.4 Gastrointestinal Disorders

Gastrointestinal (GI) disorders encompass a wide range of conditions affecting the **digestive system**, including **irritable bowel syndrome (IBS), inflammatory bowel disease (IBD)** such as **Crohn's disease** and **ulcerative colitis, gastroesophageal reflux disease (GERD), constipation**, and **diarrhea**. These disorders can significantly affect a person's quality of life, leading to **chronic pain, malnutrition**, and **poor nutrient absorption**. Nutraceuticals have emerged as valuable tools for managing gastrointestinal disorders by promoting **gut health**, supporting **digestive function**, and reducing **inflammation**. Through the use of **probiotics, prebiotics, fibers**, and **plant-based compounds**, nutraceuticals offer a natural, complementary approach to traditional medical treatments.

Several nutraceuticals have shown significant benefits in improving **gut function** and managing symptoms associated with GI disorders:

- **Probiotics:** Probiotics are live **beneficial bacteria** that play a crucial role in maintaining a healthy **gut microbiota**. They help restore the balance of good bacteria in the gut, which can be disrupted by poor diet, illness, or the use of antibiotics. Probiotics, such as **Lactobacillus** and **Bifidobacterium** species, have been shown to alleviate symptoms of **IBS**, including **bloating, diarrhea**, and **abdominal pain**. Regular intake of probiotics (typically **5 to 10 billion CFUs** per day) has been linked to reduced inflammation in conditions like **IBD** and can help support the integrity of the intestinal lining, reducing symptoms of **leaky gut syndrome**.

- **Prebiotics:** Prebiotics are **non-digestible fibers** that stimulate the growth of beneficial gut bacteria. Common prebiotics include **inulin, fructooligosaccharides (FOS)**, and **galactooligosaccharides (GOS)**, which are found in foods such as **bananas, asparagus, garlic**, and **onions**. These fibers are fermented by gut bacteria, producing **short-chain fatty acids (SCFAs)** like **butyrate**, which are essential for maintaining a healthy gut barrier and reducing inflammation. Prebiotics can be particularly beneficial for individuals with **constipation**, as they improve bowel regularity and enhance gut motility. Daily consumption of **5 to 10 grams** of prebiotic fibers has been shown to support overall digestive health and reduce symptoms of GI disorders.

- **Psyllium husk:** Psyllium is a soluble fiber that helps regulate **bowel movements** and is widely used to treat both **constipation** and **diarrhea**. Psyllium works by absorbing water in the intestines, forming a gel-like substance that promotes smoother and more regular bowel movements. It is especially effective in managing IBS symptoms by improving stool consistency and reducing discomfort. Clinical studies have demonstrated that consuming **5 to 10 grams** of psyllium husk daily can significantly improve symptoms in individuals with IBS and help manage **cholesterol levels**, which can be affected by GI conditions.

- **Glutamine: L-glutamine** is an amino acid that plays a vital role in maintaining the integrity of the intestinal lining. It serves as a primary fuel source for the **enterocytes** (intestinal cells) and helps repair the **gut barrier**, which is often compromised in individuals with **IBD** and **leaky gut syndrome**. Supplementing with glutamine (typically **5 to 10 grams** per day) can help reduce intestinal permeability, alleviate inflammation, and improve nutrient absorption. Glutamine has been particularly beneficial in individuals with **Crohn's disease** and **ulcerative colitis**, as it helps reduce symptoms like diarrhea, abdominal pain, and malnutrition.

- **Peppermint oil**: Peppermint oil, rich in **menthol**, is commonly used to relieve symptoms of **IBS**, particularly **abdominal cramps, bloating**, and **gas**. Menthol has an **antispasmodic** effect on the smooth muscles of the GI tract, which helps reduce the intensity of muscle contractions that contribute to pain and discomfort. Studies have shown that taking enteric-coated peppermint oil capsules (typically **180 to 300 mg** per day) can reduce IBS symptoms by up to **40%**, offering a natural and effective remedy for managing the condition.

- **Aloe vera**: Aloe vera has been traditionally used for its **soothing** and **anti-inflammatory** properties, making it an effective nutraceutical for individuals with **GERD, gastritis**, and other upper GI disorders. Aloe vera gel helps reduce acid production in the stomach and can soothe inflamed tissues in the digestive tract. Studies suggest that consuming **10 to 20 ml** of aloe vera gel daily can help alleviate **heartburn** and improve symptoms of **acid reflux** by coating the esophagus and reducing inflammation.

- **Turmeric (Curcumin)**: **Curcumin**, the active compound in **turmeric**, has powerful **anti-inflammatory** and **antioxidant** properties that help manage inflammatory conditions like **Crohn's disease** and **ulcerative colitis**. Curcumin reduces inflammation by inhibiting key inflammatory markers such as **NF-kB** and **COX-2**, which are overactive in individuals with IBD. Research shows that taking **500 to 2,000 mg** of curcumin per day can significantly reduce flare-ups in IBD patients and improve overall gut health. Curcumin also helps reduce oxidative damage in the gut, which is crucial for preventing further tissue damage in chronic inflammatory conditions.

- **Slippery elm**: Slippery elm (Ulmus rubra) is a traditional remedy used for its ability to coat and soothe the mucous membranes of the digestive tract. It forms a **gel-like substance** when mixed with water, which can help reduce irritation in conditions like **GERD, gastritis**, and **IBD**. Slippery elm also helps promote the healing of ulcers and inflamed tissues in the GI tract. Studies have shown that taking **2 to 4 grams** of slippery elm bark powder daily can help reduce heartburn, acid reflux, and irritation in the esophagus and stomach.

- **Ginger**: Ginger has long been used for its **anti-nausea** and **digestive-enhancing properties**. It is particularly effective in managing **nausea** and **vomiting** associated with conditions like **motion sickness**,

pregnancy, and **chemotherapy**. Ginger also helps stimulate the production of digestive enzymes and promotes **gastric motility**, making it beneficial for individuals with **dyspepsia** (indigestion). Taking **500 to 1,000 mg** of ginger extract daily can help alleviate symptoms of nausea, bloating, and discomfort in individuals with GI disorders.

Nutraceuticals are particularly valuable in managing the symptoms of gastrointestinal disorders by providing **natural solutions** that support **gut health**, reduce **inflammation**, and restore balance to the digestive system. These products can be used in conjunction with traditional therapies or as preventive measures for individuals at risk of developing GI disorders.

2.5 Study of Herbs as Health Foods

Herbs have long been recognized for their **nutritional value** and medicinal properties, making them an important component of **health foods**. Many herbs are rich sources of essential **vitamins, minerals, antioxidants**, and **bioactive compounds** that offer numerous health benefits, from boosting the immune system to supporting digestion and overall well-being. As awareness of natural health foods increases, certain herbs have gained popularity for their exceptional **nutritional profiles** and therapeutic effects. One such herb is **alfalfa**, which is well-known for its abundance of **vitamins, minerals**, and **phytonutrients**, making it a valuable addition to health-conscious diets.

2.5.1 Alfalfa – Rich Source of Vitamins and Minerals

Alfalfa (Medicago sativa) is a highly nutritious herb widely used for its health-promoting properties. Known as the "father of all foods," alfalfa has been cultivated for centuries and is revered for its dense concentration of **vitamins, minerals**, and **antioxidants**. It is often consumed as a **supplement**, in the form of **powder, tablets**, or **sprouts**, and is also used in various **herbal formulations** for its ability to support general health and vitality.

Alfalfa is particularly rich in a wide range of **vitamins**, including **vitamin A, vitamin C, vitamin E, vitamin K**, and several **B vitamins**. These vitamins play crucial roles in maintaining **vision health**, promoting **skin health**, supporting **immune function**, and aiding in **blood clotting**. For example, **vitamin K**, abundant in alfalfa, is essential for maintaining healthy **bone density** and ensuring proper blood coagulation. This makes alfalfa a valuable herb for individuals at risk of **osteoporosis** or those seeking to improve **bone health**.

In addition to vitamins, alfalfa is packed with vital **minerals**, such as **calcium**, **magnesium**, **potassium**, **iron**, **phosphorus**, and **zinc**. These minerals are essential for various physiological functions, including maintaining **electrolyte balance**, supporting **muscle and nerve function**, and promoting **bone health**. For instance, the **high calcium content** in alfalfa makes it beneficial for individuals looking to strengthen their bones and teeth, while its **iron** content supports **red blood cell production** and helps prevent **anemia**.

Alfalfa is also a rich source of **chlorophyll**, a green pigment that is thought to have **detoxifying** and **alkalizing** effects on the body. Chlorophyll supports **liver function** by aiding in the detoxification process and helping the body eliminate harmful toxins and heavy metals. Furthermore, the **antioxidant** properties of chlorophyll and other compounds found in alfalfa help protect the body from oxidative damage caused by free radicals, which can contribute to chronic diseases and aging.

The herb is also a source of **phytoestrogens**, plant compounds that mimic **estrogen** in the body. These compounds can be beneficial for **women's health**, particularly during **menopause**, as they may help alleviate symptoms such as **hot flashes** and support **hormonal balance**.

Alfalfa's **fiber content** also contributes to **digestive health** by promoting regular bowel movements and preventing **constipation**. Additionally, the herb has been studied for its ability to lower **cholesterol levels** and improve **heart health**. Research has shown that alfalfa's **saponins**, a type of plant compound, can bind to cholesterol in the intestines, preventing its absorption into the bloodstream and thereby reducing **LDL cholesterol** levels.

Regular consumption of alfalfa, whether in the form of sprouts, juice, or supplements, can offer numerous health benefits due to its **comprehensive nutrient profile**. It supports overall **immune function**, aids in **detoxification**, promotes **bone and heart health**, and contributes to maintaining healthy **blood sugar levels**. Given its impressive array of vitamins, minerals, and phytonutrients, alfalfa is considered a powerful herb that supports holistic health and wellness.:

2.5.2 Chicory – Digestive Health Benefits

Chicory (Cichorium intybus) is a herb widely known for its impressive **digestive health benefits** and has been used for centuries as a natural remedy for a variety of gastrointestinal issues. Rich in **inulin**, a type of soluble **dietary fiber**, chicory promotes **gut health** by supporting healthy digestion, improving **bowel regularity**, and aiding in the management of common digestive disorders such as **constipation** and **irritable bowel syndrome (IBS)**. In addition to its digestive benefits, chicory is also valued for its potential to support **liver health, detoxification**, and **weight management.**

One of the primary reasons chicory is so effective for digestive health is its high concentration of **inulin**, which serves as a **prebiotic**. Prebiotics are non-digestible fibers that feed the beneficial bacteria in the gut, known as the **gut microbiota**. By promoting the growth of healthy bacteria such as **Bifidobacteria** and **Lactobacilli**, inulin helps to maintain a balanced gut environment, which is essential for proper digestion and overall health. A healthy gut microbiome not only aids in breaking down food and absorbing nutrients but also plays a critical role in supporting the **immune system** and preventing inflammation.

For individuals suffering from **constipation**, chicory's fiber content helps regulate bowel movements by adding **bulk** to the stool and improving intestinal transit. Studies have shown that consuming **10-15 grams** of inulin-rich chicory root daily can increase stool frequency, improve consistency, and reduce gastrointestinal discomfort associated with constipation. This makes chicory an effective natural remedy for promoting **regularity** without the harsh effects of over-the-counter laxatives.

Chicory is also helpful in managing **IBS** and other functional digestive disorders. The **prebiotic effect** of inulin has been shown to alleviate symptoms such as **bloating, gas**, and **abdominal pain**. By nourishing beneficial gut bacteria, chicory reduces the growth of harmful bacteria that can lead to **inflammation** and **irritation** of the intestines. In people with IBS, regular consumption of chicory has been linked to improved gut health and reduced severity of symptoms, providing relief in a safe, natural way.

Beyond its effects on gut bacteria, chicory is known to support **liver health** and detoxification. Traditionally used as a **liver tonic**, chicory helps stimulate the production of **bile**, which is essential for the digestion of fats and the elimination of toxins from the body. By improving bile flow and supporting liver function, chicory aids in the body's natural detoxification processes, reducing the burden on the liver and improving overall digestive efficiency. This makes chicory a valuable herb for those looking to cleanse the digestive system and improve nutrient absorption.

Furthermore, chicory has shown potential in **weight management** due to its **fiber content**. Inulin can help promote feelings of **fullness** by slowing the absorption of food in the digestive tract, thereby reducing overall **calorie intake** and supporting weight loss efforts. By controlling appetite and helping maintain stable blood sugar levels, chicory contributes to **metabolic health** and can be beneficial for individuals trying to manage their weight.

Chicory is most commonly consumed in the form of **chicory root extract**, which can be added to beverages such as **coffee substitutes** or taken as a dietary supplement. It is also used as a natural **sweetener** in food products due to its slightly sweet taste, making it a versatile ingredient in both health foods and supplements. Chicory root powder, capsules, and teas are other popular forms of consumption, allowing individuals to easily incorporate its digestive benefits into their daily routine.

2.5.3 Ginger – Anti-inflammatory Properties

Ginger (Zingiber officinale) is one of the most widely used medicinal herbs, renowned for its powerful **anti-inflammatory properties**. For centuries, ginger has been valued in both **Ayurvedic** and **traditional Chinese medicine** for its ability to treat various ailments, especially those related to **inflammation** and **pain**. The anti-inflammatory effects of ginger are primarily attributed to its rich content of **bioactive compounds**, particularly **gingerols** and **shogaols**, which are responsible for the herb's therapeutic properties. Ginger is commonly used to manage **arthritis**, **muscle pain**, **digestive disorders**, and **inflammatory conditions** affecting various organs of the body.

One of the most notable uses of ginger is in the management of **osteoarthritis** and **rheumatoid arthritis**, two common inflammatory joint conditions. Studies have shown that ginger can significantly reduce **joint pain** and **inflammation** by inhibiting the activity of **pro-inflammatory enzymes** such as **cyclooxygenase (COX)** and **lipoxygenase (LOX)**, which are responsible for the production of inflammatory compounds like **prostaglandins** and **leukotrienes**. Clinical trials involving patients with osteoarthritis have demonstrated that taking **500 mg to 1,000 mg** of ginger extract daily for 3 to 12 weeks can lead to notable improvements in **pain** and **mobility**, comparable to the effects of non-steroidal anti-inflammatory drugs (**NSAIDs**) but without the common side effects associated with pharmaceuticals.

In addition to its effects on joint health, ginger is also beneficial for reducing **muscle soreness** and inflammation resulting from **exercise**. Athletes and individuals engaged in regular physical activity often experience muscle pain due to microscopic tears in muscle fibers, which trigger an inflammatory response. Consuming ginger, either as a supplement or in food, can reduce **delayed onset muscle soreness (DOMS)** by modulating inflammatory pathways. Research has shown that consuming **2 grams** of ginger daily for a week can lead to a significant reduction in muscle pain and faster recovery after intense exercise.

Ginger's anti-inflammatory effects extend to its ability to combat **gastrointestinal inflammation**, making it a valuable herb for managing **digestive disorders** like **irritable bowel syndrome (IBS), gastritis**, and **inflammatory bowel disease (IBD)**. Gingerols and shogaols help soothe the digestive tract by reducing inflammation and promoting healthy **gastric motility**, which can alleviate symptoms such as **bloating, cramping**, and **nausea**. For individuals suffering from **acid reflux** or GERD, ginger has been found to reduce inflammation in the esophagus, improving symptoms of heartburn and irritation.

Beyond its direct anti-inflammatory effects, ginger also provides **antioxidant protection** by neutralizing **free radicals** and reducing oxidative stress, which often accompanies chronic inflammation. This dual action of reducing inflammation while protecting cells from oxidative damage makes ginger especially beneficial for conditions where both inflammation and oxidative stress are prevalent, such as in **cardiovascular diseases** and **neurodegenerative disorders**.

In addition to managing inflammation and pain, ginger is also widely used for its **immune-boosting** properties. Chronic inflammation can weaken the immune system, and ginger's ability to modulate inflammatory pathways supports a healthier immune response. Regular consumption of ginger helps enhance **immune function** by improving the body's ability to respond to infections and reduce prolonged inflammatory reactions, which are associated with chronic diseases.

Ginger can be consumed in various forms, including **fresh ginger root, ginger tea, powdered ginger, capsules**, and **extracts**. In traditional medicine, ginger tea is commonly used to soothe **sore throats**, relieve **cold symptoms**, and reduce **inflammation** in the respiratory tract. The versatility of ginger allows it to be easily incorporated into daily diets, whether through culinary use or as a supplement.

2.5.4 Fenugreek – Anti-diabetic Effects

Fenugreek (Trigonella foenum-graecum) is a widely recognized medicinal herb with a long history of use in traditional medicine, particularly for its **anti-diabetic effects**. Native to the Mediterranean region, India, and parts of Africa, fenugreek seeds are rich in **soluble fiber, saponins**, and **alkaloids** such as **trigonelline**, which contribute to its ability to regulate **blood sugar levels** and improve **insulin sensitivity**. Fenugreek is now gaining prominence as a natural treatment option for managing **type 2 diabetes** and **prediabetes**, offering a safer and more holistic approach compared to conventional medications.

One of the primary mechanisms through which fenugreek exerts its anti-diabetic effects is by **slowing carbohydrate absorption** in the intestines. The **high soluble fiber content** in fenugreek forms a gel-like substance in the gut, which slows down the digestion and absorption of carbohydrates. This helps to **lower postprandial (after meal) blood sugar levels**, preventing spikes in **glucose levels** that are commonly observed after consuming meals rich in carbohydrates. Clinical studies have shown that consuming **5 to 15 grams** of fenugreek seeds or their extracts daily can significantly reduce post-meal blood sugar levels by up to **20-30%** in individuals with type 2 diabetes.

Another significant benefit of fenugreek is its ability to improve **insulin sensitivity**. The presence of the alkaloid **4-hydroxyisoleucine** in fenugreek seeds helps stimulate **insulin secretion** from the pancreas, improving the body's response to insulin and facilitating the uptake of glucose into the cells for energy production. This is particularly beneficial for people with **insulin resistance**, a hallmark of type 2 diabetes. Studies have shown that fenugreek supplementation can improve **fasting blood glucose** and reduce **HbA1c** levels (a marker of long-term blood sugar control), indicating improved overall glycemic management.

In addition to regulating blood sugar, fenugreek has been found to have **lipid-lowering** effects, which is crucial for individuals with diabetes who are at a higher risk of developing **cardiovascular diseases**. Fenugreek's soluble fiber helps reduce **LDL (bad) cholesterol** and **triglycerides** while maintaining or improving **HDL (good) cholesterol** levels. This contributes to better heart health and helps mitigate the cardiovascular risks associated with diabetes.

Fenugreek's **anti-inflammatory** and **antioxidant** properties also play an important role in managing diabetes. Chronic inflammation and oxidative stress are key contributors to the progression of type 2 diabetes and its complications, such as **neuropathy, nephropathy**, and **retinopathy**. The **polyphenols** and **flavonoids** present in fenugreek help neutralize **free**

radicals and reduce inflammation, thereby protecting cells and tissues from damage caused by elevated blood sugar levels.

Moreover, fenugreek seeds have been found to enhance the **glycogen storage** capacity of the liver and muscles, further aiding in glucose regulation. By increasing the body's ability to store glucose as glycogen, fenugreek helps prevent excessive glucose from circulating in the blood, thereby reducing hyperglycemia.

The anti-diabetic effects of fenugreek have been demonstrated in both **human clinical trials** and **animal studies**. In a study involving type 2 diabetic patients, those who consumed fenugreek powder (10-15 grams per day) experienced a significant reduction in fasting blood glucose levels and HbA1c after **8 to 12 weeks** of supplementation. These findings have led to the growing use of fenugreek as a complementary therapy for diabetes management, particularly for individuals looking to manage their blood sugar naturally without relying solely on pharmaceuticals.

Fenugreek is commonly consumed in various forms, including **whole seeds, powdered seeds, capsules,** and **extracts.** The seeds can be soaked in water overnight and consumed in the morning to help regulate blood sugar throughout the day. Fenugreek supplements are also widely available and are often standardized to contain high levels of soluble fiber and active compounds such as **4-hydroxyisoleucine.**

Fenugreek is a powerful herb that offers substantial benefits for managing **type 2 diabetes** and improving overall **glycemic control.** Through its ability to lower **postprandial blood sugar levels,** enhance **insulin sensitivity,** and reduce **inflammation,** fenugreek serves as a natural and effective option for individuals looking to manage their diabetes holistically. The herb's additional cardiovascular benefits, including **cholesterol regulation,** further contribute to its value in supporting long-term health for those with diabetes.

2.5.5 Garlic – Cardiovascular Benefits

Garlic (Allium sativum) is one of the most widely researched medicinal herbs, renowned for its **cardiovascular benefits** and its long-standing use in traditional medicine across various cultures. Rich in bioactive compounds such as **allicin, ajoene,** and **sulfur-containing compounds,** garlic has been shown to have a profound impact on **heart health,** particularly in reducing **high blood pressure,** lowering **cholesterol levels,** improving **circulation,** and reducing the risk of **atherosclerosis** and other cardiovascular diseases. Its potent **antioxidant** and **anti-inflammatory** properties also contribute to the overall protection of the cardiovascular system.

One of the key cardiovascular benefits of garlic is its ability to **lower blood pressure** in individuals with **hypertension**. Allicin, a compound released when garlic is crushed or chopped, helps relax the smooth muscles in the blood vessels by increasing the production of **nitric oxide** and promoting **vasodilation**. This dilation of blood vessels helps reduce **systolic** and **diastolic blood pressure**, thereby reducing the strain on the heart and lowering the risk of stroke, heart attack, and heart failure. Studies have shown that regular consumption of **600 to 1,500 mg** of garlic extract daily for 24 weeks can lead to a reduction in systolic blood pressure by up to **10 mmHg** and diastolic blood pressure by up to **6 mmHg**, making it as effective as some standard antihypertensive medications.

In addition to its effects on blood pressure, garlic is highly effective in managing **cholesterol levels**. Regular garlic consumption has been shown to lower **LDL (bad) cholesterol** and **total cholesterol** levels while modestly increasing **HDL (good) cholesterol**. Garlic's ability to reduce LDL cholesterol is particularly important because high levels of LDL contribute to the buildup of **plaque** in the arteries, leading to **atherosclerosis**. By preventing the oxidation of LDL cholesterol, garlic helps slow the progression of plaque formation and reduces the risk of **clogged arteries**, which can result in heart attacks or strokes. Studies suggest that taking **500 to 1,000 mg** of aged garlic extract daily can reduce LDL cholesterol by approximately **10-15%** over a period of 8 to 12 weeks.

Garlic also improves overall **blood circulation** by preventing **platelet aggregation**—a process in which platelets clump together and form clots that can block blood flow. This **antithrombotic** effect is largely due to the sulfur compounds in garlic, which inhibit platelet activity and reduce the risk of **thrombosis** (blood clot formation). This makes garlic beneficial for individuals at risk of **deep vein thrombosis** or **pulmonary embolism**, as well as those with a history of cardiovascular events.

Furthermore, garlic has been shown to reduce **triglyceride levels**, which are another key factor in heart disease. Elevated triglyceride levels are associated with an increased risk of coronary artery disease. Garlic's ability to lower triglycerides, in combination with its effects on cholesterol and blood pressure, provides comprehensive cardiovascular protection.

The **antioxidant properties** of garlic also contribute to its cardiovascular benefits. Garlic helps neutralize **free radicals** in the body, reducing oxidative stress, which is a significant factor in the development of cardiovascular diseases. Oxidative stress can damage the walls of blood vessels, leading to inflammation and contributing to the formation of atherosclerotic plaques. By reducing oxidative damage, garlic helps protect the heart and blood vessels from long-term damage.

Garlic's **anti-inflammatory properties** further enhance its cardiovascular benefits. Chronic inflammation is a major contributing factor to the development of heart disease, as it can lead to endothelial dysfunction, the process by which the inner lining of the blood vessels becomes damaged. By reducing the levels of inflammatory markers such as **C-reactive protein (CRP)** and **tumor necrosis factor-alpha (TNF-α)**, garlic helps protect against inflammation-related damage to the cardiovascular system.

Additionally, garlic has shown promise in improving **vascular health** by enhancing **endothelial function**. The **endothelium** is the inner lining of blood vessels, and its proper function is critical for maintaining vascular health. Garlic helps improve endothelial function, which plays a key role in preventing **arterial stiffness** and promoting healthy blood flow.

Garlic is most commonly consumed in its **raw** or **cooked** form, though garlic supplements such as **aged garlic extract** and **garlic oil** are widely available and offer a convenient way to reap its cardiovascular benefits. **Aged garlic extract**, in particular, is valued for its high concentration of bioactive compounds with reduced odor, making it a popular choice for those who want to avoid the strong taste and smell of fresh garlic. Studies suggest that a daily intake of **600 to 1,200 mg** of aged garlic extract is sufficient to provide substantial cardiovascular benefits.

In summary, **garlic** is a powerful herb that offers a wide range of **cardiovascular benefits**, including **lowering blood pressure, reducing cholesterol levels, preventing blood clots,** and protecting against **atherosclerosis.** Its **antioxidant** and **anti-inflammatory** properties further enhance its role in promoting heart health. Whether consumed raw, cooked, or in supplement form, garlic is a natural and effective way to support the cardiovascular system and reduce the risk of heart disease.

2.5.6 Honey – Antioxidant and Antimicrobial Properties

Honey is a natural sweetener produced by honeybees from the nectar of flowers, and it has been valued for its **antioxidant** and **antimicrobial** properties for centuries. Used both as a food and a medicinal remedy, honey is rich in **bioactive compounds** such as **flavonoids, phenolic acids, enzymes,** and **organic acids**, which contribute to its health benefits.

Honey's therapeutic properties make it an essential ingredient in traditional medicine for treating wounds, infections, and various health conditions. Its **antioxidant** capacity helps protect the body against oxidative stress, while its **antimicrobial** activity fights against bacterial and fungal infections, making honey a versatile natural remedy.

Honey's **antioxidant properties** are primarily due to its high content of **flavonoids** and **phenolic acids**, which help neutralize **free radicals**—unstable molecules that can cause oxidative stress and damage to cells and tissues. Oxidative stress is a contributing factor in the development of chronic diseases such as **heart disease, cancer,** and **neurodegenerative disorders.** The antioxidants in honey work to protect the body's cells from oxidative damage, reduce inflammation, and support overall health. Among the flavonoids found in honey, **quercetin, kaempferol,** and **chrysin** are particularly notable for their potent antioxidant effects. Studies have shown that consuming honey regularly can increase the levels of **antioxidant enzymes** in the body, such as **superoxide dismutase (SOD)** and **glutathione peroxidase,** helping to enhance the body's defense against oxidative damage.

Honey's **antimicrobial properties** make it an effective natural treatment for infections and wounds. These properties are primarily due to the presence of **hydrogen peroxide,** which is produced by the enzyme **glucose oxidase** found in honey. Hydrogen peroxide has strong bactericidal activity, making honey effective in killing bacteria and preventing infections. In addition, honey's **low pH** (acidic environment) and **high sugar content** create an environment that is hostile to bacterial growth. Honey also contains **methylglyoxal (MGO),** particularly in **Manuka honey,** which has been shown to have broad-spectrum antibacterial effects, even against antibiotic-resistant bacteria such as **MRSA (methicillin-resistant Staphylococcus aureus).**

Honey is commonly used to treat **wounds, burns,** and **skin infections** due to its ability to promote **healing** and prevent infection. When applied topically, honey helps to create a **moist wound environment,** which accelerates tissue regeneration and reduces scarring. Clinical studies have demonstrated that honey can speed up the healing of wounds and burns, with a significant reduction in **infection rates** and **healing time.** Its antimicrobial activity also extends to preventing and treating **oral infections** and **sore throats.** Gargling with honey or consuming honey with warm water has long been used to soothe **throat infections** and reduce irritation caused by **bacterial** and **viral infections.**

In addition to its external uses, honey's antimicrobial effects extend to the **digestive system,** where it can help manage conditions such as **gastritis, peptic ulcers,** and **irritable bowel syndrome (IBS).** Honey's ability to inhibit the growth of **Helicobacter pylori,** a bacterium linked to peptic ulcers, makes it beneficial for supporting **gastric health.** Its **prebiotic** properties also promote the growth of **beneficial gut bacteria,** improving overall **digestive function.**

Furthermore, honey's antioxidant and antimicrobial properties work synergistically to support **immune function.** Regular consumption of honey has been shown to enhance the body's ability to fight off infections by boosting **immune cell activity** and promoting the production of antibodies. The combination of antioxidant protection and antimicrobial activity makes honey an ideal natural remedy for managing colds, flu, and infections, especially when combined with other immune-boosting ingredients like **ginger** or **lemon.**

Different varieties of honey, such as **Manuka honey** from New Zealand, are particularly renowned for their high levels of **methylglyoxal** and superior antimicrobial effects. Manuka honey is often used in medical settings for treating wounds, burns, and ulcers due to its potent antibacterial properties. However, even other types of honey, including **raw** and **organic honey,** possess significant antioxidant and antimicrobial benefits, making them valuable health foods.

2.5.7 Amla – Rich in Vitamin C

Amla (Phyllanthus emblica), also known as **Indian gooseberry,** is a highly valued herb in **Ayurvedic medicine** and is recognized for being one of the richest natural sources of **vitamin C.** Amla is renowned for its wide range of **health benefits,** particularly its ability to boost **immunity,** improve **skin health,** and support overall **well-being.** The high concentration of vitamin C, along with other potent **antioxidants** such as **flavonoids, polyphenols,** and **tannins,** makes Amla a powerful tool for protecting the body against oxidative stress and enhancing **cellular function.**

Amla contains an impressive amount of vitamin C—approximately **600 to 700 mg** of vitamin C per 100 grams of fresh fruit, which is significantly higher than that found in most other fruits, such as **oranges** or **lemons.** Vitamin C is a potent **antioxidant** that plays a critical role in **neutralizing free radicals,** which are unstable molecules that can cause damage to cells, leading to inflammation and the development of chronic diseases. By counteracting oxidative stress, Amla helps protect the body from cellular damage, supports the **immune system**, and promotes **skin repair** and **collagen production.**

One of the key benefits of Amla's high vitamin C content is its ability to strengthen the **immune system.** Vitamin C is essential for the proper functioning of **white blood cells,** which are the body's first line of defense against infections. Regular consumption of Amla can boost **immune function,** making the body more resilient to **infections, colds,** and **flu.** Additionally, vitamin C promotes the production of **antibodies** and supports the function of the immune cells that help in detecting and fighting pathogens.

Amla is also beneficial for **skin health** due to its vitamin C content. Vitamin C is required for the synthesis of **collagen,** a structural protein that maintains skin elasticity and strength. Collagen production declines with age, leading to the appearance of **wrinkles** and **fine lines,** but consuming vitamin C-rich foods like Amla can help slow this process. Regular consumption of Amla can contribute to **radiant skin,** help reduce **pigmentation,** and promote **healing** of wounds and scars. Amla is often included in skin care products and treatments aimed at improving **complexion** and **youthful appearance.**

In addition to its high vitamin C content, Amla provides powerful **anti-inflammatory** benefits. Vitamin C and the other antioxidants present in Amla help reduce chronic inflammation by inhibiting the production of **pro-inflammatory cytokines.** This anti-inflammatory effect is particularly beneficial for individuals suffering from inflammatory conditions such as **arthritis, asthma,** or **autoimmune disorders.**

Amla's rich vitamin C content also plays a crucial role in supporting **cardiovascular health.** Vitamin C helps lower **cholesterol levels,** improve **blood vessel elasticity,** and prevent **atherosclerosis** (the buildup of plaque in the arteries). Amla has been shown to reduce levels of **LDL (bad cholesterol)** and increase **HDL (good cholesterol),** helping to prevent heart disease. Regular consumption of Amla, whether as a fresh fruit or as an extract, can help maintain healthy **blood pressure** and protect the heart from oxidative damage.

The antioxidant properties of Amla also contribute to its **anti-cancer** effects. By protecting cells from oxidative damage and supporting the body's natural detoxification processes, Amla helps reduce the risk of cancerous cell growth. Studies have shown that the antioxidants in Amla can inhibit the proliferation of **cancer cells** and promote **apoptosis** (programmed cell death) in certain types of cancer, including **breast cancer** and **colon cancer.**

Amla is widely consumed in different forms, including **fresh fruit, powder, juice,** and **capsules.** It is a common ingredient in traditional Ayurvedic formulations, such as **Chyawanprash,** an herbal jam known for its immune-boosting properties. Amla juice, in particular, is popular for daily consumption due to its refreshing taste and potent health benefits. Amla powder can also be mixed into smoothies, drinks, or teas for an easy way to incorporate its benefits into the diet.

Amla is a potent natural source of **vitamin C,** offering a wide array of health benefits, from **boosting immunity** and promoting **skin health** to protecting against **oxidative stress** and **inflammation.** Its high concentration of antioxidants makes it a valuable addition to the diet for overall **health maintenance** and **disease prevention.** Whether consumed fresh, as juice, or in powdered form, Amla provides an accessible and effective means of enhancing health and well-being.

2.5.8 Ginseng – Adaptogenic Herb

Ginseng (Panax ginseng) is one of the most well-known **adaptogenic herbs,** used for centuries in traditional medicine systems such as **Chinese** and **Korean medicine.** Adaptogens are a unique class of herbs that help the body adapt to **stress,** regulate **hormonal balance,** and improve overall **resilience** to physical, mental, and environmental challenges. Ginseng is revered for its ability to enhance **energy levels,** reduce **fatigue,** support **cognitive function,** and promote **immune health.** Its key bioactive compounds, known as **ginsenosides,** are responsible for many of its therapeutic effects.

As an adaptogen, ginseng helps the body maintain **homeostasis** by modulating the stress response. In today's fast-paced world, chronic stress can lead to numerous health issues such as **anxiety, depression, fatigue,** and even **hormonal imbalances.** Ginseng works by influencing the **hypothalamic-pituitary-adrenal (HPA) axis,** which is central to the body's stress response. By balancing cortisol levels (the primary stress hormone), ginseng helps reduce the negative effects of chronic stress, allowing the body to recover more efficiently from both **physical exertion** and **mental fatigue.**

One of the key benefits of ginseng is its ability to boost **physical energy** and reduce **fatigue.** Often referred to as a natural **energizer,** ginseng enhances **endurance** and **stamina** without the jittery side effects associated with stimulants like caffeine. Athletes and individuals who engage in high levels of physical activity often use ginseng to improve **performance** and recover more quickly. Studies have shown that ginseng can increase **oxygen uptake** and improve **blood circulation**, helping muscles work more efficiently and reducing overall fatigue. A typical dosage of **200 to 400 mg** of ginseng extract has been shown to improve **physical performance** and reduce fatigue over time.

Ginseng's adaptogenic properties extend to improving **cognitive function** and mental clarity, making it beneficial for those experiencing **mental fatigue** or **brain fog**. Research suggests that ginseng enhances **memory, focus,** and **concentration** by increasing the availability of neurotransmitters such as **acetylcholine** and **dopamine** in the brain. These neurotransmitters play a crucial role in **learning** and **executive function**, making ginseng useful for individuals looking to improve their cognitive performance, particularly under stressful conditions. Additionally, ginseng's ability to improve **cerebral blood flow** has been linked to its positive effects on cognitive health.

Another notable benefit of ginseng is its role in supporting the **immune system**. Ginseng has been shown to enhance the production of **immune cells**, including **T cells, natural killer (NK) cells,** and **macrophages**, all of which play a critical role in defending the body against infections. Regular consumption of ginseng has been linked to a **reduced incidence of colds and flu,** as well as faster recovery times from illness. This makes ginseng an excellent herb for individuals looking to **strengthen their immune defense,** particularly during stressful periods when immunity is often compromised.

In addition to its effects on stress and immunity, ginseng is also beneficial for **metabolic health**. It has been studied for its role in **blood sugar regulation**, with research indicating that ginseng may improve **insulin sensitivity** and help manage **blood glucose levels** in individuals with **type 2 diabetes**. By enhancing **glucose metabolism**, ginseng can help stabilize blood sugar levels and reduce **insulin resistance**, making it a valuable herb for metabolic health and weight management.

Ginseng is typically consumed in various forms, including **powder, capsules, extracts,** and **teas. Red ginseng**, which is steamed and dried, is particularly popular in East Asia and is believed to have more potent effects than raw ginseng. The recommended dosage varies depending on the form, but a standard range for ginseng extract is typically between **200 and 400**

mg per day, depending on the individual's needs and health goals.

In conclusion, **ginseng** is a powerful **adaptogenic herb** that offers a wide range of health benefits, particularly in managing **stress**, improving **energy levels**, supporting **cognitive function**, and boosting **immune health**. Its adaptogenic properties make it an ideal choice for individuals looking to enhance their overall **resilience** to both mental and physical challenges, while promoting long-term **well-being**.

2.5.9 Ashwagandha – Stress-relieving Herb

Ashwagandha (Withania somnifera), commonly known as the "Indian ginseng" or "winter cherry," is a powerful **adaptogenic herb** that has been used in **Ayurvedic medicine** for over 3,000 years. It is widely recognized for its ability to **reduce stress, promote relaxation,** and **enhance overall well-being**. The term "adaptogen" refers to substances that help the body **adapt to stress** by normalizing physiological processes and restoring balance. Ashwagandha's stress-relieving properties make it one of the most sought-after herbs for supporting **mental health**, improving **sleep quality**, and enhancing **physical resilience** in the face of stress.

The primary bioactive compounds responsible for Ashwagandha's therapeutic effects are **withanolides**, which have potent **anti-inflammatory, antioxidant**, and **anti-stress** properties. These compounds help regulate the body's response to both **physical** and **mental stressors** by modulating the **hypothalamic-pituitary-adrenal (HPA) axis**, which is involved in the release of **cortisol**, the body's primary stress hormone. Ashwagandha reduces elevated cortisol levels, helping to calm the body and mind, alleviate symptoms of **anxiety**, and prevent the harmful effects of chronic stress.

One of the key benefits of Ashwagandha is its ability to reduce **anxiety** and **stress-related disorders**. Several clinical studies have shown that regular supplementation with Ashwagandha can significantly reduce anxiety symptoms, particularly in individuals with **generalized anxiety disorder (GAD)** and those experiencing **chronic stress**. In one study, individuals who took **300 mg** of standardized Ashwagandha extract twice daily for 60 days reported a **44% reduction** in perceived stress levels compared to those in the placebo group. This effect is attributed to Ashwagandha's ability to lower cortisol and promote a more balanced response to stress.

In addition to reducing stress and anxiety, Ashwagandha is also beneficial for improving **sleep quality**. Chronic stress often leads to

insomnia or poor sleep patterns, and Ashwagandha can help promote **restful sleep** by calming the nervous system and regulating **sleep cycles**. Research has shown that Ashwagandha enhances **sleep onset** and **sleep duration**, making it a useful herb for individuals suffering from **sleep disturbances** or **insomnia** due to stress.

Ashwagandha's adaptogenic properties extend beyond stress relief, as it also helps improve **physical endurance** and **stamina** by reducing **fatigue** and promoting **energy**. Athletes and individuals who engage in intense physical activities often use Ashwagandha to enhance their performance and reduce the physical effects of exertion. Studies have shown that Ashwagandha can improve **muscle strength** and **recovery** by increasing the body's resistance to stress and reducing muscle damage caused by intense exercise. For instance, in a study involving healthy men, those who took **500 mg** of Ashwagandha extract daily showed increased **muscle mass** and strength after eight weeks of resistance training compared to the placebo group.

Furthermore, Ashwagandha supports **cognitive function** by improving **focus, memory,** and **concentration.** Stress often impairs cognitive performance, but Ashwagandha helps protect the brain from stress-induced damage and improves **mental clarity.** The herb has been shown to reduce **brain fog** and enhance **learning** and **memory** by promoting the growth of nerve cells and protecting against oxidative stress in the brain.

In addition to its benefits for stress and mental health, Ashwagandha has been shown to have a positive impact on **hormonal balance,** particularly by supporting healthy levels of **thyroid hormones** and **testosterone.** In men, Ashwagandha has been found to improve **fertility** and increase **testosterone levels,** which may be beneficial for those with stress-induced fertility issues. Additionally, Ashwagandha helps regulate the production of **thyroid hormones,** making it useful for individuals with **hypothyroidism** or suboptimal thyroid function.

Ashwagandha is typically consumed in the form of **capsules, powder,** or **liquid extracts,** with a common dosage ranging from **300 to 600 mg** of standardized extract per day, depending on the individual's needs and health goals. It can also be taken as a tea, mixed into beverages, or included in herbal formulations.

Ashwagandha is a highly effective **stress-relieving herb** that offers a range of benefits for **mental health, sleep quality, physical endurance,** and **hormonal balance.** By modulating cortisol levels and enhancing the body's response to stress, Ashwagandha helps promote relaxation, reduce anxiety, and improve overall **resilience** in the face of daily stressors. Its adaptogenic properties make it a valuable addition to any wellness routine aimed at promoting long-term **physical and mental well-being.**

2.5.10 Spirulina – Protein-rich Superfood

Spirulina is a nutrient-dense **blue-green algae** that is widely recognized as a **protein-rich superfood**, offering a remarkable range of health benefits. Known for its high content of **complete protein, vitamins, minerals,** and **antioxidants**, spirulina has gained popularity as a dietary supplement and a functional food for promoting **energy, detoxification, immune health,** and overall **well-being.** It is particularly valuable for those seeking **plant-based protein** sources, as spirulina is composed of about **60-70% protein** by dry weight, making it one of the most concentrated natural sources of protein available.

One of the key attributes of spirulina is its **high-quality protein content.** Unlike many plant-based protein sources, spirulina provides a complete profile of **essential amino acids**—those that the body cannot synthesize on its own and must obtain through the diet. This makes spirulina an excellent source of protein for **vegetarians, vegans,** and individuals looking to reduce their intake of animal products. The **amino acids** in spirulina are highly bioavailable, meaning that they are easily absorbed and utilized by the body, contributing to the growth and repair of tissues, muscle building, and overall cellular function.

In addition to its protein content, spirulina is rich in essential **vitamins and minerals** that support various bodily functions. It contains high levels of **B vitamins,** particularly **vitamin B12,** which is crucial for **energy production, brain health,** and the formation of **red blood cells.** Spirulina is also a good source of **iron,** making it beneficial for individuals at risk of **iron deficiency** or **anemia.** The iron in spirulina is highly absorbable, helping to boost hemoglobin levels and support **oxygen transport** throughout the body.

Spirulina's nutritional profile is further enhanced by its content of important **minerals** such as **magnesium, potassium,** and **calcium,** all of which are necessary for maintaining **bone health, nerve function,** and **electrolyte balance.** Additionally, spirulina is rich in **essential fatty acids,** including **gamma-linolenic acid (GLA),** which has anti-inflammatory properties and supports **heart health.**

One of the most potent benefits of spirulina is its high concentration of **antioxidants**, particularly **phycocyanin**, a pigment that gives spirulina its distinctive blue-green color. Phycocyanin has been shown to have strong **anti-inflammatory** and **antioxidant** effects, helping to neutralize **free radicals** and reduce oxidative stress in the body. This protective effect can lower the risk of chronic diseases such as **heart disease, cancer,** and **neurodegenerative disorders.** Studies have also suggested that spirulina may help boost the body's production of **immune cells,** such as **natural killer (NK) cells** and **T-cells,** enhancing the immune response to infections and illnesses.

Spirulina has also been shown to support **detoxification**, particularly in removing **heavy metals** and other toxins from the body. Its ability to bind to toxins, such as **arsenic, lead,** and **mercury,** and facilitate their elimination makes spirulina a valuable tool for detoxification programs. This detoxifying effect is particularly important for individuals exposed to environmental pollutants or those seeking to cleanse their system of toxins.

For individuals looking to manage their **weight,** spirulina can be a beneficial addition to a balanced diet due to its high protein content and **low-calorie** profile. The protein in spirulina promotes **satiety,** helping to reduce appetite and support healthy weight loss. Furthermore, spirulina's ability to stabilize **blood sugar levels** and improve **insulin sensitivity** can be beneficial for individuals with **type 2 diabetes** or those looking to manage **blood sugar spikes.**

Spirulina is typically consumed in the form of **powder, tablets,** or **capsules,** making it easy to incorporate into daily meals or supplements. Spirulina powder can be added to **smoothies, juices,** or energy bars, while tablets or capsules offer a convenient way to take spirulina as part of a daily health regimen. A typical dosage of spirulina ranges from **2 to 5 grams** per day, though higher doses (up to 10 grams) are often recommended for individuals looking to boost their protein intake or support detoxification.

In conclusion, **spirulina** is a nutrient-packed **superfood** that offers a comprehensive array of health benefits, from being an excellent source of **plant-based protein** to providing potent **antioxidants** and supporting **immune function.** Its ability to detoxify the body, enhance energy levels, and promote overall well-being makes spirulina a valuable addition to any diet, particularly for those seeking natural ways to improve health and nutrition. Whether consumed in powder form, tablets, or as an ingredient in health products, spirulina stands out as one of the most powerful

superfoods for maintaining **optimal health**.

2.6 Herbal-Drug and Herb-Food Interactions

Herbal products, widely used for their therapeutic benefits, are often combined with **prescription medications** or **food** as part of an individual's health regimen. However, the **interactions** between herbs, drugs, and foods can sometimes lead to unintended effects, either reducing the efficacy of a treatment, increasing the risk of side effects, or altering the way the body processes both the herb and the medication. Understanding **herbal-drug** and **herb-food interactions** is crucial for ensuring safety and effectiveness when using **herbal remedies** alongside conventional treatments or in everyday nutrition.

2.6.1 General Introduction to Herbal Interactions

Herbal interactions occur when the bioactive compounds in herbs influence the **pharmacokinetics** (absorption, distribution, metabolism, and excretion) or **pharmacodynamics** (the drug's effect on the body) of medications or nutrients in food. Many herbs contain complex mixtures of **alkaloids, flavonoids, terpenoids,** and other compounds that can interact with enzymes in the **liver** or **gastrointestinal tract,** leading to changes in how a drug or nutrient is metabolized. Additionally, some herbs may amplify or inhibit the effects of drugs or nutrients, potentially leading to adverse reactions or reduced therapeutic benefits.

One of the most well-known mechanisms of herbal-drug interactions is through the **cytochrome P450 enzyme system (CYP),** particularly enzymes like **CYP3A4** and **CYP2D6,** which are responsible for the metabolism of many drugs in the liver. Certain herbs, such as **St. John's Wort,** are known to induce the activity of these enzymes, increasing the metabolism of drugs and potentially reducing their efficacy. For example, St. John's Wort can significantly reduce the effectiveness of **antidepressants, oral contraceptives,** and **immunosuppressants** by accelerating their breakdown in the liver.

Conversely, some herbs may inhibit these enzymes, slowing down the metabolism of drugs and increasing their concentration in the bloodstream. This can lead to a higher risk of **toxicity** or exaggerated effects of the drug. For instance, **grapefruit** is known to inhibit CYP3A4, which can cause increased levels of certain **statins** (cholesterol-lowering drugs) and **calcium channel blockers,** leading to side effects like muscle pain or low blood pressure.

In addition to liver metabolism, herbal interactions can also occur in the **gastrointestinal tract**, where herbs may affect drug absorption. For example, **fiber-rich herbs** like **psyllium** can bind to certain medications, reducing their absorption and effectiveness. Similarly, herbs with **laxative effects** (such as **senna** or **aloe vera**) may speed up intestinal transit time, potentially reducing the absorption of nutrients or medications.

Herb-food interactions are also important to consider, as certain combinations of herbs and foods can alter the absorption or effectiveness of either component. For example, **turmeric** (rich in curcumin) has poor bioavailability on its own, but when consumed with **black pepper** (containing piperine), its absorption is significantly enhanced, boosting its therapeutic effects. On the other hand, some foods may reduce the efficacy of herbs, such as dairy products, which can interfere with the absorption of **calcium-rich herbs** or other supplements.

Moreover, interactions between herbs and medications can lead to unexpected **side effects**. For example, **ginkgo biloba**, which is commonly used for cognitive enhancement, has blood-thinning properties and can increase the risk of **bleeding** when combined with anticoagulant medications such as **warfarin** or **aspirin**. Similarly, **garlic**, another herb with cardiovascular benefits, can enhance the effects of blood thinners, leading to an increased risk of hemorrhage.

Given these potential interactions, it is essential to consider the **safety** and **efficacy** of combining herbs with drugs or certain foods. Healthcare providers and individuals using herbal supplements should be aware of these interactions to prevent adverse effects and ensure optimal therapeutic outcomes. Regular monitoring, proper dosage, and clear communication with healthcare professionals are critical when incorporating herbal products into a treatment plan or diet.

2.6.2 Classification of Herb-Drug and Herb-Food Interactions

Herb-drug and **herb-food interactions** can be classified into several categories based on their **mechanism of action** and their effect on the body. These interactions can influence how drugs are absorbed, metabolized, or excreted and how foods affect the bioavailability of herbs or drugs. Understanding these classifications helps to manage and prevent adverse effects when using **herbal products** in conjunction with **medications** or specific **foods**.

1. Pharmacokinetic Interactions

Pharmacokinetic interactions occur when herbs affect the **absorption, distribution, metabolism,** or **excretion** of drugs in the body, influencing how the drug reaches its target or how long it remains active.

- **Absorption Interactions**: Certain herbs can interfere with the absorption of drugs by altering the environment in the **gastrointestinal tract**. For instance, fiber-rich herbs like **psyllium** or **aloe vera** may slow the absorption of medications by binding to them or speeding up gastrointestinal transit time. Herbs with high levels of **tannins**, such as **green tea**, can also bind to drugs, reducing their absorption in the intestines.
- **Metabolism Interactions**: Many herb-drug interactions occur at the **metabolism** stage, particularly in the **liver**, where herbs can either induce or inhibit **cytochrome P450 enzymes**. For example:

  - **Enzyme Induction**: Herbs like **St. John's Wort** induce the **CYP3A4** enzyme, leading to increased metabolism of drugs such as **oral contraceptives, antidepressants,** and **antiretroviral drugs**. This reduces the effectiveness of these drugs.
  - **Enzyme Inhibition: Grapefruit** and certain flavonoids inhibit CYP3A4, slowing the breakdown of drugs like **statins** and **calcium channel blockers**, leading to increased drug levels and a higher risk of side effects such as **toxicity**.

- **Excretion Interactions**: Some herbs can affect how quickly drugs are excreted from the body. For instance, **diuretic herbs** like **dandelion** or **juniper** can enhance the excretion of drugs through urine, potentially lowering the drug's effectiveness. Conversely, herbs that affect kidney function can slow the excretion of medications, leading to accumulation and toxicity.

2. Pharmacodynamic Interactions

Pharmacodynamic interactions occur when herbs influence the **effects** of a drug directly at its site of action or through **additive** or **antagonistic** effects. These interactions can either **enhance** or **inhibit** the drug's therapeutic action.

- **Additive Effects**: Herbs with similar pharmacological effects to certain drugs can lead to an **additive** effect, increasing the risk of **overdosing** or **side effects**. For example:

  - **Ginkgo biloba** and **garlic** both have **anticoagulant properties** and can enhance the effects of blood-thinning medications like **warfarin** or **aspirin**, increasing the risk of **bleeding**.
  - **Valerian root** or **kava** may enhance the **sedative** effects of **benzodiazepines** or **barbiturates**, leading to excessive drowsiness or sedation.

- **Antagonistic Effects**: Conversely, some herbs may reduce the effectiveness of a drug by having **opposite effects**. For instance:

  - **Ginseng** may counteract the effects of **warfarin** by promoting **blood clotting**, thereby reducing the drug's efficacy in preventing clots.
  - **Stimulant herbs** like **guarana** or **ephedra** can antagonize the effects of **beta-blockers**, leading to increased heart rate or blood pressure.

3. Herb-Food Interactions

Herb-food interactions occur when certain foods affect the **bioavailability** or **effectiveness** of herbs or herbal supplements, either by enhancing or inhibiting their absorption or therapeutic action.

- **Enhancing Interactions**: Certain foods can improve the absorption or potency of herbs. For example:

  - **Black pepper** (which contains **piperine**) significantly enhances the bioavailability of **curcumin** from **turmeric**, increasing its **anti-inflammatory** and **antioxidant** effects.
  - **Fat-rich foods** can increase the absorption of fat-soluble herbal compounds like **carotenoids** from **calendula** or **vitamin A** from herbs like **alfalfa**.

- **Inhibiting Interactions**: Some foods can reduce the effectiveness of herbal remedies by inhibiting their absorption or metabolism. For instance:

- ◦ **Dairy products** may reduce the absorption of **calcium** and **iron** from herbal supplements by binding to these minerals and making them less bioavailable.
- ◦ **Tannins** in **tea** can reduce the absorption of **iron** from herbs or foods consumed at the same time.

4. Toxicity or Side Effect Potentiation

In some cases, combining certain herbs with drugs or foods can lead to an increased risk of **toxicity** or severe **side effects**. For example:

- Combining **ephedra** (a stimulant herb) with **caffeine** or stimulant medications can lead to **high blood pressure, heart palpitations**, or even **cardiac arrest**.
- Herbs like **kava** and **echinacea**, which affect the liver, can exacerbate liver toxicity when combined with drugs known to be **hepatotoxic**, such as **acetaminophen** or certain **statins**.

5. Herb-Herb Interactions

Sometimes, combining multiple herbs can lead to interactions that either amplify or negate their effects. For instance:

- **Ashwagandha** and **ginseng** both have **adaptogenic** properties and may have synergistic effects when taken together, enhancing the body's ability to cope with stress.
- Combining **sedative herbs** like **valerian** and **passionflower** may lead to excessive drowsiness or sedation.

The classification of **herb-drug** and **herb-food interactions** provides a comprehensive understanding of how herbal products may interact with medications and foods. These interactions can influence how drugs are metabolized, absorbed, and excreted, as well as how herbs interact with nutrients or other herbs. By understanding these classifications, individuals and healthcare professionals can better manage the use of herbal supplements alongside conventional treatments to ensure safety and optimize therapeutic outcomes.

2.6.3 Case Studies of Key Herbs and Their Side Effects

Herbal remedies are widely used for their medicinal properties, but like pharmaceuticals, certain herbs can lead to **side effects** or **adverse**

interactions when taken in conjunction with other drugs. Understanding these interactions through specific case studies of key herbs allows for better management of **herbal therapy** in clinical settings. One notable example is **St. John's Wort (Hypericum perforatum)**, a popular herb known for its antidepressant effects but also for its significant potential to interact with a wide range of medications.

2.6.3.1 Hypericum (St. John's Wort)

St. John's Wort has been used for centuries as a remedy for **depression, anxiety,** and **mood disorders**. Its primary active compounds, **hypericin** and **hyperforin**, are thought to influence **neurotransmitter levels** such as **serotonin, dopamine,** and **norepinephrine**, thereby improving mood and reducing symptoms of depression. While effective for mild to moderate depression, St. John's Wort is particularly well-known for its extensive **herb-drug interactions**, primarily due to its effect on the **cytochrome P450 enzyme system** and **P-glycoprotein (P-gp) transporters**. These interactions can reduce the effectiveness of a wide variety of medications and lead to potentially dangerous consequences.

Case Study: Antidepressant Interaction

St. John's Wort is often self-administered by individuals seeking natural alternatives to **pharmaceutical antidepressants**, but its interaction with other **antidepressant medications**, particularly **selective serotonin reuptake inhibitors (SSRIs)**, can lead to serious side effects. One well-documented side effect is the development of **serotonin syndrome**, a potentially life-threatening condition caused by excessive levels of serotonin in the brain. Symptoms of serotonin syndrome include **agitation, confusion, rapid heart rate, high blood pressure,** and in severe cases, **seizures** or **unconsciousness**.

In one case, a patient taking an SSRI for depression began using **St. John's Wort** as a complementary therapy. Within a few weeks, the patient developed **tremors, sweating,** and **elevated blood pressure**, all signs of serotonin syndrome. The symptoms were attributed to the **additive effect** of St. John's Wort increasing serotonin levels in conjunction with the SSRI. After discontinuing St. John's Wort and receiving appropriate medical care, the patient's symptoms resolved. This case underscores the dangers of combining St. John's Wort with other serotonergic drugs.

Case Study: Interaction with Oral Contraceptives

St. John's Wort is also known for its interaction with **oral contraceptives**, leading to **reduced effectiveness** of birth control pills and an increased risk of **unintended pregnancy.** This interaction occurs because St. John's Wort induces the **CYP3A4** enzyme, accelerating the metabolism of the hormones **estrogen** and **progestin** found in many oral contraceptives. The faster metabolism of these hormones reduces their concentration in the bloodstream, thereby diminishing their contraceptive effect.

In one documented case, a woman who had been taking oral contraceptives for several years without issue began using St. John's Wort to manage mild depression. After a few months, she unexpectedly became pregnant, despite no changes in her contraceptive regimen. Upon investigation, it was discovered that the induction of CYP3A4 by St. John's Wort had significantly reduced the levels of contraceptive hormones, leading to contraceptive failure.

Case Study: Organ Transplant Rejection

Another severe interaction involving St. John's Wort is with **immunosuppressant drugs,** such as **cyclosporine,** which are used to prevent **organ transplant rejection.** St. John's Wort accelerates the breakdown of cyclosporine by inducing CYP3A4 and P-glycoprotein, leading to subtherapeutic levels of the drug and a high risk of transplant rejection.

In one case, a patient who had undergone a kidney transplant was prescribed cyclosporine to suppress the immune response and prevent rejection of the transplanted organ. However, the patient began using St. John's Wort for mood enhancement without consulting their healthcare provider. After several weeks, the patient experienced signs of transplant rejection, including **elevated creatinine levels** and decreased kidney function. It was determined that the use of St. John's Wort had significantly lowered cyclosporine levels, allowing the immune system to attack the transplanted kidney. The rejection was treated, but the incident highlighted the dangers of combining St. John's Wort with immunosuppressants.

Side Effects and Contraindications

Apart from drug interactions, St. John's Wort can cause **photosensitivity,** especially in fair-skinned individuals. Prolonged sun exposure while using the herb may lead to **skin irritation, rash,** or **sunburn.** Other side effects can include **dry mouth, dizziness, fatigue,** and **gastrointestinal discomfort.** Due to its interactions and potential side effects, St. John's Wort should be used with caution and always under the guidance of a healthcare provider, particularly for individuals taking other medications.

St. John's Wort is a highly effective herb for managing mild to moderate depression, but its significant **drug interactions** make it a risky choice for individuals taking other medications, particularly **antidepressants, oral contraceptives**, and **immunosuppressants**. These case studies highlight the importance of understanding the potential side effects and interactions of herbal products to ensure safety and prevent adverse outcomes. Healthcare professionals and patients alike must be aware of the risks associated with herbal-drug interactions to avoid potentially life-threatening complications.

2.6.3.2 Kava-Kava

Kava-Kava (Piper methysticum) is a traditional **Pacific Island herb** known for its calming and **anxiolytic effects**. It has been used for centuries in cultural and medicinal practices for its ability to reduce **anxiety**, promote **relaxation**, and induce **sleep**. The active compounds in Kava-Kava, called **kavalactones**, are responsible for its psychoactive properties. These compounds interact with **gamma-aminobutyric acid (GABA)** receptors in the brain, similar to the mechanism of action of **benzodiazepines**, producing a sedative effect without the addictive potential commonly associated with conventional anxiolytics. Despite its benefits, Kava-Kava has been associated with significant **side effects** and **drug interactions**, particularly its **hepatotoxicity**, or damaging effects on the liver.

Case Study: Hepatotoxicity and Liver Failure

One of the most well-documented risks of Kava-Kava use is **liver toxicity**. While not every user experiences liver issues, numerous case studies have linked Kava-Kava to severe liver damage, including cases of **hepatitis, cirrhosis**, and even **liver failure** that required liver transplantation. It is believed that certain kavalactones in Kava-Kava can interfere with **cytochrome P450 enzymes** in the liver, leading to the accumulation of toxic metabolites.

In one case, a 45-year-old woman who had been using Kava-Kava supplements for anxiety for several months began experiencing symptoms of **fatigue, nausea, jaundice**, and **abdominal pain**. Blood tests revealed elevated liver enzymes, indicating liver dysfunction. A liver biopsy confirmed severe hepatitis, and the woman was eventually diagnosed with **acute liver failure**. Upon discontinuation of Kava-Kava, her liver function began to improve, though long-term damage remained. This case underscores the potential hepatotoxic effects of Kava-Kava, particularly when used over extended periods or in high doses.

Case Study: Interaction with Sedatives

Kava-Kava's calming effects have made it popular as a natural alternative to **benzodiazepines** and other sedative medications. However, its **additive** effects when combined with these drugs can lead to excessive sedation, **drowsiness**, and impaired motor function. Kava-Kava enhances the effects of sedatives by binding to GABA receptors, amplifying the **CNS-depressant effects** of drugs like **diazepam (Valium)** or **alprazolam (Xanax)**, which can lead to dangerous levels of sedation and an increased risk of **accidents**.

In one case, a 50-year-old man who had been prescribed a low dose of diazepam for anxiety began taking Kava-Kava supplements as well, seeking additional relief. Over the next few days, he experienced **severe drowsiness, confusion**, and **impaired coordination**, which resulted in a car accident. Medical evaluation revealed that the combination of Kava-Kava and diazepam had potentiated the sedative effects of the medication, leading to the accident. This case highlights the dangers of combining Kava-Kava with **central nervous system (CNS) depressants**, as it can significantly amplify their effects.

Case Study: Antidepressant Interaction

Kava-Kava may also interact with **antidepressants**, particularly **monoamine oxidase inhibitors (MAOIs)** and **selective serotonin reuptake inhibitors (SSRIs)**, potentially leading to serious side effects. Kava-Kava's effect on neurotransmitter systems, including **serotonin** and **dopamine**, can increase the risk of developing **serotonin syndrome** or exacerbate symptoms of **depression** or **mania** when used with certain antidepressants.

In a documented case, a woman with a history of depression, who had been prescribed **fluoxetine (Prozac)**, started using Kava-Kava to manage stress. Within a few weeks, she developed **agitation, tremors**, and **elevated heart rate**, all signs of **serotonin syndrome**, a potentially life-threatening condition caused by excessive serotonin activity in the brain. The combination of Kava-Kava and fluoxetine had led to an overload of serotonin, resulting in this dangerous interaction. The patient required hospitalization, and after discontinuing both the Kava-Kava and adjusting her medication, her symptoms subsided.

Side Effects and Contraindications

Apart from the risk of **hepatotoxicity** and its interactions with sedative medications and antidepressants, Kava-Kava has other notable side effects. Prolonged use of Kava-Kava in high doses has been associated with a condition called **kava dermopathy**, characterized by **dry, flaky skin,** particularly on the palms and soles. Additionally, Kava-Kava can cause **dizziness, headaches, nausea,** and **gastrointestinal discomfort,** particularly in individuals sensitive to its effects.

Furthermore, Kava-Kava should be avoided by individuals with pre-existing **liver conditions**, those who consume alcohol regularly, or those taking medications known to affect the liver, as the risk of liver damage is significantly increased. Pregnant and breastfeeding women are also advised against using Kava-Kava due to insufficient data on its safety in these populations.

Kava-Kava is a potent **anxiolytic herb** that offers significant benefits for managing **stress, anxiety,** and **sleep disorders**. However, it carries substantial risks, particularly its potential to cause **liver damage** and its ability to **amplify the effects** of sedative medications and antidepressants. These case studies underscore the importance of cautious use and the need for medical supervision when taking Kava-Kava, especially for individuals with pre-existing conditions or those taking other medications. Awareness of the risks and side effects of Kava-Kava is essential for ensuring safe and effective use.

2.6.3.3 Ginkgo Biloba

Ginkgo biloba is one of the oldest living tree species and is widely used in herbal medicine for its purported benefits in improving **cognitive function**, particularly in cases of **memory loss, dementia,** and **Alzheimer's disease**. The active compounds in Ginkgo, including **flavonoids** and **terpenoids**, act as **antioxidants** and **circulatory enhancers**, helping to protect neurons from oxidative stress and improve blood flow to the brain. Despite its well-documented benefits, Ginkgo biloba is also associated with various **side effects** and **herb-drug interactions**, particularly its potential to increase the risk of **bleeding** due to its **anticoagulant properties**.

Case Study: Bleeding Risk and Anticoagulants

One of the most significant risks associated with Ginkgo biloba is its ability to interfere with **blood clotting**. Ginkgo has **antiplatelet** effects, meaning it can inhibit the aggregation of platelets, which are critical for forming blood clots. While this effect can be beneficial for promoting healthy blood circulation, it can also increase the risk of **bleeding**, particularly when Ginkgo is taken alongside **anticoagulant** or **antiplatelet medications** like **warfarin, aspirin,** or **clopidogrel**.

In one case, a 72-year-old man who had been taking warfarin for a heart condition began using Ginkgo biloba to improve his memory. After a few weeks, he experienced spontaneous **nosebleeds, bruising,** and eventually developed **gastrointestinal bleeding,** requiring hospitalization. Laboratory tests revealed that his **INR (International Normalized Ratio),** a measure of blood clotting time, was significantly elevated, indicating an increased risk of hemorrhage. It was determined that the Ginkgo biloba had potentiated the anticoagulant effect of warfarin, leading to excessive thinning of the blood. The Ginkgo supplement was discontinued, and his bleeding symptoms subsided with medical treatment. This case underscores the importance of monitoring patients who take anticoagulant medications while using Ginkgo biloba, as the combination can lead to life-threatening bleeding events.

Case Study: Interaction with Antidepressants

Ginkgo biloba is sometimes used by individuals to alleviate **cognitive impairment** associated with **depression** or **age-related decline,** but when combined with **selective serotonin reuptake inhibitors (SSRIs)** or other antidepressants, it can lead to increased risk of **serotonin syndrome.** This is because Ginkgo may influence neurotransmitter activity, including **serotonin,** and when combined with SSRIs like **fluoxetine (Prozac)** or **sertraline (Zoloft),** it can amplify the effects of these medications.

In one case, a middle-aged woman taking **sertraline** for depression began using Ginkgo biloba to improve concentration and memory. After several weeks, she developed symptoms of **agitation, tremors, sweating,** and **elevated heart rate**—classic signs of **serotonin syndrome.** The interaction between Ginkgo biloba and her antidepressant medication was identified as the cause of her symptoms. After discontinuing Ginkgo and adjusting her medication, the symptoms resolved. This case highlights the potential dangers of combining Ginkgo biloba with serotonergic drugs and the need for careful monitoring in such situations.

Case Study: Seizures in Epilepsy Patients

Ginkgo biloba has been associated with **proconvulsant effects,** meaning it can lower the **seizure threshold** in individuals prone to **epileptic seizures.** While rare, there have been documented cases of individuals with **epilepsy** or those taking **anticonvulsant medications** experiencing an increase in seizure frequency after starting Ginkgo biloba supplements.

In one case, a 40-year-old man with well-controlled epilepsy who had been seizure-free for over a year began taking Ginkgo biloba to improve his memory. Within a few weeks, he experienced multiple seizures, despite maintaining his regular dose of **phenytoin,** an anticonvulsant medication.

Medical evaluation revealed that Ginkgo had likely interfered with the effectiveness of phenytoin, lowering its anticonvulsant effect and triggering the seizures. After discontinuing Ginkgo, his seizure frequency returned to normal, and his condition stabilized. This case underscores the importance of avoiding Ginkgo biloba in individuals with epilepsy or those taking anticonvulsant drugs, as it can increase the risk of seizures.

Side Effects and Contraindications

While Ginkgo biloba is generally considered safe for most people when used at recommended doses, it can cause side effects, particularly in **sensitive individuals**. Common side effects include **headaches, dizziness, upset stomach**, and **allergic skin reactions**. In rare cases, Ginkgo has been associated with more serious side effects, such as **heart palpitations** and **bleeding**.

Due to its blood-thinning properties, Ginkgo biloba is contraindicated in individuals with **bleeding disorders**, those who are about to undergo **surgery**, and those taking **anticoagulant** or **antiplatelet** medications. It should also be used with caution in individuals taking **NSAIDs** (nonsteroidal anti-inflammatory drugs), such as **ibuprofen** or **naproxen**, as these drugs can further increase the risk of bleeding.

Furthermore, because of its potential proconvulsant effects, Ginkgo should be avoided by individuals with **epilepsy** or those taking anticonvulsants. Additionally, pregnant and breastfeeding women are generally advised to avoid Ginkgo due to insufficient safety data.

Ginkgo biloba is widely used for its **cognitive-enhancing** and **circulatory benefits**, particularly in elderly individuals or those with memory concerns. However, it carries significant risks of **herb-drug interactions**, particularly its potential to increase the risk of **bleeding** when taken with anticoagulants or antiplatelet drugs, and its potential to trigger **seizures** in epilepsy patients. The documented case studies illustrate the importance of caution when using Ginkgo, especially in combination with other medications. Healthcare providers must carefully assess the risks and benefits of Ginkgo supplementation in patients with **underlying conditions** or those taking medications that affect blood clotting or neurological function.

2.6.3.4 Ginseng

Ginseng (Panax ginseng) is a popular **adaptogenic herb** that has been used in traditional medicine for centuries to enhance **energy**, improve **cognitive function**, and support **immune health**. Its active components, known as **ginsenosides**, are responsible for many of its health-promoting properties. While Ginseng is widely considered safe when used appropriately, it is also associated with various **side effects** and **herb-drug interactions**, particularly in individuals with underlying health conditions or those taking certain medications.

Case Study: Interaction with Anticoagulants

Ginseng is known to potentially interact with **anticoagulant** medications, such as **warfarin**, by affecting the **blood clotting process**. Ginseng can reduce the effectiveness of warfarin, increasing the risk of **blood clots** and reducing the therapeutic efficacy of the drug.

In one case, a 65-year-old man on long-term warfarin therapy for a heart condition began using Ginseng supplements to boost his energy. After several weeks, his **INR (International Normalized Ratio)** levels, which measure blood clotting time, were significantly lower than expected. This indicated a higher risk of **blood clot formation**. Upon discontinuation of Ginseng, his INR levels returned to the therapeutic range. This case highlights the risk of **ginseng-induced warfarin resistance**, which can lead to dangerous **clotting complications** if not properly monitored.

Case Study: Interaction with Hypoglycemic Drugs

Ginseng has been shown to have **hypoglycemic effects**, making it beneficial for individuals with **type 2 diabetes** by helping to regulate **blood sugar levels**. However, when combined with **antidiabetic medications** such as **metformin** or **insulin**, Ginseng can **enhance the glucose-lowering effects**, leading to **hypoglycemia** (dangerously low blood sugar levels).

In one case, a 58-year-old woman with type 2 diabetes was taking **metformin** to control her blood sugar. After starting Ginseng supplements to improve her overall health, she began experiencing symptoms of hypoglycemia, including **dizziness, sweating,** and **confusion**. Blood tests confirmed low glucose levels, and it was determined that the combined effects of metformin and Ginseng had caused her blood sugar to drop too low. After discontinuing Ginseng, her blood sugar levels stabilized, and the hypoglycemia resolved. This case illustrates the need for caution when using Ginseng in combination with antidiabetic drugs, as it can **amplify the blood sugar-lowering effects**.

Case Study: Interaction with Antidepressants

Ginseng is sometimes used to improve **mood** and **cognitive function**, but its use alongside **antidepressants**, particularly **monoamine oxidase inhibitors (MAOIs)**, can result in dangerous side effects. Ginseng may potentiate the effects of MAOIs, leading to **manic episodes** or **insomnia** in sensitive individuals.

In a documented case, a 45-year-old woman taking **phenelzine** (an MAOI) for depression started using Ginseng to increase her energy levels. Within a few weeks, she developed symptoms of **agitation, insomnia**, and **euphoria**, indicative of a **manic episode**. Upon discontinuation of Ginseng, her symptoms gradually subsided. This case underscores the potential for **Ginseng-induced mood alterations** when used in combination with certain **antidepressants**.

Case Study: Hypertension and Ginseng

Ginseng is often used to improve **physical stamina** and **mental clarity**, but in some individuals, it can cause an increase in **blood pressure**, especially when taken in high doses or for extended periods. While Ginseng generally has a mild **hypotensive** effect in some people, it can paradoxically cause **hypertension** in others.

In one case, a 52-year-old man who had been using Ginseng to manage fatigue began experiencing **elevated blood pressure** and **heart palpitations** after several weeks of use. He had no prior history of hypertension. After discontinuing Ginseng, his blood pressure returned to normal, and the palpitations ceased. This case demonstrates that Ginseng can have varying effects on blood pressure, and individuals with pre-existing **hypertension** or **cardiovascular conditions** should use it with caution.

Side Effects and Contraindications

While Ginseng is generally well-tolerated, some individuals may experience side effects, particularly with **high doses** or prolonged use. Common side effects include **headaches, nervousness, insomnia, gastrointestinal upset**, and **restlessness**. These effects are often more pronounced in individuals sensitive to stimulants or those who take Ginseng in combination with other **stimulants** like **caffeine**.

Ginseng is contraindicated in individuals with conditions such as **hypertension, insomnia**, or **anxiety disorders**, as it may exacerbate these conditions. Additionally, Ginseng should be used with caution in individuals taking medications that affect **blood sugar, blood clotting**, or **mood regulation**.

Pregnant and breastfeeding women are generally advised to avoid Ginseng due to insufficient safety data, and individuals undergoing surgery are cautioned against using Ginseng as it may increase the risk of bleeding.

Ginseng is a well-known **adaptogen** with a wide range of health benefits, particularly for improving **energy, cognitive function**, and **immune health**. However, it also poses risks when used in conjunction with certain medications, such as **anticoagulants, antidiabetic drugs**, and **antidepressants**. These case studies demonstrate the potential for **herb-drug interactions** and the importance of careful monitoring and consultation with a healthcare provider when using Ginseng, especially for individuals on long-term medication or those with underlying health conditions.

2.6.3.5 Garlic

Garlic (Allium sativum) is widely regarded for its health benefits, particularly for **cardiovascular health, immune system support**, and **anti-inflammatory** properties. The active compound in garlic, **allicin**, is responsible for many of its therapeutic effects, including its ability to reduce **blood pressure**, lower **cholesterol levels**, and improve **circulation**. Despite these benefits, garlic can interact with certain medications, leading to **adverse effects** and **herb-drug interactions**. It is important to understand these interactions to ensure the safe use of garlic, especially for individuals taking prescription medications.

Case Study: Interaction with Anticoagulants

Garlic's most significant herb-drug interaction is with **anticoagulant** medications, such as **warfarin, aspirin**, or **clopidogrel**, due to its **antiplatelet** effects. Garlic can thin the blood by inhibiting platelet aggregation, similar to how anticoagulants work. While this can be beneficial for cardiovascular health, it also increases the risk of **bleeding**, especially when combined with anticoagulant medications.

In one case, a 60-year-old man taking warfarin for a heart condition began consuming garlic supplements to improve his cholesterol levels. After several weeks, he experienced **excessive bruising** and **nosebleeds**, both signs of bleeding complications. Laboratory tests revealed that his **INR (International Normalized Ratio)**, which measures the time it takes for blood to clot, was significantly elevated. The interaction between garlic and warfarin had increased the blood-thinning effects of the drug, resulting in an excessive anticoagulant response. Upon discontinuation of garlic, his INR levels normalized, and the bleeding symptoms resolved. This case highlights the need for careful monitoring of individuals taking anticoagulants who also use garlic, whether as a supplement or in large dietary amounts.

Case Study: Interaction with Antihypertensive Medications

Garlic is known for its **blood pressure-lowering** properties, making it an appealing natural remedy for individuals with **hypertension.** However, when combined with **antihypertensive medications**, such as **beta-blockers, ACE inhibitors,** or **calcium channel blockers**, garlic may amplify the effects of these drugs, leading to **hypotension** (dangerously low blood pressure).

In one case, a 55-year-old woman taking **lisinopril** (an ACE inhibitor) to manage high blood pressure began consuming garlic supplements. Within a few weeks, she started experiencing symptoms of **dizziness, lightheadedness**, and **fainting spells**, especially when standing up quickly. Upon medical evaluation, it was found that her blood pressure had dropped to dangerously low levels, a result of the combined hypotensive effects of garlic and lisinopril. After discontinuing the garlic supplements, her blood pressure stabilized, and her symptoms improved. This case underscores the importance of cautious use of garlic in individuals already taking blood pressure-lowering medications to avoid excessive hypotension.

Case Study: Interaction with Antiretroviral Drugs

Garlic can interfere with the metabolism of certain medications, particularly those processed by the **cytochrome P450 enzyme system** in the liver. In the case of **antiretroviral drugs**, such as **saquinavir** used to treat **HIV/AIDS**, garlic has been shown to reduce the effectiveness of these drugs by inducing the CYP3A4 enzyme, which increases the breakdown and elimination of the drug from the body.

In one documented case, a patient with HIV began taking garlic supplements for immune support while also being treated with saquinavir. After several weeks, routine blood tests revealed a significant reduction in **saquinavir levels**, which compromised the effectiveness of the treatment. As a result, the patient's viral load increased, putting them at greater risk of HIV progression. After discontinuing the garlic supplements, saquinavir levels returned to therapeutic levels, and the patient's viral load decreased. This case demonstrates the potential for garlic to reduce the effectiveness of **antiretroviral therapy** and the importance of avoiding garlic supplementation in individuals on these medications.

Case Study: Interaction with Chemotherapy Drugs

Garlic's ability to affect the **metabolism** of drugs has also been observed in patients undergoing **chemotherapy.** Certain chemotherapy drugs, such as **cyclophosphamide** and **doxorubicin**, rely on metabolic pathways that can be influenced by garlic consumption. Garlic can alter the drug's metabolism, either by enhancing its breakdown or affecting its absorption, potentially reducing its efficacy or increasing toxicity.

In one case, a cancer patient undergoing treatment with **cyclophosphamide** began taking garlic supplements to enhance their immune system during chemotherapy. After several cycles of treatment, the patient's response to chemotherapy was suboptimal, and it was discovered that the garlic supplements were interfering with the drug's metabolism, reducing its effectiveness. Once the garlic was discontinued, the chemotherapy treatment became more effective, with better tumor suppression. This case highlights the need for caution when using garlic during **chemotherapy**, as it may impact drug efficacy.

Side Effects and Contraindications

Although garlic is generally well-tolerated in food, **garlic supplements** and large doses can cause side effects, particularly in sensitive individuals. Common side effects include **gastrointestinal discomfort**, such as **heartburn**, **gas**, and **nausea**. Garlic can also cause **allergic reactions**, including skin rashes or respiratory issues in some individuals. Additionally, due to its **anticoagulant properties**, garlic should be used with caution by individuals scheduled for surgery, as it can increase the risk of **bleeding** during and after surgical procedures.

Garlic should be avoided by individuals taking **blood-thinning medications**, and caution is advised for those on **antihypertensive** or **antiretroviral** drugs. Pregnant and breastfeeding women should consult their healthcare providers before using garlic supplements, as the safety of high doses has not been thoroughly studied in these populations.

Garlic offers a range of **health benefits**, particularly for cardiovascular health, but it is also associated with significant **herb-drug interactions**. Its **anticoagulant effects** can increase the risk of bleeding when combined with **anticoagulant** or **antiplatelet drugs**, and its ability to lower blood pressure may cause **hypotension** when used with antihypertensive medications. Additionally, garlic can reduce the effectiveness of certain drugs, such as **antiretrovirals** and **chemotherapy agents**, by altering their metabolism. These case studies highlight the importance of using garlic cautiously, particularly in individuals taking medications for chronic conditions. Consulting a healthcare provider is crucial before adding garlic supplements to any therapeutic regimen.

2.6.3.6 Pepper

Black pepper (Piper nigrum) is a commonly used spice that not only enhances the flavor of food but also offers several **health benefits**. The active compound in black pepper, **piperine**, is responsible for its **bioenhancing properties**, meaning it can increase the absorption and effectiveness of various drugs and nutrients. While this property makes pepper beneficial in many therapeutic settings, it can also lead to **herb-drug interactions** that may either enhance or reduce the efficacy of medications, leading to potential side effects. Piperine affects drug metabolism primarily by inhibiting certain enzymes in the **cytochrome P450** system and **P-glycoprotein** activity in the intestines.

Case Study: Enhanced Bioavailability of Drugs

One of the most well-known effects of piperine is its ability to increase the **bioavailability** of certain medications, particularly those that are poorly absorbed or metabolized rapidly. This is particularly true for drugs metabolized by the **CYP3A4** enzyme in the liver and intestines. By inhibiting this enzyme, piperine slows down the metabolism of the drug, allowing higher concentrations to remain in the bloodstream for a longer duration.

In one case, a patient taking **phenytoin**, an anticonvulsant medication, began consuming black pepper supplements alongside their regular medication. Piperine's inhibitory effect on the metabolism of phenytoin led to higher-than-expected drug levels in the patient's bloodstream. This resulted in **toxicity symptoms**, including **dizziness, lethargy**, and **unsteady gait**. Upon reducing the intake of pepper and adjusting the dose of phenytoin, the symptoms subsided. This case highlights the need for careful monitoring when using piperine-containing supplements with medications that have a narrow **therapeutic index**, as the increase in drug levels can lead to serious side effects.

Case Study: Interaction with Antihypertensive Drugs

Pepper's **bioenhancing properties** can also affect the metabolism of **antihypertensive medications**, such as **beta-blockers** and **calcium channel blockers**. By increasing the absorption and prolonging the effects of these drugs, piperine can lead to **hypotension** (low blood pressure) in some individuals.

In one case, a 55-year-old woman on **amlodipine**, a calcium channel blocker prescribed for high blood pressure, started taking black pepper supplements to boost the absorption of turmeric for its anti-inflammatory benefits. After a few weeks, she began experiencing symptoms of **dizziness,**

fatigue, and **fainting spells**, especially when standing up. A medical examination revealed that her blood pressure had dropped significantly due to the enhanced effect of amlodipine caused by piperine. After discontinuing the pepper supplements, her blood pressure stabilized, and the symptoms resolved. This case illustrates the importance of monitoring blood pressure and medication dosage when using pepper supplements in combination with antihypertensive drugs.

Case Study: Interaction with Curcumin

One of the most beneficial and widely studied interactions of black pepper is its ability to enhance the absorption of **curcumin**, the active compound in **turmeric**. Curcumin is poorly absorbed on its own, but when combined with piperine, its **bioavailability** increases by up to **2000%**. This interaction makes black pepper and turmeric a powerful combination in the treatment of **inflammation**, **arthritis**, and **oxidative stress**.

In one case, a 45-year-old man with **osteoarthritis** began taking a turmeric supplement combined with black pepper to reduce joint pain and inflammation. After a few weeks of use, he reported significant improvement in his pain levels and mobility, attributed to the enhanced absorption of curcumin by piperine. This positive interaction is an example of how black pepper can be used to increase the effectiveness of natural compounds like curcumin. However, the combination should still be used with caution in individuals taking medications that are also affected by the CYP450 system, as piperine's broad effect on drug metabolism can lead to unintended side effects.

Case Study: Interaction with Chemotherapy Drugs

Pepper's ability to inhibit drug metabolism can be problematic for patients undergoing **chemotherapy**, where precise drug dosages are critical for both efficacy and safety. Chemotherapy drugs such as **docetaxel** and **cyclophosphamide**, which are metabolized by the CYP450 enzymes, may have altered pharmacokinetics when taken alongside black pepper.

In one case, a cancer patient undergoing treatment with **docetaxel** started consuming black pepper supplements to enhance nutrient absorption. After several cycles of chemotherapy, the patient experienced increased side effects, including **nausea**, **fatigue**, and **suppressed immune function**, which were more severe than typically expected from the chemotherapy. It was later discovered that the piperine in black pepper had inhibited the metabolism of docetaxel, leading to higher-than-expected drug levels and toxicity. After discontinuing the pepper supplement, the side effects became more manageable, and the patient's response to chemotherapy improved. This case emphasizes the need for caution when using black pepper supplements during chemotherapy, as it can alter the effectiveness and toxicity of the treatment.

Side Effects and Contraindications

While black pepper is generally safe when used in culinary amounts, higher doses of piperine in supplement form can cause side effects, particularly in sensitive individuals. Common side effects include **gastrointestinal irritation, heartburn, and diarrhea**. Piperine's effect on the metabolism of certain drugs can lead to **drug accumulation** and **toxicity**, especially in individuals taking medications for chronic conditions such as **hypertension, diabetes,** or **cancer.**

Black pepper supplements should be used with caution by individuals taking **anticoagulant medications**, as piperine may increase the risk of bleeding by inhibiting **platelet aggregation**. Additionally, individuals undergoing **chemotherapy** or those on medications metabolized by the CYP450 enzymes should consult a healthcare provider before using black pepper supplements to avoid potential interactions.

Black pepper and its active compound **piperine** are potent bioenhancers that can significantly increase the absorption and efficacy of both **medications** and **nutrients**. While this property is beneficial in certain contexts, such as enhancing the absorption of **curcumin**, it can also lead to **herb-drug interactions** that may result in serious side effects, especially when combined with medications like **anticoagulants, antihypertensives,** or **chemotherapy drugs**. These case studies highlight the need for caution when using black pepper supplements, particularly in individuals taking **prescription medications** that are metabolized by the **CYP450 enzyme system**. Consulting with a healthcare provider is essential to ensure safe and effective use of black pepper, especially in supplement form.

2.6.3.7 Ephedra

Ephedra (Ephedra sinica), also known as **ma huang**, is a powerful herb that has been traditionally used in **Chinese medicine** for centuries to treat conditions such as **asthma, bronchitis,** and **congestion**. Its active compound, **ephedrine**, is a potent **stimulant** and **bronchodilator** that affects the **nervous system** and **cardiovascular system**. Ephedra is often used to increase **energy, enhance weight loss,** and improve **athletic performance.** However, due to its **stimulant effects**, Ephedra is associated with numerous **herb-drug interactions** and significant **side effects**, leading to restrictions on its use in many countries, including the **United States**.

Case Study: Cardiovascular Risks

Ephedra's **stimulant properties** can lead to increased **heart rate** and **blood pressure**, posing serious risks for individuals with **cardiovascular conditions** or those taking medications that affect the heart. The herb can cause **tachycardia** (rapid heart rate), **hypertension** (high blood pressure), and even **heart attacks** or **strokes** in susceptible individuals.

In one case, a 35-year-old man began taking an **Ephedra-based weight loss supplement** to boost his metabolism and aid in fat burning. He had no prior history of heart problems. After several weeks of use, he experienced **chest pain, shortness of breath**, and **dizziness**. Medical evaluation revealed **elevated blood pressure** and an **irregular heartbeat**, attributed to the stimulant effects of Ephedra. The supplement was discontinued, and his symptoms gradually improved, but the case underscored the dangerous cardiovascular risks associated with Ephedra use, even in otherwise healthy individuals.

Case Study: Interaction with Stimulants and Caffeine

Ephedra's interaction with other **stimulants**, including **caffeine** and **certain medications**, can significantly amplify its stimulant effects, leading to severe adverse reactions such as **restlessness, insomnia, nervousness,** and **severe cardiovascular complications**.

In one case, a 28-year-old woman who was taking Ephedra for weight loss also consumed high doses of **caffeinated beverages** throughout the day. After several weeks, she began experiencing **anxiety, tremors, palpitations,** and **difficulty sleeping**. A visit to the emergency room revealed **extremely elevated heart rate** and blood pressure. The combination of Ephedra and caffeine had synergistically intensified the stimulant effects, leading to these dangerous side effects. After discontinuing both Ephedra and caffeine, her symptoms resolved. This case illustrates the risks of combining Ephedra with other stimulants, which can lead to **overstimulation** of the nervous and cardiovascular systems.

Case Study: Interaction with Antihypertensive Medications

Ephedra's ability to **raise blood pressure** can negate the effects of **antihypertensive medications**, making it a dangerous herb for individuals who are trying to manage high blood pressure with medication. Ephedrine, the active stimulant in Ephedra, directly increases **vascular resistance**, which counteracts the blood pressure-lowering effects of **beta-blockers, ACE inhibitors**, or **diuretics**.

In one case, a 50-year-old man on **lisinopril** for hypertension began using an Ephedra supplement to improve his athletic performance. Within weeks, his blood pressure became increasingly difficult to control, despite adhering to his medication regimen. His doctor discovered that the Ephedra supplement was likely responsible for the spike in blood pressure, as the herb's stimulant effects were overriding the medication. After discontinuing the Ephedra, the patient's blood pressure returned to a manageable level. This case underscores the potential for Ephedra to interfere with medications used to treat **high blood pressure**, creating a dangerous situation for individuals with cardiovascular conditions.

Case Study: Stroke and Hemorrhagic Risks

Ephedra has been associated with an increased risk of **stroke** due to its ability to raise blood pressure and cause **vasoconstriction** (narrowing of the blood vessels). This effect can lead to hemorrhagic strokes, where blood vessels in the brain burst, causing internal bleeding.

In a particularly alarming case, a 42-year-old woman who had been taking Ephedra to enhance her energy and lose weight suffered a **hemorrhagic stroke**. She experienced **sudden weakness, loss of coordination**, and **severe headache**, followed by collapse. A CT scan revealed bleeding in the brain. Her medical history indicated the use of high-dose Ephedra supplements, which had significantly raised her blood pressure, leading to the rupture of a blood vessel in her brain. Although she survived the stroke, she suffered long-term neurological damage. This case highlights the extreme risks associated with Ephedra use, particularly concerning its potential to trigger **life-threatening strokes**.

Case Study: Interaction with Antidepressants

Ephedra can interact with **antidepressants**, particularly **monoamine oxidase inhibitors (MAOIs)**, leading to a dangerous condition known as **hypertensive crisis**—a sudden and severe increase in blood pressure. This occurs because both Ephedra and MAOIs can increase levels of **norepinephrine**, leading to excessive stimulation of the cardiovascular system.

In one case, a patient on **phenelzine** (an MAOI) for depression began using an Ephedra supplement for weight loss. Within days, the patient experienced **severe headaches, nausea, blurred vision**, and a dangerously high spike in blood pressure. The patient was rushed to the hospital and diagnosed with **hypertensive crisis**, which was attributed to the interaction between Ephedra and phenelzine. After emergency treatment and discontinuation of the herb, the patient's condition stabilized. This case underscores the critical risk of combining Ephedra with **MAO inhibitors**, as it can lead to **life-threatening increases in blood pressure.**

Side Effects and Contraindications

Ephedra is associated with a wide range of **side effects**, even at low doses. Common side effects include **insomnia, nervousness, headaches, dizziness, tremors,** and **gastrointestinal distress.** More severe side effects, particularly at higher doses, include **heart palpitations, arrhythmias, high blood pressure, seizures, heart attacks,** and **strokes.**

Due to these significant risks, **Ephedra is contraindicated** in individuals with:

- **Cardiovascular diseases** such as hypertension or heart disease
- **Anxiety disorders**, as it can exacerbate nervousness and agitation
- **Hyperthyroidism**, as it can overstimulate the metabolism
- **Glaucoma**, due to increased pressure in the eyes
- **Pregnant or breastfeeding women**, as its safety has not been established and it can raise the risk of miscarriage.

The use of Ephedra has been banned or heavily restricted in many countries, including the **United States**, due to its association with serious cardiovascular risks and fatalities.

Ephedra is a potent stimulant herb with significant risks, especially when used in combination with other stimulants, antidepressants, or medications for **hypertension.** The herb's effects on the **cardiovascular system** can lead to dangerous increases in **blood pressure, heart rate,** and a heightened risk of **heart attacks, strokes,** and other severe complications. These case studies highlight the importance of caution when considering the use of Ephedra, particularly for individuals with underlying cardiovascular conditions or those taking medications. Due to its serious safety concerns, Ephedra use should only be undertaken under the guidance of a healthcare professional, if at all.

CHAPTER III

Herbal Cosmetics

With a growing demand for products that are free from synthetic chemicals and rich in bioactive compounds, herbal cosmetics have gained popularity for their ability to promote skin health, reduce inflammation, and provide natural protection. The raw materials used in herbal cosmetics are derived from plants, oils, and other natural sources, offering numerous benefits due to their rich content of vitamins, antioxidants, and essential fatty acids.

3.1 Sources and Description of Raw Materials of Herbal Origin

The effectiveness of herbal cosmetics depends on the quality and properties of the **raw materials** used. These materials are primarily derived from **plant oils, waxes, herbs**, and other natural sources. Each ingredient contributes specific benefits to skin and hair care formulations. This section discusses two key categories of raw materials commonly used in herbal cosmetics: **fixed oils** and **waxes**.

3.1.1 Fixed Oils (e.g., Coconut Oil, Sesame Oil)

Fixed oils are non-volatile oils extracted from seeds, nuts, or fruits. They serve as the base or **carrier oils** in many cosmetic formulations due to their emollient properties, which help moisturize, soften, and protect the skin. These oils are rich in essential fatty acids, vitamins, and antioxidants, making them ideal for nourishing the skin and promoting overall skin health.

- **Coconut Oil: Coconut oil** is one of the most widely used fixed oils in herbal cosmetics. Extracted from the **kernel** or **meat** of mature coconuts, it is rich in **lauric acid**, which has **antibacterial, antiviral**, and **antifungal** properties. Coconut oil also contains **vitamin E**, an important antioxidant that protects the skin from free radical damage. Its high moisturizing capability makes it ideal for use in **lotions, creams**, and **hair care products**. In addition, coconut oil has excellent **penetration properties**, allowing it to deeply nourish the skin and hair without leaving a greasy residue.

- **Sesame Oil: Sesame oil** is extracted from the seeds of the **sesame plant** (Sesamum indicum). Known for its high content of **oleic acid** and **linoleic acid**, sesame oil helps maintain the **skin barrier** and locks in moisture, making it suitable for dry or sensitive skin. Sesame oil also contains **sesamol**, a powerful antioxidant that helps protect the skin from **UV-induced damage** and **environmental stressors**. Due to its **anti-inflammatory** properties, sesame oil is frequently used in formulations designed for **anti-aging** and **soothing irritated skin.**

Fixed oils such as coconut oil and sesame oil are crucial for creating **moisturizing** and **protective barriers** in the skin, making them staple ingredients in **creams, ointments,** and **balms.** Their ability to **penetrate** the skin and provide long-lasting hydration makes them highly effective in preventing **dryness, flaking,** and **rough skin.**

3.1.2 Waxes (e.g., Beeswax)

Waxes are another essential raw material in herbal cosmetics. They are used as **thickening agents** and **emulsifiers** to stabilize formulations and provide texture. Waxes also help create a **protective layer** on the skin, preventing moisture loss while adding a smooth and creamy consistency to products like lip balms, lotions, and creams.

- **Beeswax:** One of the most popular waxes in natural cosmetic formulations is **beeswax,** which is secreted by **honeybees** to build their honeycomb. Beeswax is highly valued for its **emollient** and **hydrating properties.** It forms a protective barrier on the skin's surface, locking in moisture without clogging pores. Beeswax is rich in **vitamin A,** which helps promote cell regeneration and improves skin elasticity, making it an excellent ingredient for **anti-aging** and **healing products.** Due to its natural **anti-inflammatory** and **antibacterial** properties, beeswax is also used in products designed to soothe **irritated skin** or treat **minor wounds.**

Beeswax is widely used in **lip balms, hand creams,** and **body butters** because of its ability to create a soft, smooth texture while enhancing the product's **spreadability** and **moisturizing capacity.**

3.1.3 Gums (e.g., Gum Acacia)

Gums are natural polysaccharides derived from plants that play an essential role in the formulation of **herbal cosmetics** due to their **emulsifying, thickening,** and **stabilizing properties.** These plant-based gums help enhance the texture, consistency, and performance of cosmetic products by improving their viscosity and shelf life. One of the most widely used gums in the cosmetic industry is **gum acacia**, also known as **Arabic gum**, which is derived from the **Acacia senegal** tree. Gums like acacia provide several benefits to skincare and personal care formulations, making them an important ingredient in modern herbal cosmetics.

Gum Acacia, commonly harvested in regions like Africa and India, is a water-soluble gum that has been used for centuries in various applications, including food, pharmaceuticals, and cosmetics. In cosmetics, gum acacia acts as an **emulsifier** that helps mix oil and water components, ensuring product stability and preventing separation. This is especially important in **creams, lotions**, and **serums**, where the even dispersion of ingredients is crucial for optimal performance.

As a **thickening agent**, gum acacia enhances the texture of products, giving them a smooth, creamy consistency without altering their natural feel. In herbal cosmetics, this is particularly valuable as it allows the creation of luxurious, rich textures while maintaining the **natural** and **organic** characteristics of the formulation. Gum acacia is also used in **face masks** and **exfoliants**, where it provides a binding effect, ensuring the product adheres well to the skin while delivering the intended benefits.

Beyond its emulsifying and thickening properties, gum acacia has **moisturizing** benefits as it forms a protective barrier on the skin, preventing water loss and promoting hydration. This makes it an ideal ingredient in **moisturizing creams** and **body lotions** designed for dry or sensitive skin. Gum acacia's ability to attract moisture from the environment further supports the skin's natural hydration processes, enhancing skin softness and smoothness.

Gum acacia is also gentle on the skin, making it suitable for use in formulations designed for **sensitive skin** or for individuals prone to **allergic reactions**. Its non-toxic and biodegradable nature aligns with the growing demand for **eco-friendly** and **sustainable** cosmetic ingredients. As a natural gum, acacia offers cosmetic formulators a versatile tool to improve product quality while adhering to the principles of herbal and natural beauty.

3.1.4 Colors and Perfumes Derived from Plants

In **herbal cosmetics**, the use of **colors** and **perfumes** derived from natural plant sources plays a vital role in enhancing the sensory experience of cosmetic products while avoiding synthetic additives. Plant-based **dyes** and **fragrances** are not only safer for the skin but also align with the trend towards using more **organic** and **chemical-free** ingredients in personal care products. These plant-derived colors and perfumes are obtained through natural extraction processes, ensuring they retain their **bioactive** compounds and **aromatic qualities.**

Natural Colors derived from plants offer a safe and effective alternative to synthetic dyes, which are often linked to skin irritation and allergic reactions. Some of the most commonly used plant-based colors include **turmeric, saffron, henna,** and **indigo.**

- **Turmeric** (Curcuma longa) is widely known for its vibrant **yellow pigment,** curcumin, which has been used for centuries in India not only as a spice but also as a cosmetic coloring agent. It is often incorporated into herbal face masks, soaps, and creams, giving them a warm yellow hue while also delivering **anti-inflammatory** and **antioxidant** benefits. The natural color from turmeric is gentle on the skin and has been used traditionally to enhance the complexion and improve skin tone.
- **Saffron** (Crocus sativus) provides a delicate **orange** to **red** hue and is prized for its luxurious qualities. In high-end herbal cosmetics, saffron is used in **facial serums, creams,** and **skin brightening masks** due to its ability to impart a subtle color while promoting **radiance** and **glowing skin.** The **carotenoids** in saffron contribute to its coloring and are known for their potent antioxidant properties, helping to protect the skin from environmental damage.
- **Henna** (Lawsonia inermis) has long been used as a natural **hair dye** and for body art due to its ability to stain the skin and hair with rich **reddish-brown** tones. Henna is particularly popular in **hair coloring products,** where it provides a long-lasting color without the harsh chemicals found in synthetic dyes. It is also used in natural lip stains and balms to give a warm tint while nourishing the skin.
- **Indigo** (Indigofera tinctoria) is another plant-based dye used in cosmetics, especially for **hair coloring,** where it produces deep **blue** or **black** tones. Indigo is often combined with henna to achieve various hair color shades, ranging from brown to black. Like henna, indigo is a safer alternative to chemical dyes and is frequently used in formulations catering to individuals with sensitive scalps.

Perfumes derived from plants are essential in creating **aromatic** herbal cosmetics, offering not only fragrance but also **therapeutic benefits** through **aromatherapy.** Essential oils extracted from flowers, leaves, and roots are commonly used as natural perfumes due to their soothing, uplifting, or relaxing properties. Popular plant-derived perfumes include **rose, lavender, jasmine**, and **sandalwood**.

- **Rose** essential oil, derived from **Rosa damascena**, is a highly sought-after fragrance in herbal cosmetics. Its rich, floral scent is commonly used in **facial creams, body lotions**, and **perfumed oils**. Beyond its pleasing aroma, rose oil is valued for its ability to soothe **irritated skin**, balance **moisture levels**, and reduce the appearance of **fine lines**.
- **Lavender** (Lavandula angustifolia) is known for its **calming** and **relaxing** scent, making it a popular choice in **bath products, massage oils**, and **sleep-enhancing creams**. Lavender essential oil also has **antimicrobial** properties, which are beneficial for **acne-prone** skin, making it an excellent addition to herbal facial cleansers and toners.
- **Jasmine** (Jasminum officinale) offers a sweet, exotic fragrance that is often included in luxury herbal perfumes and **body oils**. Jasmine oil is also known for its ability to improve **skin elasticity**, promote **radiance**, and reduce **stress** through its soothing scent.
- **Sandalwood** (Santalum album) provides a warm, woody fragrance that is deeply grounding and often used in **meditative** or **relaxation** products. Sandalwood essential oil is also renowned for its **anti-inflammatory** properties and is used in herbal cosmetics for **acne, eczema**, and other inflammatory skin conditions.

Plant-based perfumes and colors not only enhance the aesthetic appeal of herbal cosmetics but also contribute to the overall therapeutic value of the product. Their **natural origins** and **skin-friendly** properties make them highly suitable for individuals seeking a **clean beauty** approach, free from artificial chemicals. By leveraging the rich variety of pigments and fragrances found in nature, herbal cosmetics can offer a holistic sensory experience that nourishes the body, mind, and spirit.

3.1.5 Protective Agents and Antioxidants for Skin and Hair Care

In **herbal cosmetics**, the use of **protective agents** and **antioxidants** is essential for promoting the health and longevity of the skin and hair. These natural ingredients protect against **environmental stressors**, such as **UV radiation, pollution**, and **oxidative damage**, while also nourishing and revitalizing the skin and hair. **Antioxidants** play a key role in neutralizing **free radicals**, unstable molecules that damage cells and accelerate the aging process. Protective agents, on the other hand, create a barrier against external irritants, preserving moisture and improving resilience. This section explores common **plant-derived** protective agents and antioxidants that are widely used in **skin and hair care** formulations.

Protective Agents

Protective agents in herbal cosmetics are primarily designed to shield the skin and hair from environmental damage while promoting **hydration** and **skin barrier function**. These natural ingredients help maintain **moisture levels**, prevent **dryness**, and protect against **irritation** caused by harsh conditions.

- **Aloe Vera**: **Aloe vera** (Aloe barbadensis) is a widely used protective agent in herbal cosmetics due to its ability to soothe and hydrate the skin. Known for its **cooling** and **anti-inflammatory** properties, aloe vera is ideal for use in **sunburn relief gels, moisturizers**, and **after-sun lotions**. Aloe vera's high water content helps replenish lost moisture, while its polysaccharides form a protective layer on the skin, sealing in hydration. It is especially beneficial for sensitive or irritated skin, providing relief from redness, itching, and inflammation caused by environmental stressors like sun exposure or pollution.

- **Shea Butter**: **Shea butter** (Butyrospermum parkii) is extracted from the nuts of the **shea tree** and is highly regarded for its **emollient** properties. Rich in **vitamins A and E**, shea butter forms a protective barrier on the skin, locking in moisture and protecting it from harsh weather conditions, especially in cold or dry climates. Shea butter is often used in **body creams, lip balms**, and **hair masks** due to its ability to nourish and soften dry, flaky skin and damaged hair. Its rich fatty acid profile, including **stearic** and **oleic acids**, helps repair the skin's natural barrier and prevent trans-epidermal water loss (TEWL), keeping the skin hydrated and supple.

- **Cocoa Butter**: **Cocoa butter** (Theobroma cacao) is another effective protective agent commonly used in herbal cosmetics. Known for its deeply moisturizing and **healing properties**, cocoa butter is often used in **stretch mark creams, lip balms**, and **body butters**. It is rich in **fatty acids**, which help improve the skin's elasticity, and its thick consistency forms a long-lasting barrier, particularly useful for individuals with extremely dry skin. Cocoa butter is also a rich source of **antioxidants**, contributing to its role in protecting the skin from oxidative stress and environmental damage.

Antioxidants

Antioxidants in herbal cosmetics are critical for fighting **free radical damage**, which is a major contributor to **premature aging**, **hyperpigmentation**, and **loss of skin elasticity**. Plant-derived antioxidants help maintain the health and vibrancy of the skin and hair by reducing oxidative stress and enhancing cell renewal.

- **Green Tea Extract**: **Green tea** (Camellia sinensis) is rich in **polyphenols**, particularly **epigallocatechin gallate (EGCG)**, which is a potent antioxidant known for its ability to protect the skin from **UV-induced damage** and prevent **photoaging**. Green tea extract is widely used in **anti-aging creams, serums,** and **sunscreens** to reduce the appearance of wrinkles, fine lines, and dark spots. Its antioxidant properties help neutralize free radicals generated by sun exposure, which can damage collagen and elastin fibers, leading to sagging skin. Green tea's anti-inflammatory properties also make it suitable for individuals with **acne-prone** or **sensitive skin,** as it helps reduce redness and irritation.

- **Vitamin E**: **Vitamin E** (Tocopherol) is one of the most powerful antioxidants used in herbal cosmetics. Found in oils like **wheat germ, almond,** and **sunflower,** vitamin E protects the skin by preventing the oxidation of lipids in the skin's outer layer, which can lead to **cell damage** and **premature aging.** Its ability to neutralize free radicals makes it an essential ingredient in **moisturizers, anti-aging creams,** and **sun protection products.** Vitamin E also helps improve **skin elasticity,** reduce the appearance of scars, and promote healing, making it a valuable addition to products targeting **stretch marks** and **wound care.**

- **Vitamin C**: **Vitamin C** (Ascorbic acid) is another potent antioxidant widely used in herbal cosmetics to **brighten the skin,** improve **collagen production,** and reduce **hyperpigmentation.** Found in plant sources like **amla** (Indian gooseberry) and **citrus fruits,** vitamin C helps protect the skin from environmental damage, particularly from UV rays and pollution. Its ability to **stimulate collagen synthesis** makes it a key ingredient in **firming creams** and **serums** designed to reduce the signs of aging. Vitamin C also helps reduce **dark spots** and **uneven skin tone** by inhibiting melanin production, resulting in a more radiant complexion.

- **Grape Seed Extract**: **Grape seed extract** is rich in **proanthocyanidins,** a group of antioxidants known for their **anti-aging** benefits. These compounds help protect the skin from oxidative damage caused by free radicals, which can lead to the breakdown of collagen and elastin. Grape seed extract is commonly used in **firming creams, eye creams**, and **anti-aging serums** to help reduce the appearance of wrinkles and improve skin texture. In addition to its antioxidant properties, grape seed extract also has **anti-inflammatory** and **antimicrobial** effects, making it beneficial for individuals with acne or sensitive skin.

Antioxidants for Hair Care

In addition to their use in skin care, antioxidants also play a critical role in **hair care** formulations. Free radicals can damage hair follicles, leading to **hair thinning**, **breakage**, and **premature graying**. Antioxidants help protect the hair from environmental stressors and promote healthy hair growth.

- **Rosemary Oil: Rosemary oil** (Rosmarinus officinalis) is a powerful antioxidant that stimulates **scalp circulation** and promotes **hair growth**. It helps protect hair follicles from oxidative damage while strengthening the hair shaft, reducing breakage, and promoting overall hair health. Rosemary oil is frequently used in **scalp treatments, shampoos**, and **conditioners** to combat hair thinning and boost hair density.
- **Argan Oil: Argan oil** (Argania spinosa), often referred to as "liquid gold," is rich in antioxidants like **vitamin E** and **polyphenols**, which protect the hair from damage caused by UV rays and pollution. Argan oil is commonly used in **hair serums, leave-in conditioners**, and **heat protection sprays** to nourish dry, brittle hair and restore its natural shine and softness. Its high content of **fatty acids** also helps repair damaged hair cuticles, making it ideal for individuals with chemically treated or heat-damaged hair.

Conclusion

The inclusion of **protective agents** and **antioxidants** in herbal cosmetics is essential for maintaining the health and vitality of the **skin** and **hair**. Ingredients like **aloe vera, shea butter, green tea**, and **vitamin C** provide a natural defense against environmental damage while delivering **nourishing** and **hydrating** benefits. By incorporating these powerful natural agents, herbal cosmetics help prevent premature aging, promote a healthy complexion, and support resilient, strong hair. These natural ingredients offer a holistic approach to beauty, ensuring that both skin and hair are protected and revitalized, without the need for synthetic chemicals.

3.2 Herbal Excipients

Herbal excipients play a crucial role in the formulation of **herbal cosmetics**, providing structural support, enhancing texture, and stabilizing active ingredients. These substances, though not active in themselves, are essential for ensuring the **efficacy**, **safety**, and **stability** of herbal formulations. In contrast to synthetic excipients, **natural excipients** derived from plant sources offer multiple benefits, including better **biocompatibility, biodegradability**, and a **reduced risk of side effects**. This section covers the significance of natural excipients and details their types, such as natural binders, diluents, and viscosity builders, which are integral to herbal cosmetic products.

3.2.1 Significance of Natural Excipients

Natural excipients, sourced from plants, are increasingly favored in **herbal cosmetics** due to the growing demand for **natural** and **organic** ingredients in beauty and personal care products. The use of these excipients aligns with consumer preferences for products free from synthetic chemicals and artificial additives, which are often linked to **skin irritation**, **allergies**, and **toxicity**. Natural excipients, including **gums**, **starches**, and **celluloses**, are biodegradable and safe for the skin, making them ideal for creating formulations that are gentle yet effective.

One of the major **advantages** of using natural excipients in cosmetics is their **biocompatibility** with the skin. Plant-derived excipients often possess additional **bioactive properties**, such as **moisturizing, soothing**, and **anti-inflammatory** effects, that contribute to the overall performance of the product. For example, gums like **guar gum** and **xanthan gum** not only act as viscosity builders but also help improve skin hydration and smoothness. Additionally, natural excipients are sustainable, as they are derived from renewable resources, further supporting the **eco-friendly** and **sustainable beauty** movement.

The **safety profile** of natural excipients also makes them suitable for use in **sensitive skin** formulations, including products for **babies** and individuals with **dermatological conditions** such as **eczema** or **psoriasis**. Unlike synthetic excipients, which can sometimes cause **dermal toxicity**, natural excipients are less likely to cause adverse reactions, as they are milder and better tolerated by the skin.

Moreover, natural excipients are highly adaptable and can be used in a variety of cosmetic formulations, including **creams, lotions, gels, masks,** and **shampoos**. Their versatility allows cosmetic formulators to develop products with different textures, viscosities, and functionalities, ensuring that the final product meets the desired **application, spreadability,** and **sensory feel**.

3.2.2 Natural Binders, Diluents, and Viscosity Builders

Natural excipients in herbal cosmetics are classified into various functional categories, including **binders, diluents,** and **viscosity builders,** each of which contributes to the structure and functionality of the product.

Natural Binders

Binders are excipients that help hold the ingredients of a cosmetic formulation together, ensuring uniformity and cohesion. They are particularly important in **solid formulations** like powders, **tablets,** and **pills**. Natural binders derived from plants help in maintaining the structural integrity of these products without compromising the natural formulation.

- **Gum Acacia**: As mentioned earlier, **gum acacia** (gum Arabic) is a widely used natural binder in herbal formulations. It is sourced from the **Acacia senegal** tree and is known for its excellent binding properties. Gum acacia forms a film around particles, improving the cohesion of powdered materials in products like **face powders, compact blushes,** and **pressed eye shadows**. Its natural adhesive qualities make it ideal for ensuring that the product remains intact, even after handling or during storage.

- **Starch: Corn starch** and **potato starch** are commonly used natural binders in cosmetics. These starches, derived from plants, not only bind the formulation but also offer a **smooth texture** and **oil-absorbing properties**, making them ideal for **face powders** and **dry shampoos**. They create a soft, matte finish on the skin and help control excess oil production, contributing to a clean and fresh appearance.

Natural Diluents

Diluents are excipients used to bulk up the product, especially in formulations where the active ingredients are present in very small quantities. Natural diluents ensure the proper consistency and facilitate the even distribution of active compounds throughout the product.

- **Microcrystalline Cellulose**: Derived from plant fibers, **microcrystalline cellulose** is one of the most widely used natural diluents in herbal cosmetics. It acts as a bulking agent in **pressed powders, tablets,** and other solid formulations. Its natural origin, coupled with its **inertness** and **biocompatibility,** makes it an ideal diluent for creating lightweight, consistent formulations without affecting the efficacy of the active ingredients.

- **Rice Powder:** **Rice powder** is another natural diluent used in cosmetic formulations. Known for its **absorbent** and **smoothening properties,** rice powder is often incorporated into **facial powders, blushes,** and **foundation powders.** It provides a silky texture to the skin while absorbing excess sebum, making it suitable for oily and combination skin types.

Natural Viscosity Builders

Viscosity builders are critical for creating the desired thickness and texture in cosmetic formulations. Natural viscosity builders help thicken products, improving their application and ensuring the uniform distribution of active ingredients. These ingredients also contribute to the **stability** of emulsions, preventing the separation of oil and water phases in formulations like **creams** and **lotions.**

- **Xanthan Gum:** **Xanthan gum** is a polysaccharide derived from the fermentation of **sugar** by the bacterium **Xanthomonas campestris.** It is commonly used as a viscosity builder in **gels, lotions,** and **serums.** Xanthan gum enhances the thickness and stability of emulsions, ensuring that the water and oil phases remain evenly mixed. It also improves the spreadability of the product on the skin, making it feel smooth and non-greasy. Additionally, xanthan gum is a **natural moisturizer,** helping to hydrate the skin while giving the formulation the desired consistency.
- **Guar Gum:** **Guar gum** is another natural thickener derived from the seeds of the **guar plant** (Cyamopsis tetragonoloba). It is used in herbal cosmetics to increase viscosity in products such as **shampoos, conditioners, creams,** and **body washes.** Guar gum not only thickens the formulation but also provides a **silky** and **glossy finish,** especially in hair care products. It helps improve the texture and feel of the product, ensuring smooth application and even distribution.
- **Agar-Agar:** **Agar-agar,** extracted from red algae, is a natural gelling agent used in **face masks, hair gels,** and **body scrubs.** It forms a gel-

like consistency when mixed with water, making it ideal for creating **hydrating gels** and **firming masks**. Agar-agar's ability to form a stable gel helps trap moisture on the skin, making it highly effective in **hydrating treatments** for dry or mature skin.

3.2.3 Use of Natural Colorants, Sweeteners, Flavors, and Perfumes

In **herbal cosmetics**, the incorporation of **natural colorants, sweeteners, flavors,** and **perfumes** is essential for creating products that not only perform well but also offer a pleasant **sensory experience**. Unlike synthetic additives, which may cause **allergic reactions** or irritations, natural alternatives provide a safer, more sustainable option for cosmetic formulations. They are derived from plants and other natural sources, ensuring that the products are **biocompatible** and **eco-friendly**. This section discusses the role of natural colorants, sweeteners, flavors, and perfumes in herbal cosmetics, highlighting their benefits and uses.

Natural Colorants

Plant-based colorants are widely used in herbal cosmetics to impart color to formulations without the need for synthetic dyes, which are often associated with skin irritation and environmental concerns. These natural pigments are extracted from fruits, vegetables, flowers, and herbs and are rich in **antioxidants** and other bioactive compounds, offering both aesthetic and therapeutic benefits.

- **Annatto:** Derived from the seeds of the **achiote tree** (Bixa orellana), **annatto** provides a vibrant **orange-red** color and is often used in **lipsticks, blushes,** and **tinted creams**. Rich in carotenoids, annatto also offers antioxidant benefits, protecting the skin from free radical damage.
- **Beetroot Powder: Beetroot** (Beta vulgaris) offers a natural **reddish-pink** hue and is commonly used in **lip stains, blushes,** and **tinted moisturizers**. It also contains antioxidants like **betalains**, which help reduce inflammation and support skin health.
- **Spirulina:** This **blue-green algae** (Arthrospira platensis) provides a natural **green** or **blue** tint, commonly used in **soaps, body scrubs,** and **eyeshadows**. Spirulina is rich in **vitamins, minerals,** and **chlorophyll**, making it not only a colorant but also a nourishing ingredient in skin care formulations.

Natural Sweeteners

Although sweeteners are more commonly associated with **oral care** or **lip products**, they can also enhance the overall user experience of certain cosmetics, especially those meant to be applied around the lips or mouth. Natural sweeteners are derived from plant sources and offer a safer, more **natural alternative** to synthetic sugars or artificial sweeteners.

- **Stevia: Stevia rebaudiana**, a plant native to South America, is known for its intensely sweet leaves, which are used to extract natural **steviol glycosides**. Stevia is often used in **lip balms** and **lip glosses** to impart a touch of sweetness without calories or synthetic chemicals.
- **Honey: Honey** is not only a natural sweetener but also a **moisturizing** and **antibacterial** agent. It is frequently included in lip products and **soothing skin treatments**, providing hydration while imparting a subtle sweetness to the formulation.

Natural Flavors

Flavors play an essential role in enhancing the sensory appeal of products like **lip balms, oral care products**, and **lip glosses**. Natural flavors are extracted from fruits, herbs, and spices and are free from the harmful chemicals commonly found in synthetic flavoring agents.

- **Peppermint: Peppermint oil** (Mentha piperita) is widely used in lip care products for its refreshing **minty** flavor. It also provides a cooling sensation that soothes the lips and adds an invigorating touch to **lip balms** and **lip glosses**.
- **Vanilla: Vanilla** extract, derived from the **Vanilla planifolia** plant, offers a sweet and comforting flavor often used in **lip products**. It provides a warm, pleasant taste and aroma, enhancing the sensory appeal of cosmetic formulations.

Natural Perfumes

Natural perfumes derived from **essential oils** and **plant extracts** offer a more holistic approach to fragrance in cosmetics. These **botanical perfumes** not only provide a pleasant scent but often have **therapeutic benefits**, such as calming or energizing effects. Commonly used natural perfumes include:

- **Rose: Rose essential oil** is known for its luxurious and soothing floral scent. It is commonly used in **face creams, body lotions**, and **perfumes**, offering a calming and uplifting fragrance while providing anti-inflammatory benefits for the skin.
- **Citrus Oils:** Oils like **lemon, orange**, and **grapefruit** impart a fresh, energizing scent that is popular in **bath products, shampoos**, and **body washes**. These oils also offer **antimicrobial** and **astringent** properties, making them suitable for oily and acne-prone skin.
- **Lavender: Lavender oil** (Lavandula angustifolia) is celebrated for its calming and relaxing fragrance. It is widely used in **night creams, sleep balms**, and **aromatherapy products** to promote relaxation and reduce stress.

3.3 Herbal Formulations

Herbal formulations are an essential aspect of herbal cosmetics, combining **active herbal ingredients** with appropriate excipients to create products that are both effective and gentle on the skin. These formulations are based on traditional knowledge combined with modern science, ensuring that each product delivers its intended benefits while maintaining the integrity of the natural ingredients used. Herbal formulations come in various forms, including **syrups, creams, lotions**, and **gels**, each tailored to meet specific needs for skin or hair care.

3.3.1 Conventional Formulations

Conventional formulations in herbal cosmetics involve the use of **traditional** preparation methods to create stable, effective products. One of the most common formulations is **herbal syrups**, which are typically used for **internal consumption** to support overall health or treat specific ailments. Herbal syrups are liquid preparations made by dissolving herbal extracts in a sugar base, often combined with honey or natural sweeteners to enhance taste and stability.

3.3.1.1 Herbal Syrups

Herbal syrups are among the most widely used conventional formulations in **herbal medicine**, providing a palatable way to deliver herbal extracts to the body. These syrups are often formulated to address specific conditions such as **coughs, sore throats, digestive issues**, and **immune support**. The basic composition of herbal syrups involves a concentrated herbal extract mixed with a sugar base, which acts as both a preservative and a sweetening agent. In some cases, **honey** or **maple syrup**

is used as the base to enhance the medicinal properties of the syrup.

- **Cough Syrup with Tulsi and Honey**: One example of an herbal syrup is a cough syrup formulated with **tulsi** (Ocimum sanctum) and honey. Tulsi, known for its **antimicrobial** and **expectorant** properties, helps soothe the respiratory system, while honey acts as a natural **demulcent** to coat the throat and reduce irritation. This combination provides relief from coughs and sore throats while boosting the immune system.
- **Amla Syrup for Immune Support**: **Amla** (Phyllanthus emblica), rich in **vitamin C** and antioxidants, is another popular ingredient in herbal syrups aimed at strengthening the immune system. Amla syrup is often consumed to enhance **immunity**, promote **digestive health**, and support **skin rejuvenation**. Its high vitamin C content makes it effective in combating oxidative stress and improving overall health.

The sugar or honey base in herbal syrups not only enhances the flavor but also helps **preserve** the herbal extracts, extending the shelf life of the product. These syrups are typically consumed in **small doses** and can be easily administered to both children and adults due to their pleasant taste.

3.3.1.2 Herbal Mixtures

Herbal mixtures are an important conventional formulation in **herbal medicine**, combining various **herbs** and **natural ingredients** to create a potent remedy that addresses multiple health concerns. These mixtures can be used in both **liquid** and **powder** forms and are designed to leverage the synergistic effects of multiple herbs, enhancing their efficacy. Herbal mixtures are commonly used for treating conditions like **digestive disorders, respiratory issues, immune deficiencies**, and **skin problems**.

A well-crafted herbal mixture takes into account the **therapeutic properties** of each herb and ensures that their combined action supports the intended health benefits. Some herbs may act as the **primary therapeutic agents**, while others may serve as **supportive agents**, enhancing absorption or reducing potential side effects. These mixtures are often formulated based on **traditional knowledge** and modern scientific research, ensuring safety and effectiveness.

- **Herbal Digestive Mixture**: A popular example of an herbal mixture is a formulation designed to support **digestive health**. This could include herbs like **ginger** (Zingiber officinale), which stimulates digestion and relieves nausea, **fennel** (Foeniculum vulgare), known for its carminative properties that help reduce bloating, and **peppermint** (Mentha piperita), which soothes the digestive tract and alleviates indigestion. The combination of these herbs creates a powerful remedy for those experiencing **gas, cramping,** or **indigestion.**

- **Herbal Respiratory Mixture:** For respiratory support, a mixture may include herbs such as **eucalyptus** (Eucalyptus globulus) for its expectorant and antimicrobial properties, **licorice root** (Glycyrrhiza glabra) for soothing irritated mucous membranes, and **thyme** (Thymus vulgaris) for its ability to ease coughs and bronchial irritation. Together, these herbs work to clear congestion, reduce coughing, and promote easier breathing.

These mixtures are typically administered as **teas, tinctures,** or **decoctions,** with the dosage carefully adjusted based on the individual's condition. Liquid mixtures are especially beneficial as they allow the **active compounds** to be quickly absorbed by the body, providing rapid relief.

3.3.1.3 Herbal Tablets

Herbal tablets represent another conventional formulation, providing a **convenient** and **precise** way to deliver **herbal remedies** in a controlled dosage. Herbal tablets are created by compressing finely ground **herbal powders** or **extracts** into solid forms, making them easy to consume and transport. This formulation is particularly popular for long-term **health maintenance** and conditions that require **daily supplementation,** such as boosting immunity, supporting joint health, or improving cognitive function.

Herbal tablets offer several advantages, including **dosage accuracy, ease of storage,** and **extended shelf life.** Since they are formulated to contain a specific amount of the active ingredient, users can be confident in the consistency and reliability of the product. Tablets are also designed to dissolve slowly, allowing the herbs to be gradually absorbed by the body for sustained therapeutic effects.

- **Ashwagandha Tablets for Stress Relief: Ashwagandha** (Withania somnifera) is a well-known adaptogenic herb used to help the body cope with **stress** and **fatigue.** Ashwagandha tablets are commonly used for reducing **anxiety,** enhancing **energy levels,** and improving **cognitive function.** The standardized extract of ashwagandha in tablet form ensures consistent potency, making it an effective and reliable choice for those looking to manage stress on a daily basis.

- **Turmeric Tablets for Inflammation: Turmeric** (Curcuma longa), rich in **curcumin**, is widely used for its **anti-inflammatory** and **antioxidant** properties. Turmeric tablets are often prescribed for individuals suffering from **joint pain, arthritis, or chronic inflammation**. These tablets typically include **black pepper extract** (piperine) to enhance the bioavailability of curcumin, ensuring better absorption and greater therapeutic efficacy.

- **Amla Tablets for Immunity: Amla** (Phyllanthus emblica), known for its high **vitamin C** content and antioxidant properties, is often formulated into tablets to support **immune function** and overall health. Amla tablets provide a concentrated source of **immune-boosting nutrients**, making them a popular choice for individuals looking to enhance their body's defenses against infections.

Herbal tablets are often combined with **natural binders** and **excipients** to maintain their shape and ensure proper release of the active ingredients. **Binders** like **acacia gum** or **cellulose** ensure that the tablet remains intact during handling, while **disintegrants** help the tablet break down efficiently in the digestive system for optimal absorption.

Conclusion

Both **herbal mixtures** and **herbal tablets** play a crucial role in delivering the therapeutic benefits of herbs in conventional formulations. Herbal mixtures leverage the **synergistic effects** of multiple herbs, offering versatile treatment options for a variety of health concerns. Herbal tablets, on the other hand, provide a **convenient** and **standardized** approach to herbal supplementation, ensuring accurate dosages and **long-term stability**. By combining the wisdom of traditional herbal remedies with modern formulation techniques, these products continue to serve as effective and reliable solutions for maintaining health and wellness.

3.3.2.1 Phytosomes (Enhanced Absorption Herbal Formulations)

Introduction to Phytosomes

Phytosomes represent a significant advancement in the field of herbal formulations, offering an innovative approach to enhance the absorption and bioavailability of herbal extracts. Unlike traditional herbal extracts, which often face challenges related to poor solubility and bioavailability, phytosomes are designed to overcome these limitations by incorporating the herbal components into a phospholipid matrix. This matrix not only facilitates better absorption but also enhances the stability and effectiveness of the active ingredients.

Composition and Structure of Phytosomes

The term "phytosome" is derived from the Greek word "phyton," meaning plant, and "some," meaning body or structure. Phytosomes are essentially **phospholipid complexes** that encapsulate herbal extracts. The key components of phytosomes include:

- **Phospholipids**: These are the primary structural elements of phytosomes. Phospholipids, such as **phosphatidylcholine**, are derived from sources like **soybean lecithin** or **egg yolk**. They play a crucial role in forming a bilayer structure that mimics cell membranes, thus enhancing the compatibility and absorption of herbal ingredients.
- **Herbal Extracts**: These are the active constituents derived from plants. In phytosomes, these extracts are typically standardized to contain specific **phytochemicals** such as **flavonoids, alkaloids,** or **saponins**. The interaction between these herbal components and phospholipids significantly improves their delivery into the bloodstream.

Mechanism of Action

The efficacy of phytosomes lies in their ability to form a complex with the herbal active ingredients. This complexation process involves the following steps:

1. **Complex Formation**: Phytosomes are created through a process called **solvent evaporation**, where the herbal extract and phospholipids are dissolved in a common solvent. Upon evaporation, the phospholipids form a bilayer structure that encapsulates the herbal components.
2. **Enhanced Membrane Permeability**: The phospholipid bilayer of phytosomes is similar in composition to the cell membrane, which facilitates easier passage of the encapsulated herbal components through the gastrointestinal tract and into systemic circulation. This increased permeability is crucial for enhancing the bioavailability of the herbal extract.
3. **Stability and Protection**: The phospholipid matrix not only protects the herbal components from degradation by environmental factors like light, heat, and oxygen but also prevents their interaction with other

substances that may lead to loss of efficacy.

Advantages of Phytosomes

Phytosomes offer several advantages over traditional herbal formulations, including:

- **Improved Bioavailability**: The phospholipid complex enhances the solubility and absorption of herbal extracts, leading to higher bioavailability. Studies have shown that phytosomal formulations can increase the bioavailability of certain herbal compounds by up to **3-5 times** compared to non-phytosomal forms.
- **Enhanced Stability**: The encapsulation within phospholipids protects the herbal components from oxidative degradation and improves their shelf life.
- **Targeted Delivery**: Phytosomes can be designed to target specific tissues or organs, improving the therapeutic efficacy of the herbal extracts. This targeted delivery can result in more effective treatment with reduced side effects.

Applications of Phytosomes

Phytosomes are used in various therapeutic areas, including:

- **Anti-inflammatory and Antioxidant Treatments**: Phytosomes containing extracts from **Curcuma longa** (turmeric) and **Ginkgo biloba** are used for their anti-inflammatory and antioxidant properties. These formulations can be beneficial in managing conditions such as arthritis and neurodegenerative diseases.
- **Cardiovascular Health**: Phytosomes made from **Grapeseed extract** and **Hawthorn** are utilized for improving cardiovascular health by enhancing endothelial function and reducing oxidative stress.
- **Skin Care**: Phytosomal formulations with **Grape Seed Extract** and **Green Tea Extract** are employed in cosmetic products for their anti-aging and skin rejuvenation benefits. The enhanced absorption properties help in delivering active compounds more effectively to the skin layers.

Formulation and Manufacturing

The preparation of phytosomes involves several critical steps to ensure their effectiveness and stability:

1. **Extraction of Herbal Ingredients**: High-quality extracts are obtained from plant materials using suitable extraction methods such as **solvent extraction** or **supercritical fluid extraction**. These extracts are standardized to ensure consistent content of active ingredients.
2. **Phospholipid Complexation**: The herbal extract is mixed with phospholipids in an appropriate solvent. This mixture undergoes processes like **sonication** or **high-pressure homogenization** to ensure uniform complexation and formation of phytosomes.
3. **Drying and Powder Formation**: The solvent is removed through evaporation, and the resulting phytosome complex is often converted into a powder form. This powder can be further processed into various dosage forms such as capsules, tablets, or liquid suspensions.

Challenges and Future Directions

While phytosomes offer significant advantages, there are also challenges associated with their use. These include:

- **Cost of Production**: The complexation and formulation processes can be expensive, which may affect the cost of phytosomal products.
- **Regulatory Issues**: The regulatory framework for phytosomal products may vary by region, and obtaining approval can be a lengthy process.

Future research and technological advancements are likely to address these challenges, potentially leading to more cost-effective and widely available phytosomal formulations. Ongoing studies are exploring the use of novel phospholipid sources and more efficient manufacturing techniques to further enhance the benefits of phytosomes.

CHAPTER IV

Evaluation of Herbal Drugs

4.1 WHO & ICH Guidelines for Herbal Drug Assessment
4.1.1 WHO Guidelines

The **World Health Organization (WHO)** provides comprehensive guidelines for the evaluation and assessment of herbal drugs to ensure their safety, efficacy, and quality. These guidelines are crucial for standardizing practices and facilitating international trade and regulatory processes. The WHO guidelines are designed to address various aspects of herbal drugs, including their development, testing, and quality control.

Quality Control and Standardization

The WHO emphasizes the importance of **quality control** and **standardization** in herbal drug evaluation. The guidelines recommend the following practices:

1. **Authenticity and Purity**: Herbal drugs must be accurately identified and authenticated. This involves the use of botanical identification, **microscopic examination**, and **phytochemical analysis** to ensure the correct plant species and purity.
2. **Consistency and Potency**: The consistency of herbal drugs should be assessed to ensure that the active constituents are present in the required amounts. **Pharmacopoeial standards** and **analytical methods** like **high-performance liquid chromatography (HPLC)** are used to determine the potency of the herbal drugs.
3. **Safety Evaluation**: Safety is a critical aspect of herbal drug assessment. The WHO guidelines recommend conducting **toxicological studies**, including acute, sub-acute, and chronic toxicity tests, to identify any potential adverse effects.
4. **Stability Testing**: Herbal drugs must undergo stability testing to determine their shelf-life and ensure that they retain their quality over time. This involves evaluating the effects of various factors such as temperature, humidity, and light on the drug's stability.

Efficacy Assessment

To establish the **efficacy** of herbal drugs, the WHO guidelines suggest:

1. **Clinical Trials**: Conducting well-designed **clinical trials** is essential to demonstrate the therapeutic benefits of herbal drugs. These trials should follow rigorous protocols and include **randomized controlled trials (RCTs)** to provide reliable evidence of efficacy.
2. **Preclinical Studies: Preclinical studies**, including **in vitro** and **in vivo** experiments, are recommended to evaluate the pharmacological activities of herbal drugs and support their therapeutic claims.
3. **Traditional Use Evidence**: The WHO also acknowledges the value of traditional use evidence. Documentation of historical use and **ethnobotanical data** can provide supportive evidence for the therapeutic benefits of herbal drugs.

Regulatory and Ethical Considerations

The WHO guidelines address **regulatory** and **ethical** considerations in herbal drug assessment:

1. **Regulatory Framework**: Herbal drugs should be evaluated within a well-defined regulatory framework. This includes adherence to national and international regulations and standards to ensure uniformity and compliance.
2. **Ethical Practices**: Ethical considerations, including informed consent and the protection of human subjects in clinical trials, are paramount. The WHO guidelines stress the importance of maintaining high ethical standards throughout the evaluation process.

Documentation and Reporting

Accurate and thorough **documentation** is essential for the assessment of herbal drugs. The WHO guidelines recommend:

1. **Detailed Reports**: Comprehensive reports detailing the methods, results, and interpretations of studies should be prepared and reviewed. This ensures transparency and reproducibility of the findings.
2. **Quality Assurance**: Implementing robust quality assurance measures is necessary to maintain the integrity and reliability of the evaluation process.

4.1.2 ICH Guidelines

The **International Council for Harmonisation of Technical Requirements for Pharmaceuticals for Human Use (ICH)** provides guidelines that are critical for the development and evaluation of pharmaceutical drugs, including herbal medicines. The ICH guidelines aim to harmonize and streamline regulatory requirements across different regions, ensuring that herbal drugs meet consistent standards of quality, safety, and efficacy. Here's an overview of the ICH guidelines pertinent to herbal drug assessment:

Quality (Q) Guidelines

The ICH guidelines under the **Quality (Q) category** focus on ensuring that herbal drugs meet high standards of quality. Key aspects include:

1. **Good Manufacturing Practices (GMP)**: Herbal drugs must be manufactured according to GMP standards, which include stringent controls over production processes, equipment, and personnel to prevent contamination and ensure product consistency. Compliance with **ICH Q7** (Good Manufacturing Practice for Active Pharmaceutical Ingredients) is essential.

2. **Quality Control**: Herbal drugs must undergo rigorous quality control testing to confirm their identity, potency, purity, and quality. Techniques such as **HPLC**, **mass spectrometry (MS)**, and **thin-layer chromatography (TLC)** are used to analyze herbal constituents and ensure that they meet specified standards. **ICH Q2** (Validation of Analytical Procedures) provides guidelines for validating these analytical methods.

3. **Stability Studies**: ICH Q1 (Stability Testing) provides guidelines for stability studies, which are crucial for determining the shelf-life of herbal drugs. Stability studies assess how the quality of the herbal drug varies with environmental factors like temperature, humidity, and light over time.

Safety (S) Guidelines

Under the **Safety (S) category**, the ICH guidelines emphasize the need for thorough safety evaluation of herbal drugs:

1. **Toxicity Testing**: ICH S1 (Carcinogenicity Studies) and ICH S2 (Genotoxicity Studies) outline the requirements for conducting toxicity tests to assess potential adverse effects of herbal drugs. These include

acute, sub-chronic, and chronic toxicity studies to evaluate the safety profile of the drug.

2. **Pharmacovigilance**: ICH E2E (Pharmacovigilance) provides guidelines for monitoring and reporting adverse effects associated with herbal drugs. Effective pharmacovigilance systems are necessary for detecting, assessing, and minimizing risks related to herbal drug use.

Efficacy (E) Guidelines

The **Efficacy (E) guidelines** focus on demonstrating the therapeutic benefits of herbal drugs:

1. **Clinical Trials**: ICH E6 (Good Clinical Practice) outlines the requirements for conducting clinical trials to ensure that the studies are ethically conducted and scientifically valid. This includes obtaining informed consent from participants, maintaining trial integrity, and ensuring the accuracy of trial data.

2. **Clinical Study Reports**: ICH E3 (Structure and Content of Clinical Study Reports) provides guidelines for preparing detailed reports of clinical studies. These reports should include comprehensive data on the efficacy and safety of herbal drugs, ensuring transparency and reliability in the evidence presented.

Additional Considerations

1. **Phytopharmaceuticals**: The ICH guidelines also recognize the need for specific considerations for **phytopharmaceuticals**, which are drugs derived from plant sources but subject to pharmaceutical standards. These include adherence to both ICH guidelines and local regulatory requirements.

2. **Documentation and Record Keeping**: Proper documentation and record-keeping practices are essential to ensure compliance with ICH guidelines. This includes maintaining accurate records of manufacturing processes, quality control tests, and clinical trial results.

4.1.3 Criteria for Quality Assessment

Quality assessment of herbal drugs is essential to ensure that they are safe, effective, and meet the required standards. The criteria for quality assessment involve several critical factors, including authenticity, purity, consistency, and overall quality of the herbal products. Here are the main criteria used for quality assessment:

1. Authenticity and Identification

- **Botanical Identification**: Accurate botanical identification is crucial for verifying the authenticity of herbal drugs. This involves morphological, anatomical, and microscopic examination to confirm that the plant material used matches the specified species. Techniques such as **macroscopic examination, microscopy**, and **DNA barcoding** are commonly employed.
- **Standardization of Herbal Extracts**: The process of standardization ensures that herbal extracts contain consistent levels of active ingredients. This involves establishing **phytochemical profiles** and using analytical methods like **HPLC** to verify that the extract meets predefined standards for active compounds.

2. Purity and Contaminant Analysis

- **Microbial Contamination**: Herbal drugs must be tested for microbial contaminants to ensure they are free from harmful microorganisms. Methods such as **plate counting** and **PCR-based assays** are used to detect and quantify microbial presence.
- **Heavy Metal Testing**: Contamination with heavy metals like **lead, arsenic, cadmium**, and **mercury** can pose significant health risks. Testing methods such as **atomic absorption spectroscopy (AAS)** or **inductively coupled plasma mass spectrometry (ICP-MS)** are employed to measure heavy metal levels and ensure they are within safe limits.
- **Pesticide Residues**: Herbal drugs should be tested for pesticide residues to ensure they are within acceptable limits. Techniques such as **gas chromatography (GC)** and **liquid chromatography-mass spectrometry (LC-MS)** are used to detect and quantify pesticide residues.

3. Consistency and Potency

- **Content Uniformity**: The consistency of the herbal drug is assessed by measuring the content of active ingredients in different batches. This ensures that each batch of the product contains the same amount of active components, which is critical for maintaining efficacy. **Uniformity of Content Tests** and **HPLC** are typically used.

- **Potency**: Potency refers to the strength and effectiveness of the herbal drug, measured by its content of active ingredients. Standardization of potency is achieved through **pharmacopoeial standards** and **analytical assays** to confirm that the drug meets the required specifications.

4. Stability and Shelf-life

- **Stability Testing**: Stability testing is conducted to evaluate how the quality of the herbal drug changes over time under various storage conditions. This includes testing for changes in physical, chemical, and microbial properties. Factors such as **temperature**, **humidity**, and **light exposure** are considered during these tests.
- **Shelf-life Determination**: Based on stability testing data, the shelf-life of the herbal drug is determined, indicating the period during which the drug remains effective and safe to use. This involves analyzing data from accelerated stability studies and real-time stability studies.

5. Labeling and Documentation

- **Accurate Labeling**: Herbal drugs must be labeled accurately to provide information about the product, including its name, ingredients, dosage, usage instructions, and any precautions or warnings. Labeling should comply with regulatory standards and provide clear information to users.
- **Documentation and Record Keeping**: Proper documentation of all quality control tests, including raw material specifications, batch records, and test results, is essential for ensuring transparency and traceability. This documentation helps in regulatory compliance and quality assurance.

4.2 Stability Testing of Herbal Drugs

4.2.1 Importance of Stability Testing

Stability testing is a fundamental component in the evaluation of herbal drugs, ensuring that these products maintain their quality, safety, and efficacy throughout their shelf life. The importance of stability testing can be outlined as follows:

1. Ensuring Efficacy and Safety

- **Maintaining Potency**: Over time, herbal drugs can undergo chemical changes that may reduce their potency. Stability testing helps to confirm that the active ingredients remain effective throughout the product's shelf life. This is essential for ensuring that the herbal drug continues to provide the therapeutic benefits claimed by the manufacturer.
- **Preventing Degradation**: Herbal drugs may degrade due to factors such as exposure to light, heat, or moisture. Stability testing identifies the conditions under which degradation occurs and helps in formulating the product to minimize these effects. This is crucial for preventing the formation of potentially harmful degradation products.

2. Ensuring Quality

- **Consistency of Quality**: Stability testing assesses whether the herbal drug remains consistent in quality during its shelf life. This includes evaluating attributes such as appearance, taste, odor, and physical properties. Consistency in these attributes ensures that the product remains acceptable to consumers.
- **Compliance with Regulatory Standards**: Regulatory authorities require stability data to ensure that herbal drugs meet specific quality standards. Stability testing provides the necessary data to demonstrate compliance with these regulatory requirements, facilitating the approval and market access of herbal products.

3. Optimizing Storage and Packaging

- **Determining Storage Conditions**: Stability testing helps determine the optimal storage conditions for herbal drugs, including temperature, humidity, and light exposure. This information is critical for developing appropriate storage instructions and ensuring that the product remains stable under recommended conditions.
- **Improving Packaging**: The results from stability testing can guide the selection of packaging materials that protect the herbal drug from environmental factors that could affect its stability. Effective packaging helps in extending the product's shelf life and maintaining its quality.

4. Reducing Risk of Adverse Effects

- **Identifying Potential Issues**: Stability testing can reveal potential issues related to the stability of herbal drugs, such as the formation of toxic compounds or changes in chemical properties. Identifying these issues early helps in mitigating risks and ensuring the safety of the product.
- **Supporting Product Development**: During the development phase, stability testing provides valuable information that can influence formulation changes and improvements. This helps in designing a final product that is both effective and safe for consumer use.

4.2.2 Methods of Testing Stability in Herbal Drugs

Stability testing of herbal drugs involves various methods to assess how the product maintains its quality, efficacy, and safety over time under different conditions. These methods help in understanding the product's behavior in response to environmental factors and ensure that it meets quality standards throughout its shelf life. The main methods of testing stability in herbal drugs are:

1. Accelerated Stability Testing

- **Purpose**: Accelerated stability testing is designed to simulate long-term storage conditions in a shorter time frame. It helps in predicting the shelf life of herbal drugs by subjecting them to elevated temperatures and humidity levels.
- **Procedure**: Herbal drug samples are exposed to stress conditions such as high temperatures (e.g., $40°C \pm 2°C$) and high humidity (e.g., $75\% \pm 5\%$ RH) for specified periods (e.g., 3, 6, and 12 months). The samples are then analyzed for changes in their quality attributes, such as potency, appearance, and physical properties.
- **Benefits**: This method provides a preliminary estimate of the product's shelf life and helps in identifying potential stability issues early in the development process.

2. Long-Term Stability Testing

- **Purpose**: Long-term stability testing assesses the herbal drug's stability under typical storage conditions over its intended shelf life. It provides data on how the product performs under normal conditions.

- **Procedure**: Samples are stored at recommended storage conditions, which usually involve ambient temperatures (e.g., 25°C ± 2°C) and relative humidity (e.g., 60% ± 5% RH). The samples are tested periodically (e.g., every 3 months) for physical and chemical stability, including potency, purity, and any potential degradation products.
- **Benefits**: This method provides a comprehensive assessment of the product's stability under real-world conditions and helps in confirming the shelf life proposed for the product.

3. Stress Testing

- **Purpose**: Stress testing evaluates the herbal drug's stability under extreme conditions to understand its behavior when exposed to factors beyond normal storage conditions. This helps in identifying potential degradation pathways.
- **Procedure**: The samples are exposed to conditions such as extreme temperatures (e.g., 50°C or 60°C), high humidity (e.g., 90% RH), and light exposure (e.g., UV light) for specified durations. The samples are then analyzed for changes in active ingredients, degradation products, and overall quality.
- **Benefits**: Stress testing helps in understanding the drug's stability limits and provides insights into how it might behave under adverse conditions, aiding in the development of more robust formulations and packaging.

4. Real-Time Stability Testing

- **Purpose**: Real-time stability testing involves monitoring the herbal drug's stability over its actual shelf life under intended storage conditions. This method provides real-world data on the product's performance over time.
- **Procedure**: Samples are stored under normal conditions for the entire shelf life period as indicated on the product's packaging. Regular testing is performed to assess changes in potency, purity, and other quality attributes at specified intervals (e.g., every 6 or 12 months).
- **Benefits**: This method provides the most accurate data on the product's stability and is crucial for verifying the product's shelf life and ensuring that it remains within quality specifications throughout its intended use.

5. Microbial Testing

- **Purpose**: Microbial testing assesses the potential for microbial contamination and evaluates the efficacy of preservative systems in herbal drugs.
- **Procedure**: The herbal drug samples are tested for microbial contamination using methods such as **plate counting** and **membrane filtration**. The efficacy of preservatives is also evaluated by monitoring the growth of microorganisms over time.
- **Benefits**: Ensures that the herbal drug remains free from harmful microbial contaminants and that preservatives effectively inhibit microbial growth, thus maintaining the product's safety and quality.

6. Physical and Chemical Testing

- **Purpose**: Physical and chemical testing involves assessing changes in the physical characteristics (e.g., color, odor, texture) and chemical properties (e.g., active ingredient content, pH) of herbal drugs.
- **Procedure**: Various analytical techniques such as **HPLC, UV spectrophotometry**, and **gas chromatography (GC)** are used to monitor changes in the chemical composition and potency of the herbal drug. Physical tests include assessments of appearance, solubility, and consistency.
- **Benefits**: Provides detailed information on the drug's stability concerning its chemical and physical attributes, helping to ensure that it maintains its intended quality and efficacy over time.

4.3 Patenting and Regulatory Aspects of Natural Products
4.3.1 Definition of Key Terms
Patent

A **patent** is a legal right granted to an inventor or assignee by a government authority that provides exclusive rights to make, use, sell, and distribute an invention for a specific period, typically 20 years from the filing date. The invention must be novel, non-obvious, and useful. In the context of natural products, patents can be granted for new and innovative methods of extracting, processing, or formulating herbal substances, as well as for novel uses of natural compounds. Patents protect the inventor's innovation from unauthorized use and provide a competitive advantage in the market.

Intellectual Property Rights (IPR)

Intellectual Property Rights (IPR) refer to the legal rights granted to individuals or organizations for their creations of the mind. These rights are intended to protect and promote innovation and creativity by granting exclusive control over the use of their intellectual creations. IPR encompasses various forms of protection, including:

- **Patents**: Protect inventions and technological advancements.
- **Trademarks**: Protect distinctive signs, symbols, or logos that identify goods or services.
- **Copyright**: Protects original literary, artistic, and musical works.
- **Trade Secrets**: Protects confidential business information that provides a competitive edge.

For natural products, IPR can include patents for novel methods of processing or deriving compounds, trademarks for brand names or logos associated with herbal products, and copyrights for documentation or research publications.

Farmer's Right

Farmer's Right is a concept recognized in several international frameworks and national laws that acknowledges and protects the contributions of farmers in the conservation and development of plant genetic resources. These rights include:

- **Recognition of Contributions**: Farmers' traditional knowledge and practices related to plant breeding and seed selection are recognized and valued.
- **Benefit Sharing**: Farmers are entitled to fair and equitable sharing of benefits arising from the use of plant genetic resources that they have developed or preserved.
- **Access to Seeds**: Farmers have the right to access and use seeds of plant varieties developed through traditional methods.

Farmer's Rights aim to ensure that the contributions of local and indigenous farming communities are acknowledged and rewarded, promoting sustainable agricultural practices and conservation of genetic diversity.

Breeder's Right

Breeder's Right refers to the legal rights granted to plant breeders or developers of new plant varieties. These rights are typically established through Plant Breeder's Rights (PBR) or Plant Variety Protection (PVP) systems. Key aspects include:

- **Exclusive Rights**: Breeders have exclusive rights to propagate, sell, and distribute new plant varieties that they have developed. This includes the right to license or sell the variety to others.
- **Duration**: Breeder's rights are usually granted for a specific period, often 20-25 years, during which the breeder has exclusive control over the variety.
- **Novelty and Distinctiveness**: To qualify for breeder's rights, the plant variety must be new, distinct, uniform, and stable. This means it should differ significantly from existing varieties and consistently reproduce its characteristics.

Breeder's Rights incentivize innovation in plant breeding by providing legal protection for new and improved plant varieties, promoting agricultural research and development.

These key terms form the foundation of the regulatory and legal framework surrounding natural products, influencing how innovations in the field of herbal drugs and plant-based medicines are protected and managed.

4.3.2 Bioprospecting and Biopiracy

Bioprospecting

Bioprospecting refers to the exploration and investigation of biological resources, particularly from natural environments, to discover new compounds, genes, or materials that have potential commercial value. This process involves the collection and analysis of biological samples, such as plants, animals, and microorganisms, to identify useful substances that can be developed into products like pharmaceuticals, agricultural inputs, or industrial enzymes.

Key aspects of bioprospecting include:

- **Source Identification**: Researchers locate and identify sources of biological materials that might contain valuable compounds. This often involves exploring diverse and often under-studied ecosystems, such as tropical rainforests or marine environments.

- **Sample Collection**: Biological samples are collected with proper documentation and consent, often involving collaborations with local communities or stakeholders who have traditional knowledge about the resources.
- **Research and Development**: Collected samples are analyzed for bioactive compounds, genetic material, or other valuable substances. The findings are then used to develop new products or technologies.
- **Ethical Considerations**: Ethical bioprospecting ensures that the process is conducted responsibly, with respect for local communities, ecosystems, and indigenous knowledge. This includes obtaining informed consent and establishing fair agreements for benefit sharing.

Biopiracy

Biopiracy is the term used to describe the unauthorized or unfair exploitation of biological resources and traditional knowledge, often without proper consent or compensation to the originating communities. Biopiracy involves the following issues:

- **Unlawful Exploitation**: This occurs when companies or researchers collect biological materials or traditional knowledge without proper authorization or agreements, often violating the rights of indigenous or local communities.
- **Patent Misuse**: Biopiracy can involve the patenting of biological resources or traditional knowledge without acknowledging or compensating the original source. This includes patenting a plant compound or traditional medicine without recognizing or rewarding the contributions of local communities who have historically used or developed the resource.
- **Ethical and Legal Concerns**: Biopiracy raises significant ethical and legal issues, as it undermines the rights of indigenous peoples and local communities, often leading to disputes and conflicts. Efforts to combat biopiracy include strengthening regulations, promoting equitable benefit-sharing agreements, and ensuring respect for traditional knowledge and practices.

4.3.3 Patenting Traditional Knowledge and Natural Products
Case Study: Curcuma longa

Introduction

Curcuma longa, commonly known as **turmeric**, is a well-known herbal plant used extensively in traditional medicine, especially in Indian and Southeast Asian cultures. The rhizomes of Curcuma longa contain **curcumin**, a compound with well-documented antioxidant, anti-inflammatory, and therapeutic properties. The case of Curcuma longa provides an insightful example of the complex issues surrounding the patenting of traditional knowledge and natural products.

Traditional Use and Knowledge

Turmeric has been used for thousands of years in traditional medicine systems such as **Ayurveda** and **Traditional Chinese Medicine (TCM)**. It is utilized for its healing properties in treating various conditions, including digestive disorders, skin conditions, and joint inflammation. Traditional knowledge about the medicinal uses of turmeric is deeply rooted in indigenous practices and cultural heritage.

Patenting Issues

1. Patenting of Curcumin

- **Patents Granted**: Various patents have been granted for different formulations and uses of curcumin extracted from Curcuma longa. These patents often cover specific methods of extracting, purifying, or formulating curcumin for therapeutic applications, such as its use as an anti-inflammatory or antioxidant.
- **Challenges**: The challenge with patenting curcumin lies in balancing the protection of innovation with the recognition of traditional knowledge. Patents on curcumin or turmeric-derived products often focus on novel applications or formulations rather than the compound itself. However, issues arise when traditional uses are incorporated into patents without proper acknowledgment of their origins.

2. Biopiracy Concerns

- **Unacknowledged Knowledge**: There have been cases where patent applications for turmeric-based products did not acknowledge or compensate the traditional knowledge holders. For instance, patents were granted for turmeric's use in wound healing or cosmetic applications without giving credit to the traditional Indian medicinal practices that had long used turmeric for these purposes.

- **Legal and Ethical Disputes**: Such cases of biopiracy have led to legal and ethical disputes, as traditional knowledge holders and indigenous communities argue for recognition and fair compensation. This has prompted calls for stronger regulations and mechanisms to ensure that traditional knowledge is respected and that benefit-sharing agreements are in place.

3. Efforts to Address Issues

- **Recognition of Traditional Knowledge**: Some jurisdictions have introduced legal frameworks to protect traditional knowledge and prevent its misuse. For example, the **Convention on Biological Diversity (CBD)** and the **Nagoya Protocol** provide guidelines for the fair and equitable sharing of benefits arising from the use of biological resources and traditional knowledge.
- **Patent Regulations**: Patent offices in various countries have implemented measures to address the issues of traditional knowledge and biopiracy. This includes requiring patent applicants to disclose the source of biological material and traditional knowledge and to demonstrate that they have obtained prior informed consent from the communities involved.

Case Study: Neem (Azadirachta indica)
Introduction
Neem (Azadirachta indica), often referred to as the "village pharmacy," is a versatile plant native to the Indian subcontinent. It has been used in traditional medicine for thousands of years to treat a range of ailments due to its antimicrobial, anti-inflammatory, and antipyretic properties. The case of Neem illustrates significant issues related to the patenting of traditional knowledge and natural products, particularly in the context of biopiracy and intellectual property rights.
Traditional Use and Knowledge
Neem has been extensively used in traditional Ayurvedic medicine. Its leaves, bark, seeds, and oil have been utilized to treat conditions such as skin infections, fevers, and digestive disorders. The plant is also used in agriculture as a natural pesticide. Indigenous knowledge about Neem's uses has been passed down through generations, deeply rooted in local cultural practices.

Patenting Issues
1. Patenting of Neem Products

- **Patents Granted**: Various patents have been filed and granted for Neem-based products, including neem oil, extracts, and formulations used in agriculture and medicine. These patents often cover specific applications, such as neem oil as a natural pesticide or neem extracts in pharmaceutical formulations.
- **Challenges**: The major challenge arises when these patents cover applications or formulations of Neem that have long been known in traditional medicine. For example, in the 1990s, several patents were granted by the United States Patent and Trademark Office (USPTO) for neem-based formulations, including those used for agricultural pest control and personal care products.

2. Biopiracy Concerns

- **Unacknowledged Traditional Knowledge**: In the case of Neem, the patents granted for various uses of Neem were criticized for not recognizing or compensating the traditional knowledge holders. The knowledge of Neem's medicinal and agricultural uses had been documented in Ayurvedic texts and local practices long before these patents were filed. The lack of acknowledgment of this traditional knowledge raised concerns about biopiracy.
- **Legal and Ethical Disputes**: The controversy surrounding Neem patents led to significant legal and ethical disputes. Notably, in 1995, the Indian government challenged the USPTO's patents on Neem, arguing that the patents violated the principles of **prior art** and **traditional knowledge**. The Indian government, supported by various non-governmental organizations and advocacy groups, claimed that the patents were based on knowledge that had been freely available and widely used in India for centuries.

Resolution and Impact

- **Patent Revocation**: Following international pressure and legal challenges, some of the patents granted on Neem were eventually revoked. The case highlighted the need for integrating traditional knowledge into the patenting process and ensuring fair benefit-sharing arrangements.

- **Policy Changes**: The Neem case influenced the development of international agreements and national policies aimed at protecting traditional knowledge and ensuring that biopiracy does not occur. This includes the **Convention on Biological Diversity (CBD)** and the **Nagoya Protocol**, which emphasize the importance of obtaining informed consent and sharing benefits arising from the use of genetic resources.

4.4 Regulatory Issues in India

4.4.1 ASU DTAB and ASU DCC (Ayurveda, Siddha, and Unani Drug Technical Advisory and Consultative Committees)

In India, the regulation of herbal drugs and traditional medicines falls under the purview of various committees that oversee the quality, safety, and efficacy of these products. Two key committees involved in this regulatory framework are the **Ayurveda, Siddha, and Unani Drug Technical Advisory Board (ASU DTAB)** and the **Ayurveda, Siddha, and Unani Drug Consultative Committee (ASU DCC)**.

Ayurveda, Siddha, and Unani Drug Technical Advisory Board (ASU DTAB)

- **Role and Responsibilities**: The ASU DTAB is a regulatory body established under the Drugs and Cosmetics Act, 1940. Its primary role is to provide technical advice on matters related to the regulation and standardization of **Ayurvedic, Siddha**, and **Unani** drugs. The board is tasked with ensuring that these traditional medicines meet the required standards of quality, safety, and efficacy.
- **Functions**: The ASU DTAB performs several key functions, including:

  - **Formulating Guidelines**: Developing guidelines for the preparation, testing, and standardization of ASU drugs.
  - **Reviewing Standards**: Evaluating and updating the standards for various Ayurvedic, Siddha, and Unani medicines to keep pace with scientific advancements.
  - **Advising on Legislation**: Providing recommendations for amendments to existing laws and regulations related to ASU drugs.
  - **Examining Reports**: Reviewing reports on adverse drug reactions and other safety concerns related to traditional medicines.

- **Composition**: The board typically consists of experts in traditional medicine, pharmacology, and related fields, including representatives from various government departments and research institutions.

Ayurveda, Siddha, and Unani Drug Consultative Committee (ASU DCC)

- **Role and Responsibilities**: The ASU DCC, also established under the Drugs and Cosmetics Act, acts as a consultative body that assists in the implementation of policies and regulations concerning Ayurvedic, Siddha, and Unani drugs. It works closely with the ASU DTAB to ensure effective regulation and standardization of these medicines.
- **Functions**: The ASU DCC is responsible for:

  - **Consulting on Standards**: Providing consultation on the development and implementation of quality standards for ASU drugs.
  - **Reviewing Regulations**: Assisting in the review and modification of regulations and guidelines related to traditional medicines.
  - **Addressing Issues**: Addressing issues related to the manufacture, import, and sale of ASU drugs, including compliance with regulatory standards.
  - **Promoting Research**: Encouraging and facilitating research and development in the field of Ayurveda, Siddha, and Unani medicine to enhance the efficacy and safety of these drugs.

- **Composition**: The ASU DCC includes experts from various fields, including traditional medicine practitioners, pharmacologists, and regulatory officials. The committee often comprises representatives from the Ministry of AYUSH, which oversees the development and regulation of traditional medicine systems in India.

Regulatory Framework

The regulatory framework for Ayurveda, Siddha, and Unani drugs in India is governed by the **Drugs and Cosmetics Act, 1940**, and its associated rules. This framework ensures that traditional medicines are produced, tested, and marketed in accordance with established standards. The ASU DTAB and ASU DCC play crucial roles in implementing these regulations, ensuring that herbal and traditional medicines are safe, effective, and of high quality.

4.4.2 Schedule Z of the Drugs & Cosmetics Act for ASU Drugs

Introduction

Schedule Z of the **Drugs and Cosmetics Act, 1940** is a crucial regulatory framework governing the standards, safety, and efficacy of **Ayurvedic, Siddha,** and **Unani** (ASU) drugs in India. This schedule provides detailed guidelines for the formulation, manufacturing, testing, and marketing of ASU drugs, ensuring that these traditional medicines meet specific regulatory standards.

Key Provisions of Schedule Z

1. General Requirements

- **Standards of Quality**: Schedule Z outlines the minimum quality standards that ASU drugs must meet. It includes provisions for ensuring that herbal medicines are manufactured using standardized processes and that they contain the required levels of active ingredients.
- **Good Manufacturing Practices (GMP)**: The schedule mandates adherence to Good Manufacturing Practices for the production of ASU drugs. This includes guidelines for maintaining cleanliness, proper documentation, and quality control during manufacturing.

2. Licensing and Registration

- **Manufacturing License**: To manufacture ASU drugs, firms must obtain a license from the **Central Drugs Standard Control Organization (CDSCO)**. Schedule Z specifies the requirements for obtaining and maintaining this license, including documentation, facilities, and personnel.
- **Product Registration**: ASU drugs must be registered with the CDSCO before being marketed. The registration process requires submission of detailed information about the drug's formulation, manufacturing process, and safety data.

3. Labeling and Packaging

- **Labeling Requirements**: Schedule Z mandates specific labeling requirements for ASU drugs to ensure that consumers receive accurate information about the product. Labels must include details such as the product name, active ingredients, dosage instructions, and any potential side effects.

- **Packaging Standards**: The schedule also provides guidelines for packaging ASU drugs to protect them from contamination and degradation. Packaging materials must be suitable for preserving the integrity and efficacy of the herbal products.

4. Clinical Trials and Efficacy

- **Clinical Trials**: Schedule Z requires that clinical trials be conducted to demonstrate the safety and efficacy of ASU drugs. The trials must follow ethical guidelines and be conducted in accordance with the standards set by the ASU DTAB and ASU DCC.
- **Efficacy Data**: Manufacturers must provide evidence of the efficacy of their products based on clinical trials and traditional use. This data is essential for gaining regulatory approval and ensuring that the drugs provide the claimed therapeutic benefits.

5. Adverse Drug Reactions

- **Monitoring and Reporting**: Schedule Z mandates the monitoring and reporting of adverse drug reactions associated with ASU drugs. Manufacturers are required to establish systems for tracking adverse effects and reporting them to regulatory authorities.
- **Safety Measures**: The schedule outlines safety measures and corrective actions that must be taken if adverse effects are identified. This helps in ensuring the continued safety of the products once they are in the market.

6. Import and Export Regulations

- **Import Procedures**: Schedule Z includes regulations for the import of ASU drugs, ensuring that imported products meet the same standards as domestically produced drugs. Importers must comply with specific requirements and obtain necessary approvals from regulatory authorities.
- **Export Regulations**: The schedule also governs the export of ASU drugs, requiring that exported products adhere to international standards and

comply with the regulations of the importing country.

CHAPTER V

Introduction to the Herbal Industry

5.1 Present Scope and Future Prospects of the Herbal Drug Industry

5.1.1 Growth Drivers and Trends

The herbal drug industry has experienced significant growth over the past few decades, driven by various factors that contribute to its expanding scope and future potential. Understanding these growth drivers and trends is crucial for comprehending the current landscape and predicting future developments in the industry.

1. Increasing Consumer Awareness and Preference

- **Rising Health Consciousness**: There is a growing awareness among consumers about the benefits of natural and organic products. This shift towards health-conscious living has led to increased demand for herbal remedies as they are perceived as safer and more natural alternatives to synthetic pharmaceuticals.
- **Preference for Preventive Healthcare**: Consumers are increasingly seeking preventive healthcare solutions rather than relying solely on conventional medicine for treating illnesses. Herbal drugs, with their preventive and therapeutic benefits, align with this trend and are gaining popularity.

2. Expanding Market Opportunities

- **Global Market Expansion**: The global herbal drug market is expanding as herbal remedies gain acceptance in various countries, including those with traditionally strong pharmaceutical sectors. Markets in Asia, Europe, and North America are experiencing significant growth, driven by both increasing consumer demand and greater availability of herbal products.
- **Product Diversification**: The herbal industry is diversifying its product offerings beyond traditional forms like tablets and capsules to include functional foods, beverages, and skincare products. This diversification caters to a broader range of consumer preferences and applications.

3. Advancements in Research and Development

- **Scientific Validation**: Advances in scientific research are helping validate the efficacy and safety of herbal drugs. Clinical trials and modern analytical techniques are providing evidence-based support for traditional herbal remedies, enhancing their credibility and acceptance in mainstream medicine.
- **Innovation in Formulations**: The industry is seeing innovation in herbal formulations, including the development of standardized extracts, novel delivery systems, and combination therapies. These innovations improve the effectiveness and consumer appeal of herbal products.

4. Supportive Regulatory Framework

- **Regulatory Reforms**: Many countries are updating their regulatory frameworks to better accommodate and support the herbal drug industry. Regulations that provide clear guidelines for the quality, safety, and efficacy of herbal products contribute to industry growth by fostering consumer confidence and facilitating market access.
- **Incentives and Support**: Governments and international organizations are offering incentives and support for research, development, and commercialization of herbal products. These initiatives include grants, subsidies, and partnerships aimed at advancing the herbal industry.

5. Growing Interest in Traditional and Indigenous Knowledge

- **Cultural Revival**: There is a renewed interest in traditional and indigenous knowledge about herbal medicine. This cultural revival is not only preserving ancient practices but also integrating them into modern healthcare systems, contributing to the growth of the herbal drug industry.
- **Collaboration with Indigenous Communities**: Collaborations between herbal companies and indigenous communities are fostering the sustainable use of traditional knowledge and resources. These partnerships help in the development of new products and ensure fair benefit-sharing practices.

6. Economic and Environmental Factors

- **Cost-Effectiveness**: Herbal drugs often present a cost-effective alternative to conventional medicines, which can be expensive. This cost-effectiveness is attractive to consumers and healthcare systems, driving demand for herbal products.
- **Sustainability and Environmental Concerns**: The growing emphasis on sustainability and environmental conservation is influencing the herbal industry. Companies are adopting sustainable practices in sourcing, production, and packaging to minimize environmental impact and appeal to eco-conscious consumers.

5.1.2 Challenges in the Herbal Drug Industry

The herbal drug industry, despite its growth and potential, faces several challenges that impact its development and sustainability. Addressing these challenges is crucial for ensuring the continued success and expansion of the industry. The main challenges include:

1. Quality Control and Standardization

- **Variability in Raw Materials**: One of the primary challenges is the variability in the quality and composition of herbal raw materials. Factors such as soil conditions, climate, and cultivation practices can affect the potency and consistency of herbal ingredients. Ensuring uniform quality across batches is crucial for maintaining efficacy and consumer trust.
- **Lack of Standardization**: There is a need for standardized methods of preparation and testing to ensure that herbal products meet consistent quality and safety standards. The absence of uniform standards can lead to discrepancies in product quality and efficacy.

2. Regulatory and Compliance Issues

- **Diverse Regulatory Requirements**: The herbal drug industry faces a complex regulatory environment with varying requirements across different countries. Navigating these regulations can be challenging for companies, particularly when trying to enter international markets.
- **Lack of Harmonized Standards**: In many regions, regulations for herbal drugs are not as well-defined as those for conventional pharmaceuticals. This lack of harmonization can lead to regulatory hurdles and uncertainties in product approval and marketing.

3. Scientific Validation and Research

- **Limited Research Data**: Despite the growing body of research, there is still a limited amount of high-quality clinical data supporting the efficacy and safety of many herbal products. The need for more rigorous scientific studies is essential for gaining acceptance in mainstream medicine and for regulatory approvals.
- **Intellectual Property Issues**: The industry often faces challenges related to patenting and intellectual property rights, particularly when traditional knowledge and natural resources are involved. Ensuring fair and ethical use of traditional knowledge while protecting intellectual property can be complex.

4. Market Competition and Counterfeiting

- **High Competition**: The herbal drug market is highly competitive, with numerous players offering similar products. Differentiating products and maintaining a competitive edge can be challenging, especially for smaller companies.
- **Counterfeiting and Quality Assurance**: The herbal industry is susceptible to counterfeiting, where imitation products may be sold as authentic. Counterfeit products not only harm consumers but also damage the reputation of genuine brands. Ensuring quality assurance and implementing effective anti-counterfeiting measures are critical.

5. Supply Chain and Sustainability

- **Supply Chain Disruptions**: The herbal industry can be affected by disruptions in the supply chain, such as fluctuations in raw material availability, transportation issues, or environmental factors impacting cultivation.
- **Sustainability Concerns**: Sustainable sourcing and environmental impact are significant concerns. Overharvesting of wild plants and unsustainable farming practices can lead to depletion of natural resources and environmental damage. Promoting sustainable cultivation practices and responsible sourcing is essential for long-term industry viability.

6. Consumer Education and Perceptions

- **Misconceptions and Misinformation**: Consumers may have misconceptions or limited understanding of herbal products, leading to misinformation and potential misuse. Effective consumer education is necessary to ensure informed choices and safe use of herbal remedies.
- **Regaining Trust**: Instances of adverse reactions or quality issues can undermine consumer trust in herbal products. Building and maintaining trust through transparency, quality assurance, and effective communication is crucial for industry growth.

Addressing these challenges requires a coordinated effort from industry stakeholders, including manufacturers, regulators, researchers, and policymakers. By overcoming these obstacles, the herbal drug industry can continue to thrive and contribute to global health and wellness.

5.1.3 Future Innovations in Herbal Medicine

The herbal medicine industry is poised for significant advancements and innovations that will likely shape its future. These innovations aim to enhance the efficacy, safety, and consumer appeal of herbal products, ensuring their continued growth and integration into mainstream healthcare. Key areas of future innovation include:

1. Advanced Extraction and Formulation Technologies

- **Novel Extraction Techniques**: Innovations in extraction technologies, such as **supercritical fluid extraction (SFE)** and **ultrasound-assisted extraction (UAE)**, are improving the efficiency and efficacy of isolating active compounds from herbal materials. These methods offer enhanced yield, purity, and sustainability compared to traditional extraction techniques.
- **Targeted Formulations**: Development of **targeted formulations** that use advanced delivery systems, such as **nanoencapsulation** and **liposomal delivery**, can enhance the bioavailability and therapeutic efficacy of herbal compounds. These technologies ensure that active ingredients are delivered more effectively to their site of action in the body.

2. Integration with Modern Medicine

- **Herbal-Pharmaceutical Synergies**: Combining herbal remedies with conventional pharmaceutical treatments in **integrative medicine** approaches can provide complementary benefits. Research into synergistic effects and safe co-administration of herbal and pharmaceutical products is expanding.
- **Personalized Herbal Medicine**: Advances in **genomics** and **pharmacogenomics** are paving the way for personalized herbal medicine. By tailoring herbal treatments based on individual genetic profiles, healthcare providers can optimize therapeutic outcomes and minimize adverse effects.

3. Improved Quality Control and Standardization

- **Enhanced Analytical Techniques**: The use of **high-performance liquid chromatography (HPLC), mass spectrometry (MS),** and **genetic fingerprinting** will improve the standardization and quality control of herbal products. These techniques help ensure consistent quality and safety of herbal formulations.
- **Certification and Verification Programs**: Implementing robust **certification and verification programs** can help establish quality standards and build consumer trust. Programs that verify the authenticity and purity of herbal products through third-party testing can reduce instances of adulteration and fraud.

4. Digital Health and Technology Integration

- **Telemedicine and Digital Platforms**: The rise of **telemedicine** and **digital health platforms** enables greater access to herbal medicine consultations and products. Online platforms can facilitate virtual consultations with practitioners, personalized treatment plans, and access to a broader range of herbal remedies.
- **AI and Data Analytics**: Artificial Intelligence (AI) and **data analytics** are increasingly used to analyze large datasets from clinical trials, patient feedback, and herbal product usage. AI can assist in identifying potential new herbal formulations, optimizing treatment protocols, and predicting therapeutic outcomes.

5. Sustainable and Ethical Practices

- **Sustainable Sourcing**: The focus on **sustainable sourcing** of herbal materials is growing. Innovations in sustainable cultivation practices, such as organic farming and agroforestry, help protect biodiversity and ensure the long-term availability of herbal resources.
- **Ethical Bioprospecting**: Ensuring **ethical bioprospecting** practices, including fair compensation and benefit-sharing with indigenous communities, will become increasingly important. Efforts to integrate traditional knowledge with modern scientific research should respect the rights and contributions of local and indigenous communities.

These innovations represent exciting opportunities for the herbal medicine industry, promising advancements in product efficacy, safety, and accessibility, and driving the industry towards a more integrated and scientifically validated future.

5.2 Plant-Based Industries and Institutions in India

5.2.1 Overview of Key Plant-Based Industries

India's plant-based industries are diverse and play a significant role in the country's economy. These industries leverage the rich biodiversity of India, which is home to a vast array of medicinal, aromatic, and economic plants. The key plant-based industries in India include:

1. Herbal and Ayurvedic Medicine Industry

- **Industry Overview**: The herbal and Ayurvedic medicine industry is one of the most prominent sectors, rooted in India's ancient medical traditions. This industry involves the cultivation, processing, and marketing of herbal drugs and formulations derived from traditional knowledge.
- **Major Players**: The industry is dominated by major companies such as **Dabur, Himalaya Drug Company, Patanjali Ayurved**, and **Baidyanath**. These companies offer a wide range of products, including dietary supplements, therapeutic formulations, and personal care products.
- **Market Trends**: There is a growing demand for herbal and Ayurvedic products both domestically and internationally. Trends include increased consumer preference for natural and organic products, innovations in product formulations, and expansion into global markets.

2. Essential Oils and Aromatic Plants Industry

- **Industry Overview**: India is a leading producer of essential oils and aromatic plants, which are used in various applications, including perfumery, cosmetics, and flavorings. The essential oils sector includes the cultivation, extraction, and commercialization of oils from plants like **lemongrass, patchouli,** and **sandalwood.**
- **Major Players**: Companies like **Kama Ayurveda, Aroma Treasures**, and **NHR (Natural Health Remedies)** are key players in the essential oils sector. Additionally, several small and medium enterprises contribute to the industry's growth.
- **Market Trends**: The industry is witnessing increased demand for natural and organic essential oils. Innovations in extraction technologies and growing applications in the wellness and aromatherapy sectors are driving market growth.

3. Spices and Flavorings Industry

- **Industry Overview**: India is renowned for its spice industry, producing a variety of spices used globally. Spices such as **turmeric, black pepper, cumin**, and **cardamom** are integral to the industry, which encompasses cultivation, processing, and export.
- **Major Players**: Major companies include **MDH Spices, Everest Spices**, and **Aachi Spices**. India is also a significant exporter of spices, contributing to the global spice market.
- **Market Trends**: The demand for spices is growing due to their culinary and health benefits. Innovations in spice processing, packaging, and global trade agreements are influencing the industry's expansion.

4. Medicinal Plant Cultivation and Processing

- **Industry Overview**: Medicinal plant cultivation and processing involve growing plants used in traditional and modern medicine, including those used for phytochemical extraction and research. This sector supports the development of new herbal medicines and dietary supplements.
- **Major Players**: Institutions and companies engaged in medicinal plant cultivation include **Haryana State Agro Industries Corporation, Indian Medicinal Plant Association,** and various research institutions like the **National Institute of Ayurveda.**

- **Market Trends**: There is a growing focus on sustainable cultivation practices and research-driven development of new medicinal products. Increasing investments in research and development (R&D) and the establishment of cultivation guidelines are shaping the future of this industry.

5. Agro-Based and Biotechnology Industries

- **Industry Overview**: Agro-based industries include the cultivation of plant-based raw materials for various applications, including food, pharmaceuticals, and textiles. Biotechnology applications involve the use of plant-based materials in genetic engineering and biomanufacturing.
- **Major Players**: Companies and institutions involved in this sector include **Biocon, Syngene International**, and various agricultural research centers.
- **Market Trends**: The integration of biotechnology with traditional agriculture is leading to the development of genetically modified crops and biotechnological advancements. There is also a growing emphasis on sustainable agriculture and eco-friendly practices.

6. Natural Dyes and Pigments Industry

- **Industry Overview**: This industry focuses on the extraction and application of natural dyes and pigments derived from plant sources. Natural dyes are used in textiles, cosmetics, and other applications, providing a sustainable alternative to synthetic dyes.
- **Major Players**: Key players include **The Natural Dye Company** and **Sustainability Partners**, which specialize in producing and promoting natural dyes.
- **Market Trends**: There is an increasing consumer preference for eco-friendly and sustainable products, which is driving the demand for natural dyes. Innovations in dyeing techniques and the development of new plant-based pigments are contributing to the industry's growth.

5.2.2 Institutions Involved in Research on Medicinal and Aromatic Plants

India boasts a number of prestigious institutions dedicated to research on medicinal and aromatic plants. These institutions play a vital role in advancing scientific knowledge, developing new products, and supporting the growth of the herbal and aromatic plant industries. Key institutions involved in this research include:

1. Central Council for Research in Ayurvedic Sciences (CCRAS)

- **Overview**: The **CCRAS** is a premier research institution under the Ministry of AYUSH, focused on the scientific validation and development of Ayurvedic medicines. It conducts research on various medicinal plants used in Ayurvedic treatments.
- **Research Areas**: CCRAS's research includes the identification and standardization of medicinal plants, development of new formulations, and clinical trials to validate traditional remedies.
- **Key Initiatives**: The council is involved in various projects such as the establishment of herbal gardens, development of pharmacopoeias, and collaboration with other research institutions and universities.

2. Indian Council of Medical Research (ICMR)

- **Overview**: The **ICMR** is one of the oldest and largest medical research organizations in India, and it conducts extensive research on medicinal plants through its various research institutes and centers.
- **Research Areas**: ICMR focuses on the pharmacological evaluation, safety, and efficacy of medicinal plants. It supports projects related to the development of new drugs and therapeutic agents from plant sources.
- **Key Initiatives**: ICMR provides grants for research projects, collaborates with academic institutions, and contributes to policy development related to medicinal plants and traditional medicine.

3. National Medicinal Plants Board (NMPB)

- **Overview**: The **NMPB** is an autonomous organization under the Ministry of AYUSH, dedicated to promoting the cultivation and research of medicinal plants. It aims to enhance the production and sustainable use of medicinal plants in India.
- **Research Areas**: NMPB focuses on developing standards for medicinal plant cultivation, conducting research on plant species, and supporting initiatives for conservation and sustainable harvesting.

- **Key Initiatives**: The board implements projects for the development of medicinal plant cultivation, provides financial support for research, and facilitates the creation of herbal gardens and research centers.

4. National Botanical Research Institute (NBRI)

- **Overview**: The **NBRI** is a premier research institute under the Council of Scientific and Industrial Research (CSIR), dedicated to botanical research, including medicinal and aromatic plants.
- **Research Areas**: NBRI's research includes plant taxonomy, phytochemistry, and the development of new plant-based products. It focuses on the conservation and sustainable use of plant resources.
- **Key Initiatives**: NBRI engages in collaborative research projects, develops plant-based technologies, and contributes to the development of pharmacopoeias and herbal standards.

5. Indian Institute of Horticultural Research (IIHR)

- **Overview**: The **IIHR** is an institute under the Indian Council of Agricultural Research (ICAR), specializing in research on horticultural crops, including medicinal and aromatic plants.
- **Research Areas**: IIHR conducts research on the cultivation, breeding, and improvement of medicinal and aromatic plants. It focuses on enhancing crop yields, quality, and disease resistance.
- **Key Initiatives**: The institute develops new cultivars, provides technical support to farmers, and conducts training programs for the sustainable cultivation of medicinal plants.

6. Institute of Himalayan Bioresource Technology (IHBT)

- **Overview**: The **IHBT**, also under CSIR, is focused on the research and development of bioresources from the Himalayan region, including medicinal and aromatic plants.
- **Research Areas**: IHBT's research includes the exploration of plant biodiversity, phytochemical analysis, and the development of new therapeutic agents from Himalayan plants.
- **Key Initiatives**: The institute works on the conservation of plant species, development of value-added products, and collaborations with national

and international research organizations.

These institutions collectively contribute to advancing the knowledge, cultivation, and application of medicinal and aromatic plants in India, fostering innovation and supporting the growth of the herbal industry.

5.2.2 Institutions Involved in Research on Medicinal and Aromatic Plants

India is home to several esteemed institutions dedicated to the research and development of medicinal and aromatic plants. These institutions play a crucial role in advancing scientific knowledge, validating traditional uses, and fostering innovation in the plant-based industries. Here is an overview of some key institutions involved in this field:

1. Central Council for Research in Ayurvedic Sciences (CCRAS)

- **Overview**: The **CCRAS** is a premier research body under the Ministry of AYUSH, focusing on the scientific validation and advancement of Ayurvedic medicine. It conducts research on various medicinal plants used in Ayurvedic practices.
- **Research Areas**: CCRAS undertakes research on the efficacy, safety, and standardization of Ayurvedic medicines derived from medicinal plants. It also explores new formulations and clinical applications of traditional remedies.
- **Key Initiatives**: The council engages in the development of pharmacopoeias, establishment of herbal gardens, and collaboration with other research institutions. It supports studies on the cultivation, conservation, and sustainable use of medicinal plants.

2. Indian Council of Medical Research (ICMR)

- **Overview**: The **ICMR** is a leading medical research organization in India, known for its comprehensive research across various health domains, including medicinal plants.
- **Research Areas**: ICMR focuses on the pharmacological, toxicological, and therapeutic evaluation of medicinal plants. It supports research aimed at discovering new drugs and therapeutic agents derived from plant sources.
- **Key Initiatives**: ICMR funds research projects, conducts collaborative studies with academic institutions, and provides scientific evidence to

support the development of plant-based medicines.

3. National Medicinal Plants Board (NMPB)

- **Overview**: The **NMPB** is an autonomous organization under the Ministry of AYUSH, dedicated to the promotion and development of medicinal plants in India.
- **Research Areas**: NMPB works on improving cultivation practices, developing standards for medicinal plant quality, and supporting research on conservation and sustainable use of medicinal plants.
- **Key Initiatives**: The board implements various projects for the development of medicinal plant cultivation, offers financial support for research and development, and collaborates with state governments and research institutions.

4. Institute of Himalayan Bioresource Technology (IHBT)

- **Overview**: The **IHBT**, located in Palampur, Himachal Pradesh, is a research institute under the Council of Scientific and Industrial Research (CSIR) that specializes in the study of bioresources from the Himalayan region.
- **Research Areas**: IHBT conducts research on medicinal and aromatic plants native to the Himalayan region, focusing on their pharmacological properties, cultivation practices, and commercial applications.
- **Key Initiatives**: The institute engages in the development of high-value products from Himalayan bioresources, including herbal medicines and essential oils. It also supports conservation efforts and sustainable use of regional plant species.

5. National Institute of Ayurvedic Medicine (NIAM)

- **Overview**: The **NIAM**, located in Jaipur, is dedicated to research and development in the field of Ayurvedic medicine.
- **Research Areas**: NIAM focuses on the study of medicinal plants used in Ayurvedic formulations, including their therapeutic potential and safety profiles.
- **Key Initiatives**: The institute is involved in the development of new Ayurvedic medicines, clinical trials, and the documentation of

traditional knowledge related to medicinal plants.

6. Botanical Survey of India (BSI)

- **Overview**: The **BSI**, under the Ministry of Environment, Forest and Climate Change, is responsible for the exploration, inventorying, and documentation of plant species in India.
- **Research Areas**: BSI conducts research on the taxonomy, distribution, and conservation of medicinal and aromatic plants. It provides valuable data for the sustainable management and use of plant resources.
- **Key Initiatives**: The survey includes field surveys, herbarium maintenance, and publication of research findings on plant biodiversity, including medicinal and aromatic plants.

These institutions collectively contribute to the advancement of knowledge and innovation in the field of medicinal and aromatic plants, supporting the growth of the herbal drug industry and enhancing the value of plant-based resources.

5.3 Good Manufacturing Practices (GMP) for Indian Systems of Medicine

5.3.1 Components of GMP (Schedule T)

Schedule T of the **Drugs and Cosmetics Act, 1940** outlines the Good Manufacturing Practices (GMP) specifically for **Ayurvedic, Siddha,** and **Unani** (ASU) drugs. These guidelines are crucial for ensuring that the manufacturing of herbal medicines adheres to high standards of quality, safety, and efficacy. Schedule T encompasses several key components designed to standardize and improve the manufacturing processes. The main components include:

****1. Manufacturing Facilities and Equipment**

- **Facility Design and Layout**: Manufacturing facilities must be designed to minimize the risk of contamination and to ensure efficient production processes. This includes proper ventilation, lighting, and sanitation facilities.
- **Equipment Maintenance**: All equipment used in the manufacturing process must be well-maintained and regularly cleaned to prevent cross-contamination and ensure consistent product quality.

- **Storage Conditions**: Adequate storage conditions must be provided for raw materials, intermediate products, and finished products. Storage areas should be clean, dry, and maintained at appropriate temperatures to preserve the integrity of the products.

2. Quality Control and Assurance

- **Standard Operating Procedures (SOPs)**: SOPs must be established and followed for all manufacturing processes. These procedures include guidelines for production, quality control, and sanitation to ensure consistency and compliance with regulatory standards.
- **Testing and Quality Assurance**: Rigorous testing of raw materials, in-process materials, and finished products is required to ensure they meet quality specifications. This includes physical, chemical, and microbiological testing as per defined standards.
- **Documentation and Records**: Detailed records of all manufacturing processes, quality control tests, and product batches must be maintained. This documentation is essential for traceability and for addressing any issues that may arise.

3. Personnel Training and Hygiene

- **Training Programs**: All personnel involved in the manufacturing process must receive adequate training in GMP principles, hygiene practices, and operational procedures. Regular refresher training is also necessary to keep staff updated on best practices.
- **Personal Hygiene**: Employees must adhere to strict personal hygiene practices to prevent contamination. This includes wearing clean uniforms, using protective gear, and maintaining personal cleanliness.

4. Raw Material Control

- **Supplier Quality Management**: Raw materials should be sourced from reputable suppliers who comply with quality standards. Suppliers must be evaluated and approved based on their ability to provide consistent, high-quality materials.
- **Material Inspection and Testing**: Raw materials must be inspected and tested upon receipt to ensure they meet quality specifications. Any

materials that do not meet the required standards should be rejected and properly disposed of.

**5. Production and Process Controls

- **Process Validation**: Manufacturing processes must be validated to ensure they consistently produce products that meet quality specifications. This involves testing and documenting process parameters to verify their effectiveness.
- **Environmental Controls**: Environmental conditions in the manufacturing area, such as temperature and humidity, must be controlled and monitored to ensure they do not adversely affect the product quality.

**6. Packaging and Labeling

- **Packaging Materials**: Packaging materials must be suitable for protecting the product from contamination and degradation. The packaging should also comply with regulatory requirements and be appropriately labeled.
- **Labeling Requirements**: Labels must provide accurate and clear information about the product, including its name, ingredients, dosage instructions, and expiry date. Proper labeling ensures that consumers are well-informed and can use the product safely.

**7. Compliance and Audits

- **Regulatory Compliance**: Manufacturers must comply with all applicable regulations and guidelines set forth by regulatory authorities. Regular audits and inspections by regulatory agencies help ensure adherence to GMP standards.
- **Internal Audits**: Regular internal audits should be conducted to evaluate compliance with GMP requirements and to identify areas for improvement. These audits help maintain high standards of quality and safety in manufacturing practices.

Implementing and adhering to these components of GMP as outlined in Schedule T ensures that ASU drugs are produced consistently, safely, and effectively, maintaining the trust and confidence of

5.3.2 Objectives of Implementing GMP

The implementation of **Good Manufacturing Practices (GMP)** for Indian Systems of Medicine aims to ensure that the production of Ayurvedic, Siddha, and Unani drugs meets high standards of quality, safety, and efficacy. The key objectives of implementing GMP are:

1. Ensuring Product Quality and Safety

- **Consistency and Reliability**: GMP ensures that herbal medicines are produced consistently and reliably, with each batch meeting predefined quality standards. This consistency is crucial for maintaining the efficacy and safety of the products.
- **Minimizing Risks**: By adhering to GMP guidelines, manufacturers can minimize risks related to contamination, mix-ups, and errors during production. This helps in safeguarding the health of consumers and maintaining the integrity of the medicinal products.

2. Compliance with Regulatory Requirements

- **Adherence to Regulations**: Implementing GMP helps manufacturers comply with national and international regulations governing the production of medicinal products. This compliance is essential for obtaining necessary approvals and licenses for marketing herbal medicines.
- **Facilitating Inspections**: GMP practices make it easier for regulatory authorities to inspect and evaluate manufacturing facilities. Proper documentation and adherence to SOPs provide transparency and facilitate regulatory reviews.

3. Enhancing Consumer Confidence

- **Building Trust**: High manufacturing standards contribute to consumer trust in herbal products. When consumers know that products are manufactured under stringent GMP conditions, they are more likely to believe in their safety and efficacy.
- **Quality Assurance**: Consistent adherence to GMP practices assures consumers that they are receiving high-quality and effective products. This helps in building a positive reputation for manufacturers and their

products.

4. Improving Operational Efficiency

- **Streamlined Processes**: GMP guidelines help in streamlining manufacturing processes, reducing waste, and improving overall efficiency. Well-defined procedures and regular training lead to better management of resources and production processes.
- **Error Reduction**: By implementing systematic procedures and checks, GMP reduces the likelihood of errors during manufacturing. This leads to fewer product recalls and batch rejections, improving operational efficiency and reducing costs.

5. Supporting Research and Development

- **Facilitating Innovation**: GMP provides a solid foundation for research and development by ensuring that new formulations and processes are developed under controlled conditions. This facilitates the introduction of innovative products while maintaining high standards.
- **Regulatory Approval for New Products**: For new herbal products and formulations to gain regulatory approval, adherence to GMP is essential. This compliance helps in gaining approval from regulatory bodies and supports the commercialization of new products.

6. Promoting Sustainable Practices

- **Sustainable Manufacturing**: GMP guidelines often include provisions for environmental management and sustainability. This helps in promoting environmentally friendly practices and sustainable resource use in the production of herbal medicines.

By achieving these objectives, GMP ensures that the production of Ayurvedic, Siddha, and Unani drugs is conducted in a manner that protects consumer health, complies with regulatory standards, and supports the growth and development of the herbal medicine industry.

5.4 Infrastructural Requirements for Herbal Drug Manufacturing

5.4.1 Working Space and Design of Facilities

The design and layout of facilities for herbal drug manufacturing are critical for ensuring compliance with Good Manufacturing Practices (GMP) and for maintaining product quality, safety, and efficiency. Adequate working space and facility design play a crucial role in streamlining operations and preventing contamination. Key considerations for working space and facility design include:

1. Facility Layout and Design

- **Functional Zoning**: The facility should be designed with clearly defined zones for different stages of production, including raw material handling, processing, packaging, and storage. This zoning helps prevent cross-contamination and ensures that each area operates under appropriate conditions.
- **Flow of Materials**: The layout should facilitate a logical flow of materials and personnel to minimize the risk of contamination and mix-ups. Ideally, the layout should follow a unidirectional flow from raw material reception to final product dispatch.
- **Space Utilization**: Adequate space must be provided for each operation to ensure smooth workflow and ease of access. Overcrowding can lead to inefficiencies and increase the risk of contamination.

2. Hygiene and Sanitation

- **Clean Rooms**: Designated clean rooms or controlled environments should be established for processing and packaging operations. These areas should be equipped with appropriate ventilation, air filtration, and cleaning facilities to maintain cleanliness and prevent contamination.
- **Sanitation Facilities**: The facility should include facilities for regular cleaning and sanitation, such as sinks, hand-washing stations, and sanitation equipment. Proper sanitation protocols must be in place to ensure that all surfaces and equipment are regularly cleaned and disinfected.
- **Waste Management**: Adequate waste disposal systems should be incorporated into the facility design to handle both hazardous and non-hazardous waste. Proper waste segregation, storage, and disposal procedures are essential to prevent contamination and maintain hygiene.

3. Environmental Controls

- **Temperature and Humidity Control**: The facility must have systems in place to control temperature and humidity levels, especially in areas where sensitive raw materials or products are handled. Environmental controls help preserve the quality and efficacy of herbal products.
- **Ventilation**: Proper ventilation is essential to maintain air quality and remove any airborne contaminants or fumes. Ventilation systems should be designed to ensure adequate air circulation and exchange in all areas of the facility.

4. Equipment and Infrastructure

- **Equipment Layout**: Equipment should be arranged to optimize workflow and ensure that it is easily accessible for operation, maintenance, and cleaning. The layout should also allow for safe and efficient handling of materials.
- **Infrastructure**: The facility should be equipped with infrastructure to support manufacturing operations, including power supply, water systems, and storage facilities. These systems must be reliable and maintained regularly to avoid disruptions in production.

5. Safety and Accessibility

- **Safety Measures**: The facility design should incorporate safety features such as emergency exits, fire alarms, and safety equipment to protect personnel and minimize risks. Safety protocols should be clearly outlined and communicated to all staff.
- **Accessibility**: The facility should be designed to accommodate personnel with diverse needs, including accessibility for individuals with disabilities. This includes accessible entrances, pathways, and workstations.

5.4.2 Storage Area Considerations

The storage areas within a herbal drug manufacturing facility are critical to maintaining the quality, safety, and efficacy of herbal products. Proper design and management of these areas ensure that raw materials, intermediates, and finished products are stored under optimal conditions. Key considerations include:

1. Storage Conditions

- **Temperature and Humidity Control:** Storage areas must be equipped with systems to regulate temperature and humidity according to the requirements of different herbal materials and products. Some materials may require refrigeration or controlled room temperature, while others need low humidity to prevent degradation.
- **Ventilation:** Adequate ventilation is necessary to prevent the buildup of moisture and to ensure proper air circulation. This helps in maintaining a stable environment and prevents conditions that could lead to mold or mildew growth.

2. Segregation and Organization

- **Segregation of Materials:** Raw materials, intermediates, and finished products should be stored separately to prevent cross-contamination. Additionally, different types of materials (e.g., active ingredients, excipients) should be organized to avoid mix-ups.
- **Labeling and Tracking:** Clear and accurate labeling of all stored items is essential for traceability and inventory management. Labels should include information such as the batch number, expiry date, and storage conditions.

3. Security and Access Control

- **Restricted Access:** Storage areas should be accessible only to authorized personnel to prevent unauthorized access and potential tampering. Access control systems, such as keycards or biometric scanners, can help maintain security.
- **Inventory Management:** Implementing inventory management systems helps in tracking the quantities and conditions of stored materials. Regular inventory checks and audits are important for ensuring that materials are used within their shelf life and are replaced as needed.

4. Safety Measures

- **Fire Safety:** Storage areas should be equipped with fire safety measures, including fire extinguishers, alarms, and sprinklers. Fire exits and safety protocols must be clearly defined and accessible.

- **Pest Control**: Measures should be in place to prevent and manage pest infestations, which can compromise the quality of stored materials. Regular inspections and pest control treatments are essential.

5.4.3 Machinery and Equipment for Herbal Manufacturing

The selection and maintenance of machinery and equipment are crucial for efficient and compliant herbal drug manufacturing. Proper equipment ensures consistent product quality and adheres to GMP standards. Key considerations for machinery and equipment include:

1. Types of Machinery

- **Grinding and Milling Equipment**: Used for reducing raw materials to the required particle size. This includes **ball mills, hammer mills,** and **attrition mills**. Equipment must be designed to handle herbal materials without causing contamination or loss of active ingredients.
- **Extraction Equipment**: Includes **soxhlet extractors, supercritical fluid extractors,** and **ultrasound-assisted extractors**. These machines are used to extract active compounds from plant materials efficiently.
- **Mixing and Blending Equipment**: Equipment such as **blenders, homogenizers,** and **agitators** are used to mix herbal extracts and other ingredients to ensure uniformity in formulations.
- **Filtration and Purification Systems**: Used to filter out impurities from herbal extracts. This includes **membrane filters, centrifuges,** and **distillation units**.

2. Equipment Maintenance and Calibration

- **Regular Maintenance**: All machinery must be regularly maintained to ensure optimal performance and to prevent breakdowns. Maintenance schedules should be documented, and any repairs should be conducted promptly.
- **Calibration**: Equipment used for measuring and processing must be calibrated regularly to ensure accuracy and reliability. Calibration records should be maintained as part of quality control procedures.

3. Hygiene and Cleaning

- **Cleaning Procedures**: Equipment must be cleaned thoroughly to prevent cross-contamination between different batches of products. Cleaning procedures should be defined and validated to ensure they are effective.
- **Material Compatibility**: Equipment should be made from materials that are compatible with the herbal products being processed to prevent reactions or contamination.

4. Safety and Compliance

- **Safety Features**: Machinery should include safety features to protect operators and ensure safe operation. This includes emergency stop buttons, safety guards, and proper ventilation.
- **Regulatory Compliance**: All equipment must meet regulatory standards and GMP requirements. Compliance ensures that the equipment operates within the parameters set for herbal drug manufacturing.

5.5 Standard Operating Procedures (SOPs)
5.5.1 Importance of SOPs in Quality Control

Standard Operating Procedures (SOPs) are essential in ensuring the consistent quality and safety of herbal drugs. They provide detailed, step-by-step instructions for performing various tasks and processes within the manufacturing facility. The importance of SOPs in quality control includes:

1. Consistency and Reliability

- **Uniformity in Processes**: SOPs ensure that all processes are carried out in a consistent manner, regardless of who performs them. This uniformity helps in maintaining the quality and efficacy of herbal products across different batches.
- **Minimizing Variability**: By following standardized procedures, variability in product quality is reduced. This consistency is crucial for meeting regulatory requirements and for ensuring that products perform as expected.

2. Compliance with Regulatory Standards

- **Meeting Regulatory Requirements**: SOPs are often required by regulatory authorities to ensure compliance with Good Manufacturing

Practices (GMP) and other quality standards. Adhering to SOPs helps in meeting these regulatory requirements and facilitates inspections and audits.

- **Documentation and Traceability**: SOPs provide a documented record of procedures and practices, which is important for traceability. This documentation supports regulatory reviews and helps in addressing any issues that may arise.

3. Training and Efficiency

- **Training Tool**: SOPs serve as a valuable training resource for new employees. They provide clear instructions and guidelines, helping staff understand their roles and responsibilities and perform tasks correctly.
- **Operational Efficiency**: Standardized procedures streamline operations by reducing the need for trial-and-error and minimizing errors. This efficiency leads to smoother production processes and better resource management.

4. Risk Management and Quality Assurance

- **Preventing Errors**: SOPs help in identifying and mitigating potential risks and errors by providing detailed procedures and checks. This proactive approach contributes to overall product quality and safety.
- **Quality Assurance**: Regular reviews and updates of SOPs ensure that procedures remain current and effective in maintaining quality standards. This continuous improvement process supports ongoing quality assurance efforts.

5.5.2 Common SOPs for Manufacturing Herbal Drugs

In the manufacturing of herbal drugs, several common SOPs are essential for ensuring quality control and adherence to GMP standards. Key SOPs include:

1. SOPs for Raw Material Handling

- **Receiving and Inspection**: Procedures for the inspection, testing, and documentation of raw materials upon receipt. This includes verifying the authenticity, quality, and safety of incoming materials.

- **Storage**: Guidelines for the proper storage of raw materials, including temperature and humidity controls, segregation, and labeling requirements.

2. SOPs for Production Processes

- **Preparation and Mixing**: Detailed procedures for the preparation of raw materials and the mixing of ingredients. This includes measurements, mixing times, and techniques to ensure uniformity and consistency.
- **Extraction and Formulation**: Instructions for the extraction of active compounds from plant materials and the formulation of herbal products. This includes parameters for extraction methods, filtration, and concentration.

3. SOPs for Quality Control

- **Testing and Analysis**: Procedures for conducting quality control tests on raw materials, in-process samples, and finished products. This includes physical, chemical, and microbiological testing methods.
- **Documentation and Reporting**: Guidelines for documenting test results, recording deviations, and reporting any issues. This ensures accurate tracking and resolution of quality concerns.

4. SOPs for Cleaning and Sanitation

- **Cleaning Procedures**: Detailed instructions for the cleaning and sanitization of equipment, production areas, and storage spaces. This includes cleaning agents, methods, and frequency.
- **Sanitation Checks**: Procedures for verifying the effectiveness of cleaning and sanitation measures, including regular inspections and validation.

5. SOPs for Packaging and Labeling

- **Packaging**: Guidelines for the proper packaging of finished products to ensure their safety, integrity, and compliance with regulatory requirements. This includes packaging materials, techniques, and handling procedures.

- **Labeling**: Instructions for labeling products accurately, including information on ingredients, dosage, expiry dates, and storage conditions. This ensures clear communication of product details to consumers.

6. SOPs for Personnel Training

- **Training Programs**: Procedures for training new employees and providing ongoing education to existing staff. This includes training on SOPs, safety practices, and quality control measures.
- **Competency Evaluation**: Guidelines for evaluating the competency of personnel and ensuring they adhere to established procedures.

5.6 Health and Hygiene Requirements
5.6.1 Personnel Hygiene Guidelines

Maintaining high standards of health and hygiene among personnel in herbal drug manufacturing is essential to prevent contamination, ensure product safety, and comply with Good Manufacturing Practices (GMP). Personnel hygiene guidelines are critical for creating a safe working environment and protecting both the workers and the consumers. The key guidelines for personnel hygiene in herbal drug manufacturing include:

1. Personal Hygiene Practices

- **Hand Hygiene:**

  - Personnel must wash their hands thoroughly with soap and water before starting work, after using the restroom, and before handling raw materials or products. Hand sanitizers may also be used as an additional measure.
  - Proper handwashing techniques should be followed, including scrubbing all parts of the hands, including between the fingers and under the nails, for at least 20 seconds.

- **Uniform and Personal Protective Equipment (PPE):**

  - Employees must wear clean, appropriate uniforms and personal protective equipment (PPE) such as gloves, masks, hairnets, and goggles when handling raw materials and products.

- Uniforms should be laundered regularly to maintain cleanliness and prevent contamination.

- **Health Status:**

  - Personnel should report any illnesses or infections, particularly those that could pose a risk to product safety (e.g., gastrointestinal illnesses, skin infections). Employees showing symptoms of contagious illnesses should be excluded from the manufacturing area until they are cleared to return.

2. Workplace Behavior

- **No Eating or Drinking:**

  - Eating, drinking, smoking, or chewing gum in production areas should be strictly prohibited to prevent contamination of herbal products.

- **Limiting Personal Items:**

  - Personal items such as bags, phones, and jewelry should not be allowed in production areas to minimize contamination risks.

3. Training and Awareness

- **Regular Training:**

  - Personnel should receive regular training on hygiene practices, contamination control, and the importance of maintaining a clean working environment.
  - Training sessions should include demonstrations of proper handwashing techniques, appropriate use of PPE, and the importance of reporting health issues.

- **Hygiene Signage:**

- ○ Clear signage should be posted in relevant areas to remind personnel of hygiene practices, including handwashing stations, PPE requirements, and prohibitions on eating and drinking.

4. Facility and Equipment Hygiene

- **Sanitation Practices:**

  - ○ Personnel should be trained in the proper cleaning and sanitation procedures for equipment and production areas. Regular cleaning schedules should be established and followed.

- **Regular Inspections:**

  - ○ Regular inspections of personal hygiene practices and adherence to guidelines should be conducted by supervisory staff. Non-compliance should be addressed immediately.

5. Monitoring and Compliance

- **Health Check-ups:**

  - ○ Regular health check-ups and assessments should be conducted to monitor the health status of personnel and identify any potential health risks that could affect product safety.

- **Record Keeping:**

  - ○ Documentation of hygiene training, health status reports, and any incidents related to personnel hygiene should be maintained to ensure accountability and compliance with established guidelines.

By adhering to these personnel hygiene guidelines, herbal drug manufacturers can significantly reduce the risk of contamination, ensure the safety and efficacy of their products, and maintain compliance with regulatory requirements and industry standards.

5.6.2 Preventive Measures to Ensure Product Safety

Ensuring the safety of herbal products involves implementing preventive measures to minimize risks of contamination, maintain product integrity, and protect consumer health. These measures are critical to adhering to Good Manufacturing Practices (GMP) and safeguarding the quality of herbal drugs. Key preventive measures include:

1. Facility Design and Maintenance

- **Proper Facility Design**:

  - Manufacturing facilities should be designed to prevent cross-contamination and maintain a clean environment. This includes appropriate zoning, airflow management, and separation of different production areas (e.g., raw material handling, processing, packaging).

- **Regular Maintenance and Cleaning**:

  - Facilities and equipment must be regularly cleaned and maintained to prevent contamination. Cleaning schedules should be strictly followed, and records of cleaning activities should be maintained.

- **Preventative Maintenance**:

  - Implement a preventative maintenance program to ensure that equipment operates correctly and does not pose a risk of contamination or malfunction.

2. Controlled Environmental Conditions

- **Temperature and Humidity Control**:

  - Monitor and control environmental conditions such as temperature and humidity in storage and production areas to ensure they are within specified ranges. This prevents the growth of microorganisms and degradation of herbal materials.

- **Air Quality Management**:

- Use air filtration systems and maintain proper ventilation to reduce airborne contaminants. Regularly check and replace filters to ensure effective air quality control.

3. Quality Control and Testing

- **Raw Material Inspection:**

  - Implement strict protocols for inspecting and testing raw materials upon receipt to ensure they meet quality standards and are free from contaminants.

- **In-Process Testing:**

  - Perform in-process testing to monitor and control quality during production. This includes checking intermediate products for consistency and quality.

- **Final Product Testing:**

  - Conduct comprehensive testing of finished products for potency, purity, and safety. This includes physical, chemical, and microbiological tests to ensure that products meet specified quality standards.

4. Proper Handling and Storage

- **Handling Procedures:**

  - Establish and enforce standard operating procedures (SOPs) for the handling of raw materials, in-process materials, and finished products to prevent contamination and cross-contamination.

- **Storage Conditions:**

  - Store raw materials and finished products under controlled conditions to prevent spoilage or degradation. Use appropriate storage containers and ensure they are clean and dry.

5. Employee Training and Hygiene

- **Training Programs**:

  - Provide regular training to employees on hygiene practices, contamination control, and safe handling procedures. Ensure that employees understand the importance of their roles in maintaining product safety.

- **Health Monitoring**:

  - Implement health monitoring programs to ensure that employees who are ill or show signs of infection do not handle products or work in production areas.

6. Documentation and Record-Keeping

- **Accurate Documentation**:

  - Maintain detailed records of all manufacturing processes, quality control tests, and cleaning activities. Proper documentation helps in traceability and supports compliance with regulatory requirements.

- **Regular Audits**:

  - Conduct regular internal audits and inspections to review compliance with SOPs and GMP guidelines. Address any identified issues promptly to maintain high standards of product safety.

By implementing these preventive measures, herbal drug manufacturers can effectively manage risks, ensure product safety, and deliver high-quality products to consumers.

www.ingramcontent.com/pod-product-compliance
Lightning Source LLC
Chambersburg PA
CBHW041308120726

48005CB00014B/1922